No Man's Land

Wesleyan and Methodist Explorations

EDITORS

Daniel Castelo
Robert W. Wall

DESCRIPTION

The *Wesleyan and Methodist Explorations* series will offer some of the best Methodist Wesleyan scholarship for the church and academy by drawing from active participants in the international guilds of Methodist scholarship (Oxford Institute of Methodist Studies, Wesleyan Theological Society, American Academy of Religion—Methodist Studies Section, and others).

There is an urgent need within Wesleyan Methodist scholarship for constructive theological work that will advance the field into interdisciplinary and creative directions. The potential for the series is vast as it will seek to establish possible future directions for the field.

Another key concern of this series will be to tap the emerging field of theological interpretation of Scripture located in and for particular ecclesial traditions. Theological interpretation offers insight to historical study, especially the reception of Scripture and its effects within the Methodist church, as well as exploring the epistemic gains to particular biblical texts and themes. Theological interpretation offers insight into the holy ends of these gains for the life of the church in worship, instruction, mission, and personal devotions for a people called Methodist.

The series will seek out great monographs, while also considering superior and adapted doctoral dissertations and well-conceived and tightly focused edited volumes.

EDITORIAL BOARD

Carla Works	Hal Knight III
Karen Winslow	Priscilla Pope-Levison
Sangwoo Kim	Sharon Grant
Matt Sigler	Frederick L. Ware
Ashley Dreff	Dennis Dickerson

"Protestant equivalents to Catholic religious orders for women have rarely received the attention they deserve. In this book Priscilla Pope-Levison's diligent, wide-ranging research opens up the remarkable story of Methodist deaconesses—active in many countries from the late nineteenth century well into the twentieth, continuing today especially in African American churches, effective in a wide range of ministries, and particularly inspirational in teaching, evangelism, and social outreach among the urban poor. The book's revelations should be as important for encouraging similar services today as for rescuing a largely forgotten history."

—**Mark Noll**, co-author of *Turning Points: Decisive Moments in the History of Christianity*

"The author has lifted up for religion scholars and adherents an overlooked international arena of sacralized outreach that transcended Methodist denominational boundaries. This global movement of Methodist women revived the Wesleyan warrant to relieve the suffering of the marginalized and provided a basis for Pan Methodist ministries."

—**Dennis C. Dickerson**, Reverend James M. Lawson Chair of History Emeritus, Vanderbilt University

"This book is a true achievement, a useful and inspiring compilation of historical analysis, primary sources, international perspective, and a thoughtful and practical look forward. It is a great learning tool for the classroom but also something more. The deaconess movement's commitment to simple living, rigorous theological education, and humanitarian service is a model we still need, today perhaps more than ever."

—**Peggy Bendroth**, author of *Fundamentalism and Gender, 1875 to the Present*

"Priscilla Pope-Levison has written a ground-breaking study on the Methodist deaconess movement of the late nineteenth and early twentieth centuries. Steeped in primary sources, this work reveals the international scope of a women's religious movement often overlooked by scholars. A must-read for anyone interested in women's religious history and Methodist studies, this book will serve both scholars and students alike as an indispensable resource for years to come."

—**Christopher Evans**, Professor of the History of Christianity and Methodist Studies, Boston University School of Theology

"This book tells a captivating story of the much unknown deaconess movement worldwide, especially in the Wesleyan/Methodist context. The depth and years of research honor the legacy of trailblazing women who overcame roadblocks and questions of their authority to live out their call to ministry through service. It is a testimony of how their faith, God-given gifts, persistence, and leadership impacted the church and the world, past and present."

—**Sally Vonner**, General Secretary and CEO, United Women in Faith

No Man's Land

The International Methodist Deaconess Movement, 1874–1918

Priscilla Pope-Levison

CASCADE *Books* • Eugene, Oregon

NO MAN'S LAND
The International Methodist Deaconess Movement, 1874–1918

Wesleyan and Methodist Explorations Series

Copyright © 2025 Priscilla Pope-Levison. All rights reserved. Except for brief quotations in critical publications or reviews, no part of this book may be reproduced in any manner without prior written permission from the publisher. Write: Permissions, Wipf and Stock Publishers, 199 W. 8th Ave., Suite 3, Eugene, OR 97401.

Cascade Books
An Imprint of Wipf and Stock Publishers
199 W. 8th Ave., Suite 3
Eugene, OR 97401

www.wipfandstock.com

PAPERBACK ISBN: 978-1-6667-6250-1
HARDCOVER ISBN: 978-1-6667-6251-8
EBOOK ISBN: 978-1-6667-6252-5

Cataloguing-in-Publication data:

Names: Pope-Levison, Priscilla, 1958–, author.

Title: No man's land : the international Methodist deaconess movement, 1874–1918 / by Priscilla Pope-Levison.

Description: Eugene, OR: Cascade Books, 2025 | Series: Wesleyan and Methodist Explorations | Includes bibliographical references and index(es).

Identifiers: ISBN 978-1-6667-6250-1 (paperback) | ISBN 978-1-6667-6251-8 (hardcover) | ISBN 978-1-6667-6252-5 (ebook)

Subjects: LCSH: Deaconesses—Methodists.| Methodist women—History—19th century | Methodist women—History—20th century. | Women in church work.

Classification: BX8345.7 .P64 2025 (paperback) | BX8345.7 (ebook)

VERSION NUMBER 10/27/25

To Jack

Set me as a seal upon your heart,
as a seal upon your arm;
For love is strong as death,
passion fierce as the grave.
(Song of Songs 8:6)

CONTENTS

Permissions | ix
Photo Permissions | xi
Acknowledgments | xv
Abbreviations | xviii

Introduction | 1

Chapter I: The Emergence, Growth, and Decline of the International Methodist Deaconess Movement | 14
    Source document: "Diakonissenspiegel"/"Deaconess's Mirror" 42

Chapter II: A "Thirty Year War" and More: Exposing Complexities in the Methodist Deaconess Movement | 56
    Source document: "Experiences of a Deaconess Guitar" 73

Chapter III: Pioneers in American Women's Theological Education: Methodist Deaconess Training Schools | 79
    Source documents: "An Examination of Candidates" 94
    "A Student's View of College Life" 98

Chapter IV: "Her Distinctive Dress": Displaying the Ambiguity of the Methodist Deaconess Movement | 103
    Source documents: "Give All You Can" Hymn No. 76 118
    "Autobiography of a Bonnet" 120

"Regeln für die Diakonissen des Martha-Maria-Vereins für allgemeine Krankenpflege zu Nürnberg"/ Rules for the Deaconesses of the Martha-Maria Organization for General Nursing Care in Nuremberg"   126

Chapter V: "Mothering Not Governing": Maternalism in Late-Nineteenth Century Methodist Women's Organizations | 135
   Source documents: "Little Prayers"   153
   "Report of the Tory Street Mission"   154

Chapter VI: Male Advocates in the Early Decades of the International Methodist Deaconess Movement | 161
   Source documents: *The Deaconess and Her Vocation*   179
   The History of the Deaconess Movement in the Christian Church   183

Chapter VII: Negotiating "Andromania" and Other Disputed Borders in the Methodist Deaconess Movement | 189
   Source documents: "Ceremony of Consecration"   199
   "Special Instructions"   202

Epilogue: A Deaconess Blueprint for the Revival of Methodism Worldwide | 208

Appendix A: Diary Extracts—Elizabeth Ann Pitts | 223
Appendix B: Diary Extracts—Thirza Masters | 237
Bibliography | 253
Subject Index | 269
Scripture Index | 277

PERMISSIONS

Chapter 2 previously published as Priscilla Pope-Levison, "A 'Thirty Year War' and More: Exposing Complexities in the Methodist Deaconess Movement," *Methodist History* 47 (2009) 101–16. Used by permission.

Chapter 3 previously published as Priscilla Pope-Levison, "Pioneers in American Women's Theological Education: Methodist Deaconess Training Schools," *Methodist Review* 10 (2019) 73–91. Used by permission.

Chapter 5 previously published as Priscilla Pope-Levison, "'Mothering Not Governing': Maternalism in Late Nineteenth-Century Methodist Women's Organizations," *Methodist History* 55 (2016/2017) 32–46. Used by permission.

Chapter 6 previously published as Priscilla Pope-Levison, "Male Advocates in the Early Decades of the International Methodist Deaconess Movement" *Methodist History* 59 (2021) 215–27. Used by permission.

Chapter 7 previous published as Priscilla Pope-Levison, "Negotiating 'Andromania' and Other Disputed Borders in the Methodist Deaconess Movement," *Wesleyan Theological Journal* 54 (2019) 7–24. Used by permission.

Epilogue previously published as Priscilla Pope-Levison, "A Deaconess Blueprint for the Revival of Global Methodism." In *Thy Grace Restore, Thy Work Revive: Revival, Reform, and Revolution in Global Methodism*, edited by Sarah Lancaster, 57–82. Nashville, TN: Foundry, 2022. Used by permission.

Appendix A: Extracts from the Diary of Elizabeth Anne Pitts. Material from the Methodist collection deposited at The John Rylands Research Institute and Library is used with the permission of The John Rylands University Librarian and Director of the University of Manchester Library and The Trustees for Methodist Church Purposes (The Methodist Church in Britain).

Appendix B: Extracts from the Diary of Sister Thirza Masters. Material from the Methodist collection deposited at The John Rylands Research Institute and Library is used with the permission of The John Rylands University Librarian and Director of the University of Manchester Library and The Trustees for Methodist Church Purposes (The Methodist Church in Britain).

All Scripture quotations are from the New Revised Standard Version Bible, copyright © 1989 National Council of the Churches of Christ in the United States of America. Used by permission. All rights reserved worldwide.

PHOTO PERMISSIONS

Introduction

Sister Isabel Sinclair, Methodist Church of New Zealand
    Kei Muri Māpara/Methodist Church of New Zealand Archives Christchurch: M. A. Rugby Pratt, *The Story of the South Island Methodist Orphanage and Children's Home, Christchurch* (1934), Books of Association Collection, Box 11, Assn 80.

Sister Grace, Wesley Deaconess Order
    Material from the Methodist collection deposited at The John Rylands Research Institute and Library is used with the permission of The John Rylands University Librarian and Director of the University of Manchester Library and The Trustees for Methodist Church Purposes (The Methodist Church in Britain).

Marguerite Decker and her class at Harris Memorial Training College, Manila
    Used with permission from Harris Memorial College, Inc.

Chapter One

Rosa Simpson, Deaconess, Methodist Episcopal Church
    The Christian Advocate, May 13, 1920, 663. Methodist Library, Special Collections & Libraries, Drew University Libraries.

Sister Laura Francis, Deaconess, Methodist Church of Australia
    Copyright illuminate, Camden Theological Library.

Chapter Two

Iva May Durham (later Vennard), Deaconess, Methodist Episcopal Church
    Mary Ella Bowie, *Alabaster and Spikenard: The Life of Iva Durham Vennard, D.D., Founder of Chicago Evangelistic Institute* (Chicago: Chicago Evangelistic Institute, 1947).

Lucy Rider Meyer, Deaconess, Methodist Episcopal Church
    Portrait of Lucy Rider Meyer, 1900. Lucy Rider Meyer Digital Collection, Archives, Styberg Library, Garrett-Evangelical Theological Seminary.

Chapter Three

Scarritt Bible and Training School, Methodist Episcopal Church South
    Training School Building Photos, Undated, Container: Box 9. Scarritt Bible and Training School Collection, 2018-018. Scarritt Bennett Center—Laskey Library and Archives.

Staff of The Deaconess College, Wesley Deaconess Order
    Material from the Methodist collection deposited at The John Rylands Research Institute and Library is used with the permission of The John Rylands University Librarian and Director of the University of Manchester Library and The Trustees for Methodist Church Purposes (The Methodist Church in Britain).

Chapter Four

Seven Deaconesses in the First Training School for Colored Deaconesses in the United States
    Christian Golder, *History of the Deaconess Movement in the Christian Church* (New York: Eaton and Mains, 1908).

Early Deaconesses in Costume, Methodist Episcopal Church
    Isabelle Horton, *High Adventure: Life of Lucy Rider Meyer* (New York: Methodist Book Concern, 1928).

Hymn: "Give All You Can," *Everybody's Gospel Songs,* edited by Lucy Rider Meyer (Chicago: The Chicago Training School of Missions, 1910). Methodist Library, Special Collections & Libraries, Drew University Libraries.

Chapter Five

Children and a Deaconess
    Lucy Rider Meyer, *Deaconess Stories* (Chicago: Hope Publishing Co., 1900).

Children and a Deaconess
    Lucy Rider Meyer, *Deaconess Stories* (Chicago: Hope Publishing Co., 1900).

Chapter Six

Lucy Rider Meyer and Josiah Shelley Meyer
    Isabelle Horton, *High Adventure: Life of Lucy Rider Meyer* (New York: Methodist Book Concern, 1928).

Sister Dora Stephenson, Deaconess, Wesley Deaconess Order
    Material from the Methodist collection deposited at The John Rylands Research Institute and Library is used with the permission of The John Rylands University Librarian and Director of the University of Manchester Library and The Trustees for Methodist Church Purposes (The Methodist Church in Britain).

Chapter Seven

Anna Hall, Deaconess, Methodist Episcopal Church
> Image courtesy of the Mission Biographical Reference Files, Hall, Anna E., The General Commission on Archives and History of The United Methodist Church, Madison, New Jersey.

First Deaconesses of the Methodist Episcopal Church South
> Portraits of Methodist Leadership and Schools, 1870's, Container: Box 3. Methodist Women Collection, 2019.017. Scarritt Bennett Center–Laskey Library and Archives.

Epilogue

Sister Elise Searle, Deaconess, Wesley Deaconess Order
> Material from the Methodist collection deposited at The John Rylands Research Institute and Library is used with the permission of The John Rylands University Librarian and Director of the University of Manchester Library and The Trustees for Methodist Church Purposes (The Methodist Church in Britain).

Sister Olive Jeffrey, Methodist Church of New Zealand
> Kei Muri Māpara/Methodist Church of New Zealand Archives Christchurch: Sister Olive Jeffrey [b.1875–d.1973], Collection: Portraits–New Zealand Methodist Deaconesses, 1902. Special Collections Box 1, Item No. Z.

ACKNOWLEDGMENTS

THIS BOOK HAS BEEN thirty years in the making. In 1994, as I wrote my first lecture for a course on the history of evangelism in the United States, I came across my first-ever reference to a Methodist deaconess. Despite growing up in the United Methodist Church (UMC), despite earning bachelor's and master's degrees at UMC institutions, I had never heard of a Methodist deaconess. And I only came across the reference by happenstance while on the hunt for women evangelists to counter the standard, historical trajectory of male evangelists, from Jonathan Edwards to Charles Finney, from Dwight L. Moody to Billy Sunday, and finally to the other Billy (Graham). The question I pursued as I prepared this lecture was simple yet monumental: Were there any women evangelists? That question led me to Iva Durham Vennard, an evangelist who began her ministry as a Methodist deaconess.

Since that day, I have published articles on the Methodist deaconess movement. At first, these studies had a focus only on the United States. Subsequent travel for research altered my perspective. I had the opportunity to spend time in the Wesley Deaconess Order Archives at the John Rylands Library in Manchester, England, as well as the Oxford Centre for Methodism and Church History at Oxford Brookes University. While on sabbatical in Germany, I researched the deaconess movement in the Martha-Maria Deaconess Organization Archives in Nuremberg. Increasingly but inevitably, I grasped the international reach of the Methodist deaconess movement, which is the perspective that shapes and suffuses this book.

Generous funding from a number of sources made possible travel to archives, as well as photocopy and translation costs. These include the following: several Sam Taylor Grants from the UMC's General

Board of Higher Education and Ministry; a Research Fellowship at the former Oxford Centre for Methodism and Church History; a Research Fellowship at the Manchester Wesley Research Centre; a Florence Ellen Bell Scholar Award from the Department of Special Collections and University Archives of the Drew University Library; several Perkins School of Theology Faculty Travel Grants; and a Southern Methodist University Travel Grant.

Many chapters were delivered first as keynote lectures for these organizations: Australasian Wesleyan Research Centre, Oxford Institute for Methodist Theological Studies, European Methodist Historical Society, John Wesley Theological Institute, Office of Deaconess and Home Missioner of the United Methodist Church, and the Wesleyan Theological Society.

I am delighted, as I look back over these thirty years, to thank a host of dear people for the immense help they provided. A remarkable coterie of scholars from across the globe graciously took their time to offer immensely beneficial feedback on my persistent questions. For their expertise and collegial support, I am grateful to Ted Campbell; Paul Chilcote; Charlie Collier; Dennis Dickerson; Chris Evans; Peter Forsaith; Bill Gibson; Trevor Hoggard; Steve Hoskins; Fred Jordan; ST Kimbrough; John Lenton; Tim Macquiban; Randy Maddox; Jenny McGill; Christy Mesaros-Winckles; Lars-Erik Nordby; Carol Noren; Glen O'Brien; Ulrike Schuler; Lynne Taylor; Geoff Treloar; Paul Trebilco; and Martin Wellings.

This book would not have come to fruition, particularly with its international reach, without the extraordinary assistance of archivists and librarians around the world. I am extremely grateful to Sarah Blair; Karis Blaker; Thomas Dobson; Jane Elder; Anthony Elia; Ellen Frost; Janet Hauck; Sally Hoover; Renate Horn; Harriet Lightman; Gareth Lloyd; Frances Lyons; Arvid Nelsen; Alex Parrish; Steve Perisho; Joon Powell; David Schmersal; Daniel Smith; Robert Tifft; and LaDonna Riddle Weber.

A handful of undergraduate and graduate students contributed their time and talent to this project in various ways. I am grateful to Andrew Klumpp and Heather Ogilvie for transcribing the deaconess diaries; Allie Shulman for writing the reflection questions and providing valuable technical assistance in the manuscript's final stages; Maddie Wiltse for editing the bibliographies and finalizing the photos; Becky Stegman for turning the printed source documents into Word documents; and Anna Lowery for translating the German source documents.

ACKNOWLEDGMENTS xvii

Methodist deaconesses maintain today their vital work of serving the church and the world, and they too have assisted and encouraged me with this project. I thank Sister Roswitha Müller for welcoming me so warmly to the Martha-Maria Archives; Leah Wandera, the first African deaconess in the UMC, for our phone conversation; Mj Andes, Sheila Faye D. Binuya, Cristina Mañabat, and Liwliwa T. Robledo for photos and statistics on Filipino UMC deaconesses; and Megan Hale, UMC deaconess in Fort Worth, Texas, for our coffee conversation, during which she turned my attention from historical deaconess documents to the current deaconess movement worldwide.

Writing a book is principally a solitary endeavor, which makes the tangible and loving support from others that much sweeter. Cherished friends, some of whom I have known since our teenage years, cheered me on to the finish line: Emily Cramer; Leslie Fight; Dustin Grabsch; Lisa Hancock; Judi Zink; my "Seattle sisters"—Jayne Engle, Beth Gerlach, Karen Henricksen, Connie Jacobson, Becky Overland, Chris Penner, and Ruth Stiling–with whom I have met monthly (now on zoom) for ten years to practice Lectio Divina together; Rob Wall and Daniel Castelo, co-editors of the Wesleyan and Methodist Exploration Book Series for Wipf & Stock and former colleagues at Seattle Pacific University; and our longtime friend and retired German Methodist pastor, Reiner Kanzleiter, who helped with several thorny translation questions.

Our cherished children, Chloe and Jeremy, fill me with such delight in their company, whether grabbing a latte with Jeremy during a writing break or having him stop by our campus apartment (we lived in a dorm as Faculty in Residence) after a videography shoot at SMU or traveling with Chloe to run a 10K race in Acadia National Park or working amiably alongside her at the dining room table when she is home from Chicago for a visit. Their love, support, and pride in who I am and what I do fills me full.

In closing, I dedicate this book to Jack, my forever love, my huckleberry friend, and my closest colleague in all that I do. Your love and companionship held me close as I worked on this book, as we talked about it *ad nauseum*, as we traveled to research it, as I told you stories about the women in it, and as you improved it significantly with your editorial prowess. After more than forty years of marriage, I fall deeper in love with you each new day. We truly are two drifters off to see the world!

ABBREVIATIONS

AME	African Methodist Episcopal Church
AMEZ	African Methodist Episcopal Zion Church
CTS	Chicago Training School
EEI	Epworth Evangelistic Institute
MEC	Methodist Episcopal Church
MECS	Methodist Episcopal Church South
MPC	Methodist Protestant Church
UK	United Kingdom
UMC	United Methodist Church
US	United States
WDO	Wesley Deaconess Order
WFMS	Woman's Foreign Missionary Society
WHMS	Woman's Home Missionary Society

OUR FIRST ORPHANAGE FAMILY
(SISTER ISABEL AND SISTER DORA IN CHARGE).

Sister Isabel Sinclair, Methodist Church of New Zealand

Sister Grace, Wesley Deaconess Order

Marguerite Decker and her class at Harris Memorial Training College, Manila

INTRODUCTION

Even before the Panama Canal opened in 1914, New Zealand native Isabel Sinclair made several steamship journeys across unforgiving seas to train and serve as a Methodist deaconess. Records are scant, but we can be sure that she spent months of her life—fifty to one hundred days per journey—waiting and wondering, as she traveled at least once to the United Kingdom and twice to the United States between 1900 and her death in 1922.[1] These arduous journeys made it possible for Sinclair to complete deaconess training in London and then to labor as a deaconess in no less than four countries—New Zealand, the United Kingdom, the United States, and Australia.

Although she was an intrepid traveler, Sinclair was by no means a pioneer. Her itinerary traced a well-oiled international Methodist deaconess pipeline, across which ideas, personnel, and communication flowed in the late nineteenth and early twentieth centuries. Sinclair's journeys, in short, illustrate the international network that characterized the early Methodist deaconess movement.

Born in South Otago in 1868, Sinclair worked for four years with Trinity Methodist Church in Dunedin as a Sister. (At the time, New Zealand Methodist deaconesses were called Sisters.) In 1900, she took her first trans-oceanic trip to London to enroll in deaconess training at Mewburn House, the newly established training school of the Wesley Deaconess Order (WDO). One of her classmates was Elizabeth Ann Pitts, whose diary in Appendix A traces daily duties, lectures, essays,

---

1. Affordability of steamship travel contributed to the international emergence of this movement. "As the century advanced, more and more people were able to go abroad, and by the 1890's they sometimes totaled 100,000 a year." Dulles, "Historical View of Americans Abroad," 13–14. I am grateful to Lynne Taylor for finding information on Isabel Sinclair.

and practical work settings she experienced while a student at Mewburn House. Pitts mentions Sinclair several times when they went out on visitation rounds together, and once when they led a missionary meeting together and prayed specifically for New Zealand and the WDO deaconess stationed there.

After completing her training, Sinclair served a three-year appointment in London at the newly built Sunfields Methodist Church in the Blackheath neighborhood. On April 24, 1903, she was consecrated as a deaconess at the Deaconess College at Ilkley, the WDO training school recently opened in the Yorkshires.[2] When she returned home to New Zealand, her WDO consecration remained intact, thanks to a committee's decision that she and her fellow New Zealander, Frances Cannon, could remain WDO deaconesses on three conditions: "(1) That they write a report of their work to the [WDO] Warden twice a year; (2) That a yearly report be received from the Superintendent minister of the circuit in which they reside; and (3) That they neither pay into nor receive benefit from the Superannuation Fund."[3] With this decision, through which the WDO extended its reach by forming a bridge between the UK and New Zealand, we see firsthand the international character of the early deaconess movement.

When she returned to New Zealand, Sinclair's next deaconess appointment was to Taranaki Street Methodist Church in Wellington and the newly opened Tory Street Mission. Here, as outlined in her 1908 report (see the source document in chapter 5), she did what deaconesses everywhere did when assigned to a city mission; she went on daily visitation rounds to minister to people struggling with addiction, unemployment, and poverty and led religious meetings, often as many as twelve a week.

In 1913, Sinclair once again took advantage of the international deaconess network and spent a year in residency at the Chicago Training School (CTS), founded and run by its longtime principal, Lucy Rider Meyer. Sinclair then returned to New Zealand to work at the South Island

---

2. Aitchison, "Overseas Mission of the Wesley Deaconess Order," 217. For more on the opening of the Deaconess College at Ilkley, see Graham, *Saved to Serve*, 244–47.

3. "Minutes of the First Meeting of Executive Committee," 204; quoted in Graham, *Saved to Serve*, 217. According to Aitchison, "For deaconesses in Australia & New Zealand, the WDO was still the goal to which many strove. Their influence and the quality of the training provided at Ilkley seem to have given them a higher profile and acceptance in the churches." Aitchison, "Overseas Mission of the Wesley Deaconess Order," 43–44.

Methodist Orphanage and Children's Home in Christchurch. When the position of Superintendent opened on July 1, 1914, she temporarily filled it, before being appointed Field Canvasser, or ambassador, on behalf of the home.[4] In 1917, she traveled back to the US to work first at a settlement house, the Neighborhood House, in New York City. Then, from 1919 to 1921, she served at the Pottsville Children's Mission in Schuylkill County, Pennsylvania. This shift required of her the capacity to work both in the impoverished conditions of a major urban center and among children in a rural setting. Such adaptation was common for deaconesses as they moved from serving in one context to another. Sinclair then made one final oceanic trip to Sydney, Australia, where she worked with the Young Women's Christian Association until her death on August 5, 1922. Her obituary captured the international character of her deaconess work in three words—she had a "singularly peripatetic career."[5]

Sinclair's travel, training, and numerous deaconess appointments in different countries were made possible by a groundbreaking *international* Methodist women's movement in the late nineteenth and early twentieth centuries, known as the Methodist deaconess movement. The purpose of this book is to identify and illuminate pivotal aspects of this international women's movement. Prior studies of this movement, which are few in number, follow the common trajectory of focusing on "the narrow confines of *national* historical traditions" that David Hempton has justifiably critiqued.[6] These studies overlooked the reality that the

---

4. Pratt, *Story of the South Island Methodist Orphanage*, 7.

5. W. J. W., "Sister Isabel Sinclair," 14.

6. Hempton, *Methodism*, 4. Italics added. Margaret McFadden expresses similar sentiments concerning the nineteenth-century transatlantic feminist movement: "Like chronological eras, national borders too often delimit the study of history, and thus a resolutely international focus creates difficulties." McFadden, *Golden Cables of Sympathy*, 7. For a selective list of resources on the Methodist deaconess movement, country by country, see the following: on Australia, Hancock, *History of the Methodist Deaconess Order* and O'Brien, *God's Willing Workers*, 99–106; on Canada, Thomas, "Servants of the Church," and McConnell, "Canadian Deaconess;" on Germany (in English), Bloedt, "Pioneering Deaconess Movement," and Herfarth, "European Roots"; on New Zealand, Chambers, *Not Self-But Others*, Tennant, "Sisterly Ministrations," and Tennant, "Pakeha Deaconesses"; on the Philippines, Robledo, "Gender, Religion, and Social Change," and Robledo and Crismo, *Celebrating A Century of God's Faithfulness*; on the UK, Graham, *Saved to Serve*; and on the US, see bibliographical entries by Dougherty, Gifford, Hartley, Keller, and Warner. See also chapters 2, 3, 5, and 7 in this book, which were published previously. Exceptions to this single-country pattern are Chilcote and Schuler, *Women Pioneers in European Continental Methodism*; Lee, *As Among the Methodists*; and Warner, "Methodist Episcopal and Wesleyan Methodist Deaconess Work."

deaconess movement, like Methodism itself, was international, with resilient connective strands stretching across many oceans and continents. In this regard, it mirrored other international late-nineteenth and early-twentieth century movements that linked multiple nations. Margaret McFadden, for instance, outlines a similar international pattern in the late nineteenth-century feminist movement, "The gradual building up of international relationships and contacts . . . across borders of nations, languages, ethnic groups, and sometimes class, intensified throughout the nineteenth century. Although this process had been going on even earlier, the transformation of travel, magazine and book dissemination, and the international post combined with nineteenth-century advances in literacy and education to create a virtual explosion in the number of physical and verbal connections between women."[7] Methodist deaconess leaders from many countries also drew on such advances to lend a distinctly international tenor to their fledgling movement.

An International Lens

Viewing the Methodist deaconess movement through an international lens allows us to comprehend two of its defining features. The first is its international character from the start, and the second is the uniformity of the movement despite its international character. These might seem to conflict with one another; in reality, the international and uniform character combination was part of its genius.

International from the Start

From the outset, Methodist leaders envisioned the deaconess movement as an international network that transcended geographical and political boundaries. This vision was evident at the Second Ecumenical Methodist Conference held in 1891 and attended by hundreds of delegates representing international Methodism, including the United Kingdom, Europe, Jamaica, New Zealand, Australia, India, South Africa, United States, and Canada. An entire session on the sixth day, under the topic of "The Church and Her Agencies," headlined deaconesses working in multiple countries. This scheduling decision underscores the import of Methodist deaconesses already at work by 1891 in many countries.

7. McFadden, *Golden Cables of Sympathy*, 3.

Further, in the major address during this session, Methodist Episcopal Church (MEC) Bishop W. X. Ninde set out in grandiose terms the global as well as the divine significance of this movement: "I am convinced of another thing—that God never will save *this world* without the large instrumentality of woman. We all believe in that."[8]

The international character at the start of the movement is also evident in three books written between 1890 and 1903 by Methodist leaders. The first book, Jane Bancroft Robinson's *Deaconesses in Europe and Their Lessons for America*, published in 1890, was a detailed study of deaconess work throughout Europe and the UK. Robinson first encountered deaconesses at the beginning of an extended sabbatical in Europe from her faculty position in history at Bryn Mawr College. Recognizing the groundbreaking possibilities for women in the MEC, she detailed her observations in a letter to several leaders of the Woman's Home Missionary Society (WHMS). With their positive response in hand, she spent her remaining sabbatical days traveling from one European deaconess community to another.

The second book, published in 1892 on the heels of Robinson's, was Lucy Rider Meyer's *Deaconesses, Biblical, Early Church, European, American*. While her summary of the international scene was briefer than Robinson's because she did not travel as widely, Meyer still presented information on deaconess work in Germany, Switzerland, France, and the UK.

The third international exposé was authored by Rev. Christian Golder, General Superintendent of German Methodist deaconess work in the US. At five hundred pages, his book, *The History of the Deaconess Movement in the Christian Church*, was the gold standard, with full, geographic coverage of Europe, the UK, and the US, as well as some locations of deaconess missionary work. Along with the international focus, he also included several significant paragraphs on Black Methodist deaconesses in the US.

Now, more than a century later, *No Man's Land* pays particular attention, like the three studies just outlined, to the international reach of the deaconess movement. In this regard, it is more comprehensive than the intervening studies, since 1903, that focus upon a single context, country, or continent. Further, following the lead of Golder, *No Man's Land* offers an analysis of Black Methodist deaconesses. There

---

8. Ninde, "Deaconess Movement," 278. Italics added.

is still much we do not know about Black deaconesses in Methodist denominations, but this book offers entrée to the topic through an analysis of data recovered principally from archives. Similarly, while this book is international in scope, it is not exhaustive in detail, and there remain archives and church collections with material relating to the international Methodist deaconess movement that still need to be consulted. My hope is that this book will prompt further publications on the movement from an international perspective.

A Uniform Character

Analyzing the deaconess movement with a particular eye to its international character allows us to grasp as well how uniform the movement was and how little it varied from country to country. This uniform character is evident in four areas: 1) a similar launch pattern in each locale (as we will see in chapter 1); 2) a similar training curriculum with a strong emphasis on biblical studies coupled with theology, church history, and evangelism (as we will see in chapter 3); 3) a similar uniform with only slight variations in the bonnet design (as we will see in chapter 4); and 4) a similar consecration service with prayers, questions for the candidates, and the laying on of hands along with the Trinitarian invocation (as we will see in chapter 7). The source of this uniformity is not difficult to pinpoint, since Methodist deaconess leaders in every country corresponded frequently with each other, visited each other's institutions, republished each other's articles with carte blanche permission, and shared fundraising techniques.

Illustrations of this international camaraderie show up in the "World-Wide Deaconess Notes" column published in the monthly CTS newsletter. The following example comes from July 1894, where the worldwide notes encompass three countries—Canada, the US, and the UK. The column begins with the introduction of Alice Thompson and Sarah King, both graduates of CTS in the US, who were sent to Canada to help open the deaconess training school in Toronto. Their assignment came about through conversations between CTS principal, Lucy Rider Meyer, and Canadian Methodist leaders about which US-trained deaconesses to tap for launching the Canadian deaconess movement. In the column, this sentence is included: "Dr. Stephenson, of London, was there and made a fine address." This one line is remarkable because it states that

Rev. Dr. Thomas Bowman Stephenson, a Wesleyan Methodist minister who founded the Wesleyan Deaconess Order in the UK, was there in Toronto observing the onset of Methodist deaconess work in Canada. The note's closing comment brings it back to the US: "Mrs. Meyer is spoken of lovingly by a great many people here." So, here at this one gathering, we see Methodist deaconess leaders from three countries assisting with each country's deaconess work.[9]

This priority of establishing an international exchange to learn from and help deaconess work to prosper everywhere bolstered the early efforts of Methodist deaconesses. As we will see in the epilogue, this international association has implications for today, because such sharing of knowledge and experiences via an international network is one of five vital practices I lift up to promote a revival in our time in Methodism worldwide.

The International Movement Then and Now

No Man's Land begins with the first initiative in German Methodism towards deaconess work as early as 1874. It then follows the movement's exponential growth in numbers and geographical expansion from the mid-1880s through the mid-1910s. Its ending point in 1918 coincides not only with the end of the First World War but also with the war's impact on women's employment and educational patterns, both of which had an appreciable impact on the deaconess movement.[10]

If we fast forward more than a century, the Methodist deaconess movement today looks vastly different from how it appeared in 1918. While there remains a remnant of Methodist deaconesses in a few European countries, including Germany and Switzerland, the Wesleyan

---

9. "World-Wide Deaconess Notes," 7.

10. Given the time frame from the deaconess movement's beginning in 1874 to its decline by 1918, the book does not include churches that had not yet merged with a Methodist church, like the Church of the United Brethren in Christ and the Evangelical Association, even though they had deaconesses. (For information on deaconesses in these two churches, see Dougherty, *My Calling to Fulfill*, 57–63 and 82–87.) Similarly, Wesleyan Holiness churches are not included, since they formed as denominations separate from Methodist churches during this time period. For information on deaconesses in the Church of the Nazarene, see Wood, "Diaconal-Dilemmas" and Ingersol, "Deaconess in Nazarene History." For information on deaconesses in the Free Methodist Church, see Mesaros-Winckles, *Silenced*, 137–41, 145–47.

Deaconess Order in the UK no longer exists.[11] Similarly, the Methodist deaconess movement launched in the late nineteenth and early twentieth centuries in New Zealand, Australia, and Canada met the same fate.[12]

In the United Methodist Church in the US, 250 active deaconesses continue their longstanding service in such varied professions as teaching, nursing, social justice ministries, hospital and hospice chaplaincy, and many aspects of local church ministry. For instance, the president and CEO of the United Way in Yellowstone County in Montana, as well as the pastoral care coordinator and organist for a United Methodist Church in Iowa, are deaconesses. In the African Methodist Episcopal Zion Church (AMEZ), deaconesses are set apart for visitation and assisting in worship in their local church. Their visitation extends to church members as well as to hospitals, jails, and nursing homes. Their tasks related to the worship service range from dressing the altar in each liturgical season to assisting in the celebration of Communion and Baptism.[13] Deaconesses in the African Methodist Episcopal Church (AME) are selected by the pastor and official board of their local church and complete a two-year deaconess training course. Following the same order of service with nearly identical wording from 1900, when the Office of Deaconess was first established (see the source document in chapter 7), AME deaconesses are consecrated. In 125 years, only one significant change has been made to the service. The AME General Conference in 2000 voted to add Rosa Parks's name to a paragraph listing "holy women." Parks, best known as a civil rights pioneer, was consecrated as a deaconess in 1964 in Saint Matthew AME in Detroit.[14]

The Philippines Annual Conference of the UMC has the highest number of deaconesses, currently at more than 550.[15] A Filipino dea-

---

11. "After a period of considerable uncertainty and widespread debate within the Methodist Church in Britain about its continued existence, the female-only Wesley Deaconess Order was reformed by the Methodist Conference of 1986 into what became known from 1988 as the Methodist Diaconal Order." Orton, "Diverse and Contested Diaconate," 267.

12. Methodism's merger with other Protestant churches, such as in Australia, precipitated the decline of Methodist deaconesses. As Bethany Hancock explains, "The Joint Commission on Church Union failed to make an acceptable proposal for a renewed diaconate before the inauguration of the Uniting Church in Australia in 1977." Hancock, *History of the Methodist Deaconess Order*, 25.

13. Hunt, *Walking in the Power of Purpose*, 32.

14. AMEC Sunday School Union, *Doctrine and Discipline*, 685. See also Dickerson, "Theologizing Rosa Parks," 35–36.

15. Email to the author from Sheila Binuya and Cristy Mañabat.

coness, Norma P. Dollaga, received the World Methodist Council's 2024 Peace Award for four decades of service focusing on peace and justice. The award recognized in particular Dollaga's efforts to establish safe havens for those targeted by extrajudicial killings in the Philippines. When expressing appreciation for her experience as a deaconess, Dollaga said, "The training and the practical ministries that nurture our spiritual and social connections with people became a helpful strength in embracing the ministry of compassion, solidarity, and action. Over time, the blending of deaconess work with social justice advocacies becomes a process of embracing prophetic witness."[16]

The Philippines is also the site of Harris Memorial College, in Manila, which continues to offer deaconess training both to Filipino and international students. The college, founded in 1903 by the Woman's Foreign Missionary Society of the Methodist Episcopal Church, welcomed its first international student, Linares Manullang, an Indonesian from Medan, Sumatra, in 1934. Soon after, it became "a multi-cultural educational institution preparing the first deaconesses for Malaysia, Indonesia, Taiwan, Okinawa, Japan, Singapore, and Sawarawk."[17] Harris Memorial College recently extended its geographic reach with the enrollment of its first African students. Their deaconess training will be pivotal to the newly launched Methodist deaconess movement in Africa. The first deaconess from an African region, Leah Wandera, was consecrated in 2022; several more African deaconesses were consecrated in 2024.[18] In these current realities, we see a geographical shift in the international deaconess movement, from its origin in Western countries to its continued emergence and strengthening in Asian and African countries. Even more, there is a change in direction from the early years when deaconesses in Western countries were sent out to serve in Asia and Africa. Now, the direction is reversed with United Methodist Filipino deaconesses working in the US and Canada.

Despite the decline of the deaconess movement in many countries, this international network of women, which shared so much from one continent to another at a time when communication was slow and travel slower still, has much to teach the contemporary church. While the lion's share of *No Man's Land* consists of historical analysis, I have opted in the epilogue to elucidate five elements from the deaconess movement that

16. Mangiduyos, "Filipino Deaconess Receives Peace Award."
17. Robledo, "Gender, Religion, and Social Change," 212.
18. Author's conversation with Deaconess Leah Wandera.

can enliven the contemporary Western church, particularly churches that share Wesleyan roots. Yet, I encourage readers not to jump there too quickly because so much that is fascinating and instructive lies in the first seven chapters as well as in the two deaconess diaries in the appendices. To help readers navigate the rest of the book, it may be useful to ascertain the lay of the land.

Reading the Chapters

Readers can approach *No Man's Land* from the beginning or the end. On the one hand, if they begin with chapter 1, they will grasp the international landscape, influential leaders, and important institutions that shaped the deaconess movement from the start. This chapter is a combination of archival work and historical analysis of the movement's broad sweep alongside illustrative anecdotes. On the other hand, if readers begin with the appendices, both of which contain annotated transcriptions of diaries written by Wesley Deaconess Order deaconesses in the UK, they will enter the quotidian existence of actual deaconesses; from this vantage point, readers will hear first from the deaconesses themselves. These diaries, which are among the only extant deaconess diaries in the world, invite readers to experience first-hand their deep emotions, their successes and failures, their courage, and their consecration to serve God, humanity, and the church.

Chapters 2 through 7, which are discrete studies that take on a different topic in each, can be read in any order. All but chapter 4 have been previously published. Chapter 2 considers the internal conflict between three deaconess leaders in the US over what activities should be prioritized and what authority should oversee the deaconess movement. Chapter 3 looks in-depth at the theological education offered to deaconesses long before women were welcomed into seminaries. Chapter 4 compares the deaconess uniform to the dress worn by Salvation Army slum sisters, Roman Catholic nuns, and fashionable women volunteering in urban ministry centers. Chapter 5 analyzes the ideology of maternalism, a strategy of mothering embraced by leading Methodist women, especially Lucy Rider Meyer, to characterize the deaconess vocation. Chapter 6 turns from women to men and examines the ways they supported the movement as bishops, benefactors, founders, authors, and husbands. Chapter 7, whose main point gives this book its title, keys in on why deaconesses existed in no man's land, despite their consecration into a recognized church office. Reflection questions at the end of each chapter will help readers assess the historical information and apply it to the contemporary context.

An Archival Adventure

No Man's Land offers a wide range of source documents curated from boxes and folders housed in an array of international archives. Alongside chapters I have written on the Methodist deaconess movement, readers will have ready access to the writings of deaconesses themselves, as well as a prayer and hymn they spoke and sang, and the original writings of two men who lent their unalloyed support to the early movement. These documents, like the movement itself, transcend geographical and national boundaries. Their points of origin cross the prime meridian and the equator. This is, to be clear, the first collection of its kind, which contains a careful and annotated curation of original writings that encompass an international perspective on this generative movement.

To engage fully these primary sources, I suggest readers follow the three-step strategy—observe, reflect, and question—recommended by the US Library of Congress.[19] First, *observe* the document. As you observe, be attentive to what you notice first, to what surprises you, or to what seems out of place. Second, *reflect* on the document. As you reflect, consider its source by asking where it came from and who the intended audience was; reflect too on what you, living in a completely different time and context, can learn from engaging with it. Third, *question* the document. As you question, consider why it was written, for what purpose, and whether you think it accomplished that purpose. In addition, reflection questions following each source document will assist readers in engaging and applying these unique writings to their context.

---

19. Library of Congress, "Teacher's Guides and Analysis Tools."

Rosa Simpson, Deaconess, Methodist Episcopal Church

Sister Laura Francis, Deaconess, Methodist Church in Australia

Chapter I

THE EMERGENCE, GROWTH, AND DECLINE OF THE INTERNATIONAL METHODIST DEACONESS MOVEMENT

Overview

THE INTERNATIONAL METHODIST DEACONESS movement—its patterns, people, and places—comes into focus through the wide-angle lens of this chapter. From Germany to the US, from Canada to the Philippines, this chapter traces the arc of its modest, almost imperceptible emergence, to its growth which became exponential in some countries, then monitors its swift decline after the First World War. It also provides a deep dive into Black Methodist deaconesses and the very different arc that unfolded for them compared to White Methodist deaconesses. The source document, aptly titled "Deaconess Mirror," comprises a list of 116 self-examination questions. A deaconess was to look in the mirror, so to speak, by reading "a few questions continuously on a daily basis and bring[ing] them prayerfully before God." These questions from the Martha-Maria Deaconess Organization in Nuremberg, Germany, take us on a deep dive into the spirituality, stability, and uniformity expected by these consecrated women in every moment of each day, even on holidays and sick days, as well as in all relationships both inside and beyond the deaconess home.

Decades before most Methodist churches had established a clear path to the ordination of women, thousands of single women in their twenties and thirties, the daughters of farmers and skilled workers, traveled from their rural homes and small towns in Europe, North America, and Australasia to a deaconess home or training school, where they received theological and practical training in preparation for becoming a Methodist deaconess.[1] Upon the church's approval, they were consecrated to the Office of Deaconess by the laying on of hands by a bishop or minister during a public worship service. They lived in community with other deaconesses and devoted themselves to service (*diakonia* in Greek, hence the term deaconess),[2] particularly with the urban poor, as teachers, nurses, evangelists, pastors, administrators, missionaries, and social service workers.[3]

1. The path to women's ordination in a Methodist church opened first in the Methodist Protestant Church (MPC) in the US when Helenor M. Davisson was ordained in 1866. In the Primitive Methodist Connexion (1807-1934) and the Bible Christian Connexion (1815-1907) in the UK, there were itinerant women preachers active before the emergence of the deaconess movement; however, these women were not ordained. "Throughout the nineteenth century, even at the height of female evangelism in the 1820s and 1830s, women were excluded from the official ministry, first informally, and then by denying them access to the education and training necessary for reception into 'full Connexion,' the term used for recognition of professional ministerial status." Lloyd, *Women and the Shaping of British Methodism*, 4.

In her expansive study of the ecumenical deaconess movement in the US, Jenny Legath claims that "the deaconess story is not the story of women's ordination," and she critiques those who would make it so. "In their search for a usable past, clergywomen and women's historians have looked to the deaconesses as early advocates for the ordination of women.... In contrast, this book argues from the sources that the vast majority of women who became deaconesses were not terribly interested in ordination." Still, Legath assesses that "the history of deaconesses helps us to understand women's complicated struggle for ecclesiastical equality..." Legath, *Sanctified Sisters*, 5. I agree that shining a spotlight on deaconesses displays an array of gender inequities in the church in the late nineteenth and early twentieth centuries. I question, however, her claim that deaconesses simply were not interested in ordination because it is impossible to know precisely why. How does one assess why they did not more readily pursue an option unavailable to them? Perhaps it was not disinterest, as Legath claims, as much as their being frightened by the relentless persecution that fell on those few women who did pursue ordination, like Anna Howard Shaw, as explained in chapter 3.

2. The key biblical text for the deaconess movement as it emerged in the nineteenth century was Rom 16:1-2: "I commend to you our sister Phoebe, a deacon (*diakonos*) of the church at Cenchreae, so that you may welcome her in the Lord as is fitting for the saints, and help her in whatever she may require from you, for she has been a benefactor of many and of myself as well."

3. The majority of deaconess work occurred in cities. According to Legath, "almost 75 percent of all deaconess institutions, and all but two of the institutions that trained deaconesses, were in cities." Legath, *Sanctified Sisters*, 38. For this reason, some

Methodist deaconesses in every country fit the profile outlined by Methodist Episcopal Church (MEC) Bishop James Thoburn: "a Christian woman who is providentially disentangled from all other matters and can give all her time and talent to the Christian church. She offers herself to the church without any reservation. If she be given food and clothing and work, she will give all her energies in return. She does not stipulate in what direction she will work."[4] Each Methodist deaconess, while embodying Thoburn's generic description, placed her own stamp on this work.

> **Louise Schneider** was a deaconess in the Martha-Maria Organization, founded in 1889 in Nuremberg, Germany, under the auspices of the German Wesleyan Methodists. She, along with Elise Heidner, began the work, and within four years, they were able to purchase their own property. A decade later, they built a clinic on the property; then, in 1907, it had to be doubled in size.[5] Schneider served as Mother Superior in Nuremberg for several decades.
>
> **Laura Francis** penned a letter to Rev. W. G. Taylor of the Central Methodist Mission in Sydney, Australia, offering to work for the mission. The story goes that she threatened to join the Salvation Army, "if there was no avenue of service for her in her own Church."[6] Taylor responded favorably, and in 1890, Francis entered the first Sisters of the People home, the early name for Methodist deaconesses in Australia.[7] After several

---

historians situate the deaconess movement in the US as integral to the Social Gospel Movement. See Dougherty, "Social Gospel According to Phoebe," 356–68; Legath, *Sanctified Sisters*, 23–30; Schmidt, *Grace Sufficient*, 206–8; and Shaver, "Deaconess Identity," 216–19. Still, there were Methodist deaconesses assigned to work on river boats and in mining towns, lumber camps, seaports, small towns, and villages.

4. Thoburn, "Deaconesses and the Church," 6. It is important to note, however, that there were Methodist women in other organizations doing similar work as deaconesses who also fit Thoburn's description. One example was the Sisters of the People, an organization founded by Katherine Hughes under the auspices of the Wesleyan West London Mission while her spouse, the Rev. Hugh Price Hughes, was head of the mission. For a comparison of deaconesses and Sisters of the People, see Lloyd, *Women and the Shaping of British Methodism*, 250–55, 259–60, and Walters, "Methodist Brotherhoods and Sisterhoods," 278.

5. *50 Jahre Diakonissenarbeit*, 6.

6. Chambers, *Not Self–But Others*, 14.

7. An article about Francis and other Australian deaconesses in the CTS newsletter explained that "they are called Methodist 'Sisters,' but their work and indeed organization is very similar to that of deaconesses in America." "World-Wide Deaconess Notes. Deaconesses in Australia," 4.

years in Sydney, she went to Auckland, New Zealand, to work with the Helping Hand Mission. There, she founded Door of Hope, a hostel on Cook Street, where prostitutes and unwed mothers could stay.

Jane Blakeley was the first Methodist deaconess in New Zealand. In 1890, she began visiting the poor in conjunction with the Helping Hand Mission at Freeman's Bay, a work started by Pitt Street Methodist Church, known as the Cathedral of Auckland Methodism.[8] Methodist deaconess work in New Zealand expanded over the next decade into other cities, such as Dunedin, Christchurch, and Wellington. Blakeley and her sister deaconesses were inspired by their order's motto, *Non Sibi Sed Aliis*–"Not for self, but for others."[9]

Alice Thompson, an 1894 Chicago Training School (CTS) graduate, became the first Superintendent of the Toronto Deaconess Home and Training School when it opened at 28 McGill Street in 1894; her classmate, Sarah King, joined her as a resident deaconess in the new home. The connection between the two schools remained strong; CTS supplied seven of the first twenty-seven deaconesses in Canadian Methodism.[10]

Louise Golder, as a teenager growing up in Germany, visited her aunt, who was a deaconess in Stuttgart. After that experience, she dreamed of becoming a deaconess nurse. Before coming to the US to join the Christ Hospital staff in Cincinnati, Ohio, in 1895, she had already studied nursing in five European institutions. Later, with six other nurses from Germany, "she formed the nucleus of Bethesda Hospital [in Cincinnati], which developed to be the greatest single institution in German [-speaking] Methodism."[11]

Elise Searle was elected to the Board of Guardians in 1895 in Norwich, England. As a member of the relief committee, she worked to change the diet of those classified as "infirm" to nourish them with better food. She also increased the supply of towels

---

8. Fry, *Out of the Silence*, 99. For the Pitt Street nomenclature, see Morley, *History of Methodism in New Zealand*, 206. For more on the Freeman's Bay Mission, see Morley, *History of Methodism in New Zealand*, 219–20.

9. Chambers, *Not Self–But Others*, 16.

10. Thomas, "Servants of the Church," 378.

11. Douglass, *Story of German Methodism*, 143. For more on Louise Golder, see Dougherty, *My Calling To Fulfill*, 49–54.

at the local hospital and improved food at the workhouse.[12] As a Wesley Deaconess Order (WDO) deaconess entrusted with providing spiritual care, she would slip out of board meetings and lead those waiting in line for monetary help in a familiar hymn, like "Jesu, lover of my soul," and "Safe in the arms of Jesus."[13]

Jeanie Banks became a WDO deaconess evangelist in 1896 after working in the East London Mission for several years. She traveled to preach the gospel throughout the UK, including summers in the Scottish Isles, where she preached and provided medical care. Everywhere she went, she worked to revitalize Methodist class meetings.[14]

Marie Bagger was one of three women tapped to start a Methodist deaconess work in Oslo, Norway, in 1897. Born in Denmark, she took nursing courses in Copenhagen and traveled to the US to work with the mentally ill and to the UK to work with people living in impoverished communities. She brought this vast experience to her deaconess work at the *Søsterhjemmet Bethanien* in Oslo. Then, in 1903, she moved into a slum area of Oslo and cared "for the most vulnerable children and their mothers in the District."[15]

Mattie Wright was an 1897 graduate of Scarritt Bible and Training School in Kansas City, Missouri. She was consecrated in 1903 in the first class of Methodist Episcopal Church, South deaconesses. In a 1904 report, she proudly claimed that the time spent "playing snowball and skating on the ice with these boys were as profitably spent as any I have given to visiting the sick" because such "innocent enjoyment" is vital in the Christian life.[16]

Anna E. Hall was one of the first Black women to complete a one-year certificate at the New England Training School in Boston. The following year, in 1902, she was consecrated as a deaconess by Bishop Walden in Atlanta. She served for several years at her alma mater, the Thayer Industrial School, an institution of the Woman's Home Missionary Society (WHMS) of the

---

12. Searle, "Notes from Norwich," 118–19.

13. Searle, "Unique Congregation," 136.

14. Integral to the development and discipleship of the early Methodist movement were the class meetings, which consisted of twelve to fifteen members of a Methodist society meeting weekly with their class leader for spiritual assessment, direction, challenge, and encouragement.

15. Nordby, "Marie Bagger," 206.

16. Dougherty, *My Calling To Fulfill*, 73.

Methodist Episcopal Church (MEC). When a training school for Black deaconesses opened in Atlanta in 1904, she was sent to assist until influenza broke out and the school closed. In 1906, she left the US to become a missionary in Liberia, where she remained for twenty-five years.[17]

Rosa Simpson, the longest-serving Black Methodist deaconess in the US, was consecrated in 1904. She worked as the WHMS Organizer in the Texas Annual Conference of the MEC for 32 years until her retirement in 1936. For seven MEC General Conferences from 1908–1932, she was elected as a lay delegate from the Texas Annual Conference.

Fidela Gatdula, a Filipino deaconess in the first graduating class, in 1907, of Harris Memorial Training School in Manila, undertook an arduous journey to a remote town, San Jose, Nueva Ecija, to serve in four-month stays. "She journeyed by train up to the town of Cabanatuan, the end of the railway line, and from there began a forty-mile trek on 'carabao [a domestic farm animal] back' through deep mud and water."[18] Gatdula engaged in visitation in the town, taught Sunday School and weekly classes for women and children, assisted the pastor, and trained the pastor's wife how to teach the Bible.

Grace Crump sailed on the *SS Oranto* from the UK in 1914 to take charge of the Training Home for Deaconesses in Christchurch, New Zealand. She transformed the home to become not only a home for deaconesses but also a hostel for women students and a meeting place for women's groups and mission-based organizations. Before returning to the UK two years later, she instituted the first Deaconess Convocation in New Zealand.[19]

This miscellany of Methodist deaconesses, whose greatest influence spanned a half-century and more than half the globe, documents a sliver of the thousands of women who took up the mantle—the curriculum, the commitment, and the costume—of the Methodist deaconess movement. While they shared a common vocation, they exercised that vocation, that calling, that mission in countless ways and myriad places. The studies in this book expose and explore the stories, many still untold, of this international women's movement.

---

17. For more on Hall, see McGill, "Legacy of Anna E. Hall," 92–103.
18. Robledo, "Gender, Religion and Social Change," 120–21.
19. Chambers, *Not Self–But Others*, 25.

The Emergence of the International Methodist Deaconess Movement

The association between Methodism and deaconesses originated during John Wesley's brief sojourn in Georgia, where, according to Paul Chilcote, "Wesley conducted his initial experiments in the use of women in the life of that infant, colonial church." Chilcote asserts that a "particularly controversial practice" among these experiments, which included extemporaneous prayer and preaching and the utilization of lay leaders, was his provision for deaconesses.[20] Methodist historians puzzle over whether Wesley ever appointed deaconesses, but they agree that he *intended* to appoint women as deaconesses so they could assist in the immersion baptism of female converts. Geordan Hammond finds strong evidence that Wesley mentored his close friend, Margaret Bovey, in deaconess work so that she could minister to Native American women.[21]

Upon his return to England, Wesley encouraged women to be visitors of the sick, perhaps as a means to reinstitute what he considered to be the early church's ministry of deaconesses. In his sermon, "On Visiting the Sick," we see this connection in detail. "8. It is well known, that, in the primitive Church, there were women particularly appointed for this work. Indeed there was one or more such in every Christian congregation under heaven. They were then termed Deaconesses, that is, servants; servants of the Church, and of its great Master."[22]

Visitation of the sick for Wesley extended beyond the physical to encompass the domain of soul care, which he considered to be of "infinitely greater importance." He suggested this two-pronged approach:

---

20. Chilcote, *John Wesley and the Women Preachers of Early Methodism*, 22. See also Hammond, *John Wesley in America*, 136–39.

21. Hammond, *John Wesley in America*, 137. In a summary statement about Wesley's intention to include women in his work in Georgia, Hammond declares, "He was taking advantage of the lack of episcopal oversight in Georgia to encourage women to engage in ministry to an extent that was far from customary within the Church of England." Hammond, *John Wesley in America*, 138–39. Wesley found precedent for developing an order of deaconesses from the Moravian church, a group with whom he fellowshipped while sailing onboard the *Simmonds* and continued to while in the Georgia colony. Moravian deaconesses held substantial leadership roles, particularly for the spiritual nurture and oversight of women and girls. Even beyond their work with women, Moravian deaconesses, for a time, "shared top governing responsibility in the many settlements and missions that Moravians developed around the world during the mid-1700s by serving on local Elders Conferences along with men." Smaby, "'Only Brothers,'" 135.

22. Wesley, "On Visiting the Sick."

First, care for the body, then "inquire concerning their souls. And here you have a large field before you; you have scope for exercising all the talents God has given you." Later in his sermon, Wesley called on all to visit the sick, especially women. To emphasize his point, he cited Gal 3:28 (in which Paul declared "There is no longer male and female; for all of you are one in Christ Jesus"). Wesley appealed as well to Phoebe in Rom 16:1 (in which Paul declared "I commend to you our sister Phoebe, a deacon of the church at Cenchreae") and the early church's practice to appoint women to this work.[23] Despite Wesley's continued interest in deaconesses, however, nothing formal or official developed along these lines within Methodism for more than a century.

Not until 1874 did the Methodist deaconess movement finally begin with the founding of the *Bethanienverein, Diakonissenverein für allgemeine Krankenpflege* (Bethany Association, Deaconess Society for Medical Care and Nursing) under the auspices of the MEC in Germany. Two years later, the Motherhouse of the Bethany Association established the first permanent deaconess station in Frankfurt am Main. In total, three separate German Methodist deaconess organizations, each with headquarters in a different city—Frankfurt am Main, Elberfeld, and Nuremberg—were launched between 1874 and 1889.[24] All three expanded Methodist deaconess work into more cities and more European countries in the ensuing years. For instance, the Martha-Maria Deaconess Organization, founded in Nuremberg in 1889, expanded within three years to Munich (1889), Vienna (1890), and Magdeburg (1892).[25]

The emergence of the Methodist deaconess movement in Germany, rather than elsewhere in the world, can be traced to the influence of Kaiserswerth, where the modern Protestant deaconess movement commenced several decades earlier in 1836. In Kaiserswerth, a small town on the Rhine River six miles from Düsseldorf, Rev. Theodore Fliedner, a Lutheran minister, founded a deaconess Motherhouse with a wide-ranging outreach, particularly in nursing. Kaiserswerth grew exponentially in size, stature, and influence. By 1910, the numbers associated with the Kaiserswerth Conference were staggering: 84 mother-houses, 7,216 substations, and close to 20,000 deaconesses.[26]

23. Wesley, "On Visiting the Sick." See Rowe, "Ministry of Deacons in Methodism," 343–46.
24. Bloedt, "Pioneering Deaconess Movement in Germany," 50.
25. Bloedt, "Pioneering Deaconess Movement in Germany," 54.
26. Briggs, "Restoration of the Order of Deaconesses," 382–83.

Kaiserswerth's reputation as a "transnational space" stems from the number of international visitors who spent time there to observe deaconesses at work.[27] Florence Nightingale, for example, first observed deaconesses as nurses when she visited in 1850 and again in 1851. Her pamphlet, *The Institution of Kaiserswerth on the Rhine for the Training of Deaconesses*, published anonymously in 1851, broadcast widely the existence of this deaconess institution.[28] International Methodist luminaries who visited Kaiserwserth included a host of Americans, such as Belle Harris Bennett, Lucy Rider Meyer, Josiah Meyer, Jane Bancroft Robinson, Bishop Matthew Simpson, Isabella Thoburn, Bishop James Thoburn, and Annie Wittenmyer. Methodists from other countries also stayed there to learn about deaconess work, including the Rev. Dr. Thomas Bowman Stephenson, founder of the Wesley Deaconess Order (WDO) in the UK;[29] the Rev. W. G. Taylor, an Australian Methodist minister who initiated deaconess work in Sydney; and Louise Golder, the first German Methodist deaconess in the US, who studied nursing at Kaiserswerth.

From Germany, the Methodist deaconess movement crossed the Atlantic to Chicago, where Lucy Rider Meyer, founder of the Chicago Training School for City, Home, and Foreign Missions and the Chicago Deaconess Home (CTS), welcomed the school's first students in October 1885. Three years later, the Methodist Episcopal Church (MEC) established the Office of Deaconess by a vote of General Conference, the highest legislative body of the denomination. By the end of the decade, new Methodist deaconess ventures in the US were set up to reach non-English speakers. In 1888, when English-speaking Methodists opened the Elizabeth Gamble Deaconess Home in Cincinnati, Ohio, they also requested assistance from native German speakers, since the city's German-speaking population at the turn of the twentieth century exceeded 50 percent. Louise Golder volunteered, and within a short time, fifteen more German-speaking deaconesses were admitted to the Elizabeth Gamble Deaconess Home.[30]

27. Kreutzer and Nolte, "Deaconesses in Nursing Care," 8.

28. Nightingale, *Institution of Kaiserswerth*. See Dietz, "Deaconess Movement and Professional Nursing," 117.

29. Stephenson returned home and developed a deaconess work after being "deeply impressed" with Kaiserswerth deaconesses. Bradfield, *Life of the Reverend Thomas Bowman Stephenson*, 284–85. For more on Kaiserswerth's influence on the Methodist deaconess movement, see Herfarth, "European Roots," 65–82, and Aitchison, "Overseas Mission of the Wesley Deaconess Order," 36–37.

30. Douglass, *Story of German Methodism*, 141.

Over the next decade, Methodist deaconess work began in other countries, for instance, in Australia (1890), New Zealand (1890), the UK (1890), Canada (1893), Norway (1897), Sweden (1900), the Philippines (1903), and Denmark (1907).[31] In the US, two additional Methodist churches—the African Methodist Episcopal Church (AME) in 1900 and the Methodist Episcopal Church South (MECS) in 1902—each authorized an Office of Deaconess.

The expansion of this international movement coincided with seismic changes for women in all areas of society, from higher education to increased professional opportunities to women's right to vote. More women than ever, nearly six million in the United States Census of 1900, earned wages outside the home. "Between 1890 and 1900 the number of women in industry increased faster than the number of men in industry. *It increased faster than the birth rate.*"[32] As to suffrage—the right to vote—New Zealand was the first country to grant women's suffrage in 1893. The following year, suffrage passed in South Australia for White women. In 1906, Finland became the first European country to grant women's suffrage, and by 1915, the vote for women's suffrage had passed in most Scandinavian countries.[33] In the UK, despite the publicly disruptive, sometimes violent, tactics of the suffrage movement under the motto, "Deeds not words," women's suffrage did not pass until 1918. The following year, women's suffrage became law in the US with the passing of the Nineteenth Amendment.

---

31. I am grateful to Lars-Erik Nordby for information on Methodist deaconesses in Scandinavian countries. India is not included in this country list, despite Bishop Thoburn's claim that Methodist deaconesses were established there by the late nineteenth century. Elizabeth Meredith Lee dismissed his claim and offered this explanation: "At the 1889 Annual Conference of North India the deaconess work was discussed. At that meeting, Miss Lucy Sullivan 'was recognized as a deaconess,' and also Miss Phoebe Rowe, who had been born and brought up in India and became a missionary of the Woman's Foreign Missionary Society in that field. These women could not have been authorized deaconesses for in 1889 no deaconesses had been commissioned by the Methodist Episcopal Church. The four women, thus named in India, are officially listed as foreign missionaries ... Evidently, Bishop Thoburn, in his zeal for the cause, had given the title 'deaconess' to the foreign missionaries as an unofficial act. The 1888 General Conference had declined his plea to have deaconesses ordained in India." Lee ends her lengthy discussion with this statement: "deaconess work never became an indigenous movement in India.... Many Indian women were trained and engaged in church work, but 'Bible Woman' was the title given them." Lee, *As Among the Methodists*, 104.

32. Dorr, *What Eight Million Women Want*; quoted in Hofstadter, *Progressive Movement*, 84.

33. Sulkunen, "International Comparison of Women's Suffrage," 89.

The impact on women of the suffrage movement exceeded that of the right to vote, as Anne O'Brien explains for the Australian context: it "inspired women to become involved outside of their usual social spheres. At the same time, churches were experiencing a need for labor within the church because men were drifting away from church jobs. Protestant churches began to employ women to work independently as missionaries and deaconesses to fulfill labor needs without completely usurping male clergy."[34]

Methodist deaconesses were heavily recruited during this era, in which Protestant churches attempted "to solve the *social question*," particularly for the urban poor, whose already dire living conditions worsened with rampant industrialization.[35] In Germany, for example, a seismic migration from rural to urban industrial areas took place, and by 1910, only 40 percent of the population remained in the countryside.[36] In the UK, innovations in technology, science, and industry arrived in company with urban pollution, child labor abuses, poverty, and disease.[37] Across the Atlantic, in the US, the rate of immigration reached 800,000 people annually. Immigrants arrived with their own "dress, language, customs, and religions," which seemed "threatening to older-stock Americans."[38] In reaction, Congregational minister and one-time General Secretary of the Evangelical Alliance, Josiah Strong, ranked immigration as the first of seven perils facing America.[39]

These complex realities raised a pivotal question for Methodist churches about how, particularly in urban areas, to keep their membership intact while simultaneously serving and evangelizing so many people, many from other countries, with pressing needs.[40] The answer, for

---

34. O'Brien, *God's Willing Workers*, 31–32.

35. Kreutzer and Nolte, "Deaconesses in Nursing Care," 8.

36. Geary, "Germany."

37. Two contributing factors that gave rise to the deaconess movement in the UK were "crowded conditions in cities especially in the slum areas; [and] catastrophes in agriculture 1875–1899 which drove people from the land to seek work in expanding manufacturing industries." Staton, "Development of Diaconal Ministry," 3.2.

38. Buenker, "Introduction to Chapter Six," 300. See also Bennett, *Party of Fear*, 163–79.

39. Strong, *Our Country*, 52. See also Deichmann, "Forging an Ideology for American Missions," 163–91.

40. This book focuses on Methodist deaconesses working in home mission as opposed to foreign mission. For resources on Methodist deaconesses who served as foreign missionaries, see Graham, *Saved to Serve*, 98–211, McGill, "Legacy of Anna E. Hall," Pope-Levison, "Role of Deaconess Training Schools," and Robert, *American Women in Mission*, 152–59.

visionary leaders, lay in a previously untapped resource—single Methodist women ready and eager to engage full-time in religious work. One such leader, Bishop James Thoburn, boasted that Methodist deaconesses were the solution to urban evangelism and ministry.

> Only last Tuesday I received a letter from England inviting me to turn aside for a day on my way back to India and preach to a congregation of a thousand persons gathered together by a band of deaconess sisters in the city of Brighton. The churches of that city are discussing the question which is discussed in every great city in England and America, as to what we can do for the masses. While they are discussing these women are working. What they have done in Brighton can be repeated in New York. The New Testament gift of prophecy is coming back again in its fullness to the Christian Church, and by the time that you have two or three hundred anointed deaconesses in this city [New York City], with hearts all aglow and lips touched with living flame, going among the people and speaking for Jesus, you will hear less of the despairing question, "How can we reach the masses?"[41]

A coalescence of the groundswell of women's activity outside of the traditional, familial sphere, the predominance of women involved in church activities, and pressing social needs combined to make becoming a deaconess, particularly for women from the lower to middle classes, an attractive option, with its educational and practical training in a profession. As Ruth Esther Meeker notes in her decades-long study of the Woman's Home Missionary Society (WMHS), "The [deaconess] movement was timely. The church was ready for an emphasis on the evangelism of the city. It was a new career field for women. And it offered special training."[42] In return, being a deaconess helped women achieve social and economic advancement. Mareike Bloedt explains for the German context that becoming a deaconess provided a way for single women to be "equal in status to a married woman"; with this opportunity, such women "attained financial security."[43]

MEC deaconess and training school founder, Iva Durham Vennard, picked up on similar themes. She expressed the hope that with the

---

41. Thoburn, *Deaconess and Her Vocation*, 113–14.
42. Meeker, *Six Decades of Service*, 93.
43. Bloedt, "Pioneering Deaconess Movement in Germany," 49.

dawning of a new century, there would be wider opportunities, through which women, particularly in the church, would finally move beyond their "very narrow sphere."

> The nineteenth century will stand out in history as "the discoverer of woman" and it is for the womanhood of this twentieth century to prove what this discovery shall mean. No longer cramped by the old time notions of a woman's very narrow sphere, our girls today find wide open doors for culture and education and travel. They may enter business if they choose, and the professions are inviting them. But in no realm of activity does the door swing wider than to Christian service. The Church is recognizing the necessity of the labor of trained, capable, spiritual women, and today she offers a magnificent opening for her consecrated daughters.[44]

The Growth of the International Methodist Deaconess Movement

It is possible to discern an emergent, if provisional, pattern for the inauguration and growth of the movement. This pattern includes early advocates, modest beginnings, and a dramatic impact. While this pattern is not airtight, it is characteristic of the sequence in many countries and, consequently, worthy of illustration.

Early Advocates

Typically, an advocate or group of advocates stepped up to introduce the idea of deaconesses to their constituencies. Some were clergymen, like Thomas Bowman Stephenson, a Wesleyan Methodist minister, who created the Wesley Deaconess Order (WDO) in 1890 after realizing the need for more trained women workers to staff the Children's Home in south London, which he had founded two decades earlier. Chicago pastors in the Norwegian-Danish Conference of the MEC launched a committee to explore deaconess work in 1892, and they appointed Dina Mellum to begin visiting the poor and the sick.[45] Under the leadership of the Rev. Christian Golder, deaconess work began in 1896 among German

---

44. Vennard, "Appeal to Young Women," 8.
45. Andersen, *Salt of the Earth*, 174.

Methodists in Cincinnati, and in the African Methodist Episcopal Church (AME), Rev. Reverdy Ransom's impassioned pleas and advocacy first brought deaconesses to the church's attention.

Another source of advocacy, particularly in the US, were Methodist laywomen. Jane Bancroft Robinson and Lucy Rider Meyer, for example, were leading advocates of the MEC deaconess movement, although they championed conflicting visions of how it should be developed, which we will discuss in chapter 2. In the Methodist Episcopal Church South (MECS), Belle Harris Bennett, President of the Woman's Foreign Missionary Society (WFMS) and Woman's Home Missionary Society (WHMS) used her stature and influence to help pass legislation to establish the MECS Office of Deaconess at the 1902 General Conference.

Modest Beginnings

Advocacy, when successful, invariably led to the establishment of a deaconess home or training school. Such beginnings were modest. The oldest Motherhouse of Methodist deaconesses in Germany, in Frankfurt am Main, began in April 1876 with one deaconess, who lived in the minister's study in the Methodist church on the Kornmarkt.[46] The Chicago Training School (CTS) commenced with five students in 1885. In Sydney, Australia, a home opened on August 9, 1890, with four women: Sisters Mary Bibby (Sister in Charge), Emily Gannon, Ada Atkins, and Laura Francis.[47] When the MECS approved the Order of Deaconess in 1902, it had the advantage of tapping Scarritt Bible & Training School, founded more than a decade earlier, as the approved school, along with its intact student body. The first class of five MECS deaconesses—Mattie M. Wright, Amy Rice, Annie Heath, Elizabeth R. Davis, and Anabel Weigel—consecrated by Bishop Eugene R. Hendrix on April 19, 1903, consisted exclusively of Scarritt alumnae. That same year, the Methodist deaconess movement began in the Philippines when the Woman's Foreign Missionary Society (WFMS) of the MEC purchased an old Spanish house and established a training school in Manila. It too had a modest beginning with an initial enrollment of four girls between the ages of 14 and 16, who came from Tagalog-speaking towns around Manila.

---

46. *50 Jahre Diakonissenarbeit*, 4.
47. Chambers, *Not Self-But Others*, 14.

A Dramatic Impact

Despite modest beginnings, the movement's growth in some cases would prove to be astonishing. As noted earlier, by 1891, the Martha-Maria Deaconess Organization, founded only three years earlier in Nuremberg, had already expanded to three more cities in Germany and Austria. In a year's report from ten deaconess nurses sent out in private nursing from Martha-Maria, they reported these statistics: "551 days; 899 days and nights; and 813 nights spent in nursing from July 1891 to July 1892; of this time 202 days, 596 days and nights and 217 nights, besides 321 hours and 1921 visits to the sick poor were given free."[48]

Across the ocean, in the US, the Woman's Home Missionary Society (WHMS) of the MEC in 1900 reported "under its direction 32 deaconess institutions—homes, schools, and hospitals. It has more than 300 deaconesses and students preparing for the work, and property valued at $321,000."[49] This amounts to over eleven million dollars in 2025. In 1908, fourteen years after German-speaking Methodist deaconess work began in Cincinnati, Ohio, Sisters Gross and Schuster tallied these statistics for the year: "1050 visits and 150 house-to-house calls in Cincinnati; they distributed 600 tracts and pieces of Christian literature, 250 pieces of clothing, 60 bouquets of flowers, 8 Bibles, 50 baskets of eatables and $10 in cash. They nursed the poor for 40 days and 6 nights, and spent 110 hours at the Milk Station."[50]

In Dunedin, New Zealand, Sister Alice, the Central Mission Nursing Sister, made a staggering number of visits—1,650—in 1907 to the poor and the sick; this number averages out to 31 visits per week. "All her [Sister Alice's] mornings, and frequently whole days, have been devoted to sick visiting and nursing. Chronic cases have been attended to as a rule once a day, and acute cases oftener.... The telephone at 4 Fernhill Street is kept ringing all day by applicants for aid from Sister Alice."[51]

The statistics compiled below by the Superintendent of the Toronto Methodist deaconess work illuminate not only extensive numerical statistics, but also an expansive breadth of work, including religious visitation for prayer and Bible study in homes, hospitals, and jails, nursing

---

48. Dreyer, "German Deaconess Echoes," 7.
49. Lee, *As Among the Methodists*, 38.
50. *German Methodist Deaconess Home and Bethesda Hospital*, 26.
51. Chambers, *Not Self-But Others*, 20.

the sick, and taking children for homestays or day-long outings to the countryside in what was known as Fresh Air work.[52]

Superintendent's Statistics
May 1, 1909, to April 30, 1910
There are twenty-two Deaconesses working in this Conference, twenty-one in Toronto and one in Collingwood.

Number of	Canvassing calls	10,950
	Missionary and parish calls	16,219
	Calls upon the sick	9,816
	Business calls	2,606
	Calls received at the Home	1,871
Total number of calls		41,462
Number of papers and tracts distributed		7,012
	...	
	New garments distributed	2,503
	Half-worn garments distributed	10,258
	...	
	Bouquets of flowers distributed	1,075
	Families supplied with fuel	57
	Children taken to Whitby	472
	Persons given a day's outing	1,055
Persons for whom work was secured		423
Number of times teaching in the Sunday School		1,398
	Teaching in Kitchen Garden	116
	In Sewing School	917
	Meetings in hospitals, prisons or infirmaries	27
	Mothers' or cottage meetings	270

52. The Montreal Conference's deaconess report included this description of their Fresh Air work: "A fifty-acre farm, sixty-five miles from Montreal, fourteen hundred feet up in the Laurentian Mountains, will give this summer to one thousand women and children, in parties of two hundred, a two weeks' holiday, without a cent of expense to any one of them, and a Boys' Club of some sixty lads, whose homes are non too bright or happy, and who have been busy with gymnasium, games and the gospel during the winter, will have a free two weeks' outing." *Annual Report of the Deaconess Society of the Methodist Church*, 75. For another firsthand account of Fresh Air Work, see Masters's diary in Appendix B.

Children's or temperance meetings	185
...	
Hours spent in nursing	2,296
In sewing	12
In class work	18,458[53]

Again, this is not a fixed pattern, but it reflects a common international experience. Advocates led to the founding of institutions, which led, in ways both dramatic and modest, to an impact that extended well beyond the comparatively few women who populated these earliest Methodist deaconess institutions.

Black Methodist Deaconesses in the US

The Methodist deaconess movement in the US, in particular, ought not to be seen exclusively as a movement of White women. It also unfolded, though with a divergent narrative, among Black women, including those within the predominantly White Methodist Episcopal Church. Black women already had to endure horrific Jim Crow laws that emboldened racism to operate freely in every sphere of daily and national life. In addition, specific to the deaconess movement, there was never established even one permanent training school for Black women who aspired to become a deaconess. While White women were able to study at many institutions across the country dedicated to their preparatory deaconess training, Black women did not have access to one training school that stayed open for longer than two to three years before it closed.

Every attempt to establish a Black deaconess training school remained underfunded. For instance, Rev. Walter Riley, a graduate of Gammon Theological Seminary and pastor of Mount Zion Church in Cincinnati, Ohio, and his wife began a training school in their living room at 1033 E. McMillan St. Riley described the school he administered to the audience gathered for the 1901 national Woman's Home Missionary Society (WHMS) meeting. He reported that seven young women "were at work during the day, and had to study and recite in the evenings." Despite working double shifts—during the day as an employee, then as a student at night—these seven women still compiled these statistics in the

---

53. *Annual Report of the Deaconess Society of the Methodist Church*, 9.

school's first year: "Over one thousand missionary calls were made, help was given to twenty-five needy families, employment found for seventy-five persons, and more than one hundred people brought to the Church and Sunday-school."[54] Four women were graduated from Riley's school: Dixie Malissa Riley, Mary E. Poindexter, Rowena Howard, and Martha Jane Joiner. When WHMS funds waned, to make up the financial gap, Riley even donated two hundred dollars of his own to keep the fledgling school in existence. Nevertheless, the home-grown training school closed in 1904 due to lack of funding.

The WHMS attempted another training school for Black women in Atlanta in 1904. Anna E. Hall, along with her classmate from the New England Training School, Martha Drummer, were sent to help out, but, shortly after they arrived, influenza broke out. Within two years, both Hall and Drummer had left the US to become missionaries in Africa.[55] The lack of a training school no doubt had an impact on the numerical growth of Black Methodist deaconesses. In 1904, the year Riley's school closed and the training school in Atlanta opened, the number of Black deaconesses in the MEC reached its apex at twelve.[56] Available data suggest something startling: though there were only twelve Black deaconesses in the MEC in 1904, this was significantly more than in any other Black Methodist denomination.

Without a dedicated deaconess training school, three Black Methodist women "with splendid literary preparation and religious devotion" were sent in 1913 by the WHMS to study at the Lucy Webb Hayes National Training School in Washington, DC. "Lucy Webb Hayes students all boarded at the Training School, a living arrangement that defied the social norms in the rigidly segregated environment of the nation's capital."[57] Yet those who were able to do this were few; the lion's share of potential Black deaconesses had little or no access to training. The obstacles Black Methodist deaconesses faced are evident in a WHMS report, which mentions that "a training school for Negro women was in the talking stage year in and year out." The *talking* stage was as far as they got.

54. "Deaconess Training-School for Colored Girls," 151.

55. Dougherty, *My Calling To Fulfill*, 65.

56. Jones, "Colored Deaconess Work," 150. Legath confirms the whiteness of the deaconess movement in all US churches: "Demographic research reveals a diaconate that was almost exclusively white, ethnically rooted in Northern and Western Europe, and based primarily in cities of the Midwest." Legath, *Sanctified Sisters*, 30.

57. Dougherty, *My Calling To Fulfill*, 65.

A vague explanation follows, citing "unexpected hindrances" that kept postponing its permanent establishment.[58]

Despite this herculean obstacle, the few Black Methodist women who were consecrated as deaconesses worked tirelessly and effectively with minimal resources and training. Consider the statistics for MEC deaconess, Rosa Simpson. In 1914, as WHMS Conference Organizer for the Texas Annual Conference, she traveled between one and two thousand miles to and from her home in Galveston on the Gulf of Mexico as far as Paris, Texas, north of Dallas, and east, as far as Texarkana, nearly to the Louisiana border. She recounted: "I have made 6479 visits to homes, hospitals, and jails during the year, and performed duties in visiting, reorganizing, and organizing local auxiliaries."[59] Her report in 1918, the year of the "Spanish flu" epidemic, seemed particularly joyful, even as she acknowledged "disasters, epidemics, and dangers, seen and unseen." She declared, "Never have the women received me more cordially, never have they listened more attentively to my humble message than this year . . . This is the best year's work of my life. Doors have opened to me, hands have been extended as never before."[60]

In addition, Simpson was elected seven times consecutively, from 1908–1932, as a Texas Annual Conference lay delegate to the MEC General Conference. Yet, although she garnered the respect of Texas Methodists to elect her repeatedly to this influential position, she relied on others for financial assistance. At the 1908 General Conference, Lucy Rider Meyer invited her to lunch and afterward gave Simpson her second-best white silk ties for her deaconess uniform. Meyer recalled the encounter in these words, "When we had become quite friendly, I persuaded her to accept a pair of my fluffy, new, white silk ties. May the Lord forgive me! I didn't offer my very best pair. She was so pleased and grateful. I pinned them into her bonnet and tied them under her chin myself. Several other of our deaconesses are interested in her wardrobe and she will go home better clothed than when she came."[61] For her to attend the 1912 General Conference in Minneapolis, John (Jack) Arthur Johnson, the first Black world heavyweight boxing champion, nicknamed the Galveston Giant, paid her expenses.[62] Unfortunately, however, despite her significant

58. Meeker, *Six Decades*, 99.
59. *Journal of the Forty-Ninth Annual Session of the Texas Conference*, 48.
60. *Minutes of the Fifty-Third Session of the Texas Annual Conference*, 88–89.
61. Meyer, "Assorted Writings of Lucy Rider Meyer."
62. "Afro-American Cullings," n.d.

contribution to Methodism in Texas, what Simpson did during the decade between her retirement in 1936 and her death in 1945 in obscurity in a mental hospital in Austin remains a mystery.

The deaconess movement failed, in its early years, to prosper as well in Black churches and denominations other than the MEC. The African Methodist Episcopal Church (AME), as we noted earlier, sanctioned the Office of Deaconess at its 1900 General Conference. The denomination then purchased for $5,000 a substantial property, which covered over two city blocks in Roanoke, Virginia, to serve as a deaconess home and school. This property included "a three-story brick building, covered with slate, ninety-one feet by forty-one feet; a good frame dwelling with four rooms, and all necessary out-buildings."[63] AME deaconesses were expected to take a year's training, preferably at this school. However, it is unclear whether it ever functioned as a training school for AME deaconesses. The school's name appeared alongside a list of its trustees in three consecutive annual conference summaries (1902–1904) for the AME Church in Virginia. Of those three mentions, only in 1902 and 1903 did the school's name include the word, deaconess: the Deaconess Home and Girls' Training School. In 1904, the name appeared and was listed simply as the Girls' Training School. The following year, there was no citation at all of the school in the annual conference session summary.[64]

The scarcity of information on AME deaconesses is enigmatic, given the advocacy of influential AME pastor Rev. Reverdy Ransom. Several years before the General Conference vote in 1900, Ransom had set up a Board of Deaconesses in St. John's AME, in Cleveland, Ohio. "In 1894," he explained, "I organized and consecrated the first Board of Deaconesses in the A. M. E. Church, or perhaps, in any other Negro denomination at that time."[65] In his next pastorate, Bethel AME, situated on the corner of 30th and Dearborn Streets, in "the heart of the black ghetto" in Chicago, he once again instituted a Board of Deaconesses.[66] In 1898, in an article for the church's newspaper, *Christian Recorder*, he called for women serving in the church to be recognized as deaconesses. "It is conceded that there are certain kinds of work in the church which women can do better than men; a deaconess is a minister of the church called upon to exercise her

63. Weaver, "Roanoke Deaconess Home," n.d.
64. Butt, *History of African Methodism in Virginia*, 197, 203, 207. I am grateful to Dennis Dickerson for his assistance with this resource.
65. Ransom, *Pilgrimage of Harriet Ransom's Son*, 69.
66. Gomez-Jefferson, *Sage of Tawawa*, 54.

special gift of teaching, nursing, or whatever it may be in the service of the church for the purpose of extending the Kingdom of the Lord Jesus."[67] Yet only one woman in his congregation is on record for having gone on to be trained as a deaconess within the AME church at large. Sarah Slater, the lone woman listed in the *AME Deaconess Manual*, published in 1902, completed the deaconess training course, but she did so at Meyer's training school in Chicago, close to where Slater lived, rather than in Roanoke, Virginia, at the designated AME deaconess training school.[68]

Although Ransom did not populate the AME church with deaconesses, he did encourage and authorize their work in the congregations he served. In a *Christian Recorder* article, Ida B. Wells-Barnett explained that he created "an order of deaconesses, twelve women, who cover that district seeking strangers, visiting the sick and feeding, clothing and making warm the poor and needy." She regarded this initiative to be integral to Ransom's "new gospel to the city . . . that whatever was of moral or racial or educational value to the community; whatever was of an elevating or intellectual character, should be fostered and encouraged and established by the church."[69]

The Decline of the International Methodist Deaconess Movement

Nearly as rapid as the emergence of this international women's movement was its decline. The movement deteriorated precipitously after the First World War, as many deaconesses left their dark, serge uniforms hanging in the closet and joined the nursing, social work, and teaching professions. What factors prompted the decline? Among many, we will consider three: the professionalization of work that supplanted deaconess work following the First World War; the on-the-ground reality that deaconesses remained in no man's land as neither clergy nor laity; and the vexing problem of a Protestant religious order, which looked to many too much like Roman Catholicism.

---

67. Ransom, *AME Christian Recorder*, cited in Morris, *Reverdy C. Ransom*, 119.
68. Grant, *Deaconess Manual*, 17.
69. Wells-Barnett, "Rev. R. C. Ransom, D.D.," 1.

The Professionalization of Women's Labor

The First World War had a significant impact on women's moving in vast numbers into secular professions, prompted primarily in support of the war effort. "With the men off to war (WWI), women entered the workforce in unprecedented numbers. . . . Although many of these women returned to housewifery after the war, they had gained the vote in the United States and elsewhere. There was no going back to what had been before."[70] Women looked increasingly to professions outside the church for employment. To train for these professions, women's enrollment increased in other types of educational institutions, instead of deaconess training schools, which led to secular careers. This situation had a deleterious impact, for instance, on a school like CTS, the flagship deaconess training school in the US, where the Methodist deaconess movement was arguably the most robust. The impact showed up in the acceleration of the downward decline in enrollment as well as in the decision in 1919 to admit male students. This recruiting decision, made to keep the school financially solvent, meant the end of CTS as a women-only educational institution. What happened at CTS, therefore, portended the inexorable decline of the movement internationally.

Even from within the church itself came the push for professionally trained workers to do what deaconesses had been doing, such as teaching Sunday School. According to MEC deaconess Alice Robertson, writing in 1919, "The Board of Sunday Schools appeals for directors of religious education and insists upon a high grade of specialization." Her comment points to the growing professionalization in the field of religious education, marked by the founding of the Religious Education Association in 1904.[71] She found the same to be true of the Board of Home Missions and Church Extension of the MEC, which issued a "challenge for [hiring] trained leaders. In both instances, the work is practically the same as some deaconesses are doing." She then raised a fundamental question, if in somewhat turgid prose, "what shall be called deaconess and what shall be designated as nondeaconess . . . just how the work of the nondeaconess church secretary differs from that of the church secretary who is a deaconess. The same question may be asked of religious education,

---

70. Olson, *Deacons and Deaconesses*, 305–6.

71. See Furnish, "Women in Religious Education," 3:310–17 and Brereton, "Protestant Sunday Schools and Religious Education," 2:906–12.

the social and immigrant work."[72] This realization, which women even at the time had, that for professional status and a salary they could do the same work that deaconesses had done before and during the war for neither, contributed to the movement's decline.[73]

Even more, in some Western countries, the rise of the welfare state exacerbated tensions between deaconesses and secular social service providers to the detriment of the church workers. A Wesley Deaconess Order pamphlet notes that the expanded role of the UK government in providing the sort of social and philanthropic services restricted the sphere of deaconess duties.[74] New Zealand experienced a similar situation, and deaconesses in that country confronted head-on these sorts of questions, according to Margaret Tennant: "Was the deaconess a social worker, or was she more properly a parish assistant, religious educator or preacher? Could she be all these things and how adequately was she any of them? . . . The question of the deaconess's proper role was never resolved, and was still debated within the Presbyterian and Methodist churches 30 years later. As a result, at least in part, "in 1979 the Methodist order ended."[75]

Neither Clergy Nor Laity

A second factor leading to their reduced numbers was that deaconesses were neither clergy nor laity; they remained in limbo, in no man's land, even though they were consecrated into an established office of the church. It was simply not clear who they were in terms of a church position or role, or to whom they were to report. This challenge faced deaconesses in many countries. For instance, an historian of the Canadian Methodist deaconess movement documents "a maze of conflicting commitments. The demands of their clients notwithstanding, deaconesses answered to the pastor, the ladies' aids and the church boards that employed and supervised them, the General Board of Management which stationed them, and the deaconess superintendents of the local Homes who governed their off-duty lives."[76] Given this labyrinth

---

72. Robertson, "What Is Deaconess Work?" 360.

73. For more on the issue of a salary (or allowance) for deaconesses, see Legath, *Sanctified Sisters*, 109–30.

74. Wesley Deaconess Order Pamphlet, No. 7, n.d.

75. Tennant, "Sisterly Ministrations," 20.

76. Thomas, "Servants of the Church," 388.

of conflicting commitments and lines of authority, the decline in the number of Canadian Methodist deaconesses began to emerge in 1910, only sixteen years after its initial launch in Toronto.

In the New Zealand Methodist Church, there was a lack of clarity about which women serving in the church as full-time workers were deaconesses. Despite their formal recognition in 1912, "as late as 1929," according to Wesley Chambers, "all women workers at home and overseas were listed in the Minutes of Conference as Deaconesses. Not until 1952 do the Minutes of Conference differentiate between Deaconesses and Missionary Sisters, in the overseas mission field." Chambers extrapolates from this official imprecision that deaconesses occupied an "anomalous position."[77]

In the US, the deaconess occupation of a place in no man's land can be traced directly to General Conference legislative debates. In 1880, the MEC General Conference voted to rescind all local preacher licenses previously issued to women, including popular evangelists Jennie Fowler Willing and Maggie Newton Van Cott. The same vote slammed the door shut on women's ordination, as well as banning women from most church leadership positions, except for Sunday School superintendent, class leader, and steward.[78] Then, in 1888, in an apparent effort to backtrack from the previous conference's hard line, the General Conference voted to sanction the Office of Deaconess. From the start, then, the deaconess movement was a compromise—offering with one hand what the church had already taken with the other.

Similarly, many clergymen in the Methodist Episcopal Church South (MECS) were loath to open the door to women as church officers in any capacity. In a bishop's address during the 1902 General Conference, those voting on the deaconess legislation were encouraged to approach it as a "very grave matter," because "no more delicate and difficult problem will be before you for solution."[79] There was a tie in the standing committee, with thirteen in favor and thirteen against, which nearly derailed the legislation. Eventually, however, when it was brought to the full legislative body, the vote in favor of deaconesses passed.[80]

At issue among Methodists worldwide was the overlap of responsibilities, even authority, between clergymen and deaconesses. Deaconess

77. Chambers, *Not Self–But Others*, 7.
78. Curts, *General Conferences of the Methodist Episcopal Church*, 201.
79. Tigert, *Journal of the 14th General Conference of the MEC, South*, 30–31.
80. Tigert, *Journal of the 14th General Conference of the MEC, South*, 217.

evangelists, for example, itinerated from venue to venue, preaching the gospel. The Rev. Henry Smith, Warden of the United Methodist Deaconess Institute in the UK, explained clergymen's objection: "As might be expected, there were many who objected to the evangelistic side of the deaconess work. They said that they were glad to see the Sisters giving themselves to ministries in the home and the Sunday School, and there was singular appropriateness in their doing so; but that they should conduct evangelistic services was improper and unbecoming, probably unscriptural."[81] In other words, when deaconess labors intersected directly with that of the clergy, as happened in evangelistic services where preaching was involved, conflict increased between deaconesses and the clergy, as we will see in the next chapter with MEC deaconess Iva Durham Vennard.

Perhaps in an effort to mitigate the tension inherent in this overlap, the *AME Deaconess Manual*, as one example, articulated the duties of a deaconess versus the clergyman's when tending to the sick. According to the manual, deaconesses were to follow these instructions: "Acquaint your pastor of all cases needing his attention. He can do his work much better than you. And do not argue about religion with the pastor as to what you do, or, do not believe, in the sick room; be quiet and let him have 'the right of way.'" So, what *could* the deaconess do in the sick room? "Arrange the disordered room and the bedclothes; if the bedding require it, try and effect a change."[82] The lines of authority in this manual are clearly drawn, with the deaconess retreating on every potentially contested occasion.

The difficulty with this line in the sand is that precisely there, in the sick room, the deaconess could, and perhaps should, cross the line into pastoral care. After all, as noted previously, Wesley himself had encouraged women to "inquire concerning their souls" when visiting the sick. Further, the exigencies of the sick room demanded both physical and pastoral care. "Since the pastor could not always be present," explains a historian of German Methodist deaconesses, "very often the deaconesses were in charge of providing the patients and the dying with spiritual support.... the sisters also provided care for the soul by themselves when the pastor could not be there. In other words, the boundary between the spiritual guidance the pastors provided and the deaconesses'

---

81. Smith, *Ministering Women*, 114–15.
82. Grant, *Deaconess Manual*, 29.

care for the soul was not very distinct in everyday practice."[83] In still further haziness vis-à-vis these lines, clergymen tended to expect that "deaconesses were supposed to be able to interpret biblical texts and apply them to the specific situation of the patient. However, the pastors wished that they would do that only to a limited degree in order to differentiate clearly between their care for the soul and the spiritual guidance provided by pastors."[84] Such a neat distinction was not always—or even often—possible. The need both to hold the line and to cross it, especially in the sick room, proved to be untenable.

The Resemblance to Roman Catholicism

The very idea of a religious order in Protestantism disturbed many clergy and laity because it veered, as they perceived it, too close to Roman Catholicism.[85] This critique, expressed from the beginning, was relentless; not even the best efforts of deaconess advocates could silence such unremitting opposition. Like Roman Catholic nuns, deaconesses were single women who turned aside from what was considered the norm for women—to aspire to become a wife and mother. Like nuns in a convent, deaconesses lived in community with other women. They wore a uniform that approximated a nun's habit, and many deaconesses remained unmarried, like nuns called to a vocation of celibacy. Understandably, to outside observers, deaconesses and nuns were identical. Deaconesses countered that they did not take a lifetime vow, so they could leave the order at any time, and many did leave to marry, to care for aged parents, to recuperate from illness, or to do something else entirely. They also explained that they were called by God to be mothers of humanity's orphans.[86] Deaconesses stood behind this catchy phrase repeated frequently in deaconess literature: The Roman Catholic Church has nuns. The Methodist Church has NONE! Nevertheless, their attempts, whether

83. Nolte, "Deaconesses' Self-Understanding," 33.

84. Nolte, "Deaconesses' Self-Understanding," 23. Janet West expresses for the Australian context the sentiment that was true in many countries at the time, "Another problem for sisters and deaconesses in Protestant churches was that their fellow churchmen and women were often uneasy about their role. There was a lurking suspicion that women in orders were undermining the authority of the family—as well as the male hierarchy—because of their autonomous role." West, "Recipe for Confrontation," 72.

85. For a detailed account of anti-Catholic sentiment and its impact on the ecumenical deaconess movement in the US, see Legath, *Sanctified Sisters*, 78–108.

86. For more on maternalism in the deaconess movement, see chapter 5.

lighthearted or serious, to neutralize the criticism of being "too Catholic" never prevailed. Methodist clergy and laity could not be persuaded otherwise, given their communal life, their dress, and their commitment, even their *provisional* commitment, to a religious vocation that kept them from birthing and nurturing their own children.

Conclusion

The international Methodist deaconess movement was the fulfillment of John Wesley's dream of an organized group of women who visited the sick, offering physical and spiritual comfort. Yet the deaconess movement did much more than this; it provided opportunities for women to teach, preach, lead institutions, and provide social, religious, and economic resources to those in need. The deaconess movement also fulfilled Wesley's vision of Methodism moving beyond the shores of the UK; before he died, he had sent Thomas Coke and Francis Asbury to the US in 1784 to gain a foothold for Methodism on new shores. In this chapter alone, we have documented the reach of the Methodist deaconess movement with examples from the US, Canada, Europe, Australia, New Zealand, and the Philippines.

Still, what did the movement mean for the women who populated the ranks of the deaconess movement? In other words, did the hope expressed by Iva Durham Vennard—that church doors would swing wider for Methodist women in the early twentieth century—come to pass in the establishment of the international Methodist deaconess movement? The answer? "Yes" and "No." Yes, because the Office of Deaconess was an established church office, created and confirmed by legislative action. No, because this same legislative action was fraught with misperception and confusion, with unclarity and suspicion. Such imprecision, due in part to the threat deaconesses posed to the authority of clergymen, upon whom the continued existence of the deaconess order depended, led to a near-constant renegotiation of boundaries for deaconess activity and authority.

The lack of clarity that characterized the role of the deaconess extended as well to the question of whether being a deaconess was a vocation or a profession. In Germany, for instance, Methodist deaconess work was largely nursing. Was this a vocation or a profession? This conundrum was never cracked. Such vagueness at the heart of the movement would prove not just demoralizing to deaconesses but also damaging to its continued existence, particularly once the door for women's access to various professions in the wake of the First World War flung open. These challenges proved insurmountable, and Methodist deaconesses never did find a way out of no man's land.

Reflection Questions

1. What factors made becoming a deaconess an appealing decision for women in the late nineteenth and early twentieth centuries?

2. How did the broader societal shifts, such as urbanization and women's increasing participation in the workforce, shape the development and appeal of the Methodist deaconess movement? How do these historical dynamics compare to current trends in church-based social outreach and ministry?

3. The chapter demonstrates how Black Methodist deaconesses struggled to obtain training and recognition in the church. How do these challenges demonstrate the impact of systemic barriers in the church in their day? What connections can we make to similar issues in the church today?

"DIAKONISSENSPIEGEL"/ "DEACONESS'S MIRROR"[1]

I know, my God, that you test the heart, and honesty is pleasing to you.[2] Search me, God, and discover my heart; test me and learn, what I think. And see if I am on an evil path, and lead me to the eternal path.[3]

Could you read a few questions continuously on a daily basis and bring them prayerfully before God?

I.

My First Morning Time

1. Upon waking, have I first thought upon God with praise and thanks (Ps 63:7),[4] or first on earthly things?

2. Have I asked for new mercy and charity, for new love, patience, gentleness, humility, and wisdom for my service in the name of my Savior?

3. Have I not forgotten, in prayer like the Apostle Paul (Eph. 1:16–19)[5] to think of those commended to my care in body and soul, my

---

1. I am grateful to Anna Lowery, with additional help from Reiner Kanzleiter, for the German translation of this document, "Diakonissenspiegel." Used with permission from the Martha-Maria Deaconess Organization Archives.
2. 1 Chr 29:17a.
3. Ps 139:23–24.
4. "For you have been my help, and in the shadow of your wings I sing for joy."
5. "I do not cease to give thanks for you as I remember you in my prayers. I pray that

fellow sisters, my other companions, my relatives, my work and house parents, my chairman and my country? (1 Tim 2:1–3)⁶

4. Have I not forgotten to ask that I may do all of my work for the entire day in God's face, to please my Savior and not people with work before their eyes? (Col 3:17)⁷

5. Have I gotten up punctually at the determined hour, have I dressed myself fully and orderly as quickly as possible, without serving vanity?

6. Have I gathered and prepared myself for the shared prayer in silence? Have I never missed it without emergency, always participated with my entire heart and tried at first to make it fruitful for me?

7. Have I used my quiet hour so that the Lord can speak to me, and with prayer and Bible reading searched and found his face?⁸

II.

My Attitude to God

1. Do I have peace of heart with God? Has no hidden spell come up between him and me through some unknown, denied, or un-regretted sin?

2. Have I admitted sins, when they have been told to me and I recognized them, and humbled myself under them instead of excusing them and explaining them? Have I ordered what there was to order, and received forgiveness from the Lord?

---

the God of our Lord Jesus Christ, the Father of glory, may give you a spirit of wisdom and revelation as you come to know him, so that, with the eyes of your heart enlightened, you may know what is the hope to which he has called you, what are the riches of his glorious inheritance among the saints, and what is the immeasurable greatness of his power for us who believe, according to the working of his great power."

6. "First of all, then, I urge that supplications, prayers, intercessions, and thanksgivings should be made for everyone, for kings and all who are in high positions, so that we may lead a quiet and peaceable life in all godliness and dignity. This is right and is acceptable in the sight of God our Savior."

7. "And whatever you do, in word or deed, do everything in the name of the Lord Jesus, giving thanks to God the Father through him."

8. At this point in the document, these biblical passages are written out: Ps 63:7, Eph 1:16–19, 1 Tim 2:1–3, and Col 3:17.

3. Have I all the time and in everything that I have done stood in the awareness of his presence? Could his nearness protect and heal me, or have I driven away servility?

4. I do perform all of my assignments in childlike reverence to my crucified Savior and in inner gratitude for his unending love and forbearance, or have I been hypocritical?

5. Do I accept his mercy not out of willfulness, but rather thinking on the word of Scripture: "In the Lord I have justice and strength"[9] and "With you is forgiveness, so that man fears you"?[10]

6. Do I belong to the happy, voluntary people who bring the Lord holy sacrifices in holy ornament, and am I determined daily to prove to the world as a saved child of God through brave testimonies of Christ, that children of God are happy children and their belief is the victory that overcomes the world?

7. Am I through all of my worries childlike and trusting before the Lord?

8. Does the Lord Jesus stand in the first place in my life?

9. Is his word very dear to me, so that I read and listen with truthful desire, and do not misuse it as a cold duty?

10. Do I practice thanking my Lord for everyday incidents at all times and for everything?

11. Is it of holy seriousness to stand in everything decided and without cowardice on the side of my Lord?

12. Have I not said any conscious lies? Have I also not gone around the truth with cunning and silence?

13. Have I denied the Lord at no opportunity?

14. Do I gladly let myself be humbled by God, or do I defend myself against it?

15. Am I moody, and do I attempt to excuse myself with the mistakes of others and through this wash myself clean?

16. Do I let myself be lightly provoked to anger? Am I sensitive and agitated?

---

9. Mic 3:8.
10. Ps 130:4.

17. Do I strive to get my way through cunning and obstinacy?

III.

My Attitude to My Occupation

1. Do I take all of my strength for work and suffering happily and faithful from the wealth of his free mercy? Or do I try to work in my own strength, do I drive justice in my work?
2. Do I not imagine myself to be a finished sister?
3. Do I try by my work in order to receive thanks, recognition, and reputation?
4. By all work, do I maintain a gathered heart, which rests in the peace of the Lord? Do I also not miss the quiet and reading of the Bible daily?
5. Do I work with the right sense of a pilgrim, who knows: "Here we have no permanent city, rather we search for the future one?"[11] Have I built no little nest in my work?
6. Am I *ready* for *every* path and for *every* assignment, do I take *every* command from the hand of the Lord and not from humans?
7. Am I internally aware of my calling to be a Deaconess, and do I serve the Lord with unshared heart?
8. Am I a merciful servant to the poor, the sick, the lost, the suffering, in the love and the patience that the Savior has for me?
9. Do I practice being *faithful* in everything, even in the *little* things?
10. Do I endeavor to achieve cleanliness, order, and punctuality?
11. Do I practice using my time well? Do I not waste it on superfluous things, that the Lord did not offer me?
12. Have I accepted invitations to eat and drink against the order of our House?
13. Have I avoided misusing the necessary departures from the city for vanity, my eye's desires, and for useless going about, and avoided the gathering and playing places of the world during my recovery time?

---

11. Heb 13:14.

14. Am I vain about my Deaconess vocation? Do I search for no special features in myself regarding it?

15. Have I accustomed myself to unnecessary needs?

IV.

My Attitude to the Motherhouse

1. Do I recognize the blessing of the Motherhouse, and do I stand like a child without inner reservation in it as a true member of the family of God?

2. Am I gladly obedient to the orders of the Motherhouse? Have I stood under the discipline of the Holy Spirit by waking, going to bed, eating, drinking, by work and rest as well as with traveling?

3. Do I bear the needs of my Motherhouse as my own? Am I prepared to alleviate them through my strengths, and also in prayer to ask for them?

4. Do I gladly judge the institutions and public figures of the Mother-House, or do I hold them dear to my heart?

5. Do I recognize the leaders of the Motherhouse as those given to me by the Lord, so that I "do not despise or anger [them], but rather hold them in honor, serve them, obey them, hold them dear and worthy?"[12] Do I stand in a childlike relationship of trust to them?

6. Have I kept not only my heavenly, but also my earthly accounts in such an order, that I won't be scared and surprised by the message "Do the accounts for your household"?

7. Have I been faithful and dependable in small things, as well as with my own things, and have I not forgotten, how many widow's contributions[13] have been trusted to us in God's gift?

8. Have I not let out or betrayed all sorts of internal affairs of the Motherhouse to those who stand outside of it, or exposed afflictions of the Motherhouse?

9. Have I written the Sister's letters punctually and prayerfully?

---

12. This phrase quotes Martin Luther's comment on the Fourth Commandment—"Honor thy father and mother"—found in his *Small Catechism*.

13. The widow's mite in Mark 12:41–44 and Luke 21:1–4.

10. Have I regularly held silent prayer with my Sisters and visited on the Sister's Day?
11. Have I read the entirety of our circular [letter] with inner participation?

V.

My Attitude to the Sisters

1. Do I make an example for my younger sisters in everything good, especially in obedience to the House order? Do I try to lead them and carry them away through loving word and example, and thank the Lord for everything unanimously with them in humility, obedience, and faithfulness?
2. Have I been for my fellow sisters an interceding, helpful, humble companion, who helps to bear their cross, encouraged her despondent heart in all needs through truthful, loyal love, and raised her up to believing trust?
3. Do I happily let my fellow sisters say things to me? Have I recognized and taken on rebukes that seem unfriendly as love of the Lord?
4. Have I had the courage of truth, not only towards subordinates but also towards older sisters, when the Lord reminds me, or will the blood of my fellow sister be challenged because out of cowardice I allowed her to go unwarned?
5. Have I first brought the needs of my fellow sisters in my little chamber in interceding love before the Lord and received from him what I should say to them?
6. Have I let my tongue be protected by the Lord and not without need spread the sins and afflictions of my fellow sisters?
7. When my fellow sister gives me something to bear, do I consider the admonition of the Apostle: "One bears the burden of another, so she fulfills the law of Christ"?[14]

---

14. Gal 6:2.

8. Am I really happy not to lead, but to serve and to have the lowest place under the others after the word of David: "I want to become even lower therefore and want to be lowly in my eyes"?[15]

9. Do I recognize the blessing of the sister's community for my inner life? Do I let myself be worn down in going around with the others? Am I glad and friendly in speaking with my fellow sisters?

10. Am I gladly obedient to the leading sister?

11. Am I prying with questions into the personal affairs of my fellow sisters? But do I also help to bear the personal suffering of my fellow sisters through heartfelt participation and intercession?

12. Do I complain about my fellow sisters? Do I see one or the other as a burden?

13. Have I begun a tired[16] connection? Is it still a holy thing of the conscience not to recognize anybody according to the flesh?

14. Am I taciturn and cold in intercourse with my fellow sisters?

15. Do I gladly seek out true community with my fellow sisters, and am I not a stop to them by being swept up and unquiet?

16. Is it a holy matter to me to lead my fellow sisters on all sides in outer efficiency as well as in inner connection to the Lord?

17. In my letters about my fellow sisters, do I write only that which the holy eye of God would not shy away from?

VI.

My Attitude to the Parents and Relatives

1. Have I remained an obedient daughter and loving sister to my parents and siblings? Do I also write to them regularly?

2. Have I not raised myself above anyone in my family, who have perhaps led an oppressed life in poverty and seclusion?

---

15. Dan 4:7.

16. This German word, *hängerisch*, is difficult to translate because it is archaic. It describes the feeling of being tired, listless, depressed, lacking in energy.

3. Have I gone after those in my family who are lost and astray with interceding and active love? Have I not withheld the testimony of my Savior from them?

4. But have I also not neglected my duties and tasks in the service of my Lord due to natural, worldly devotion to my blood relatives?

VII.

My Attitude to the Patients

1. Will the poor, sick, fallen, children and most of all my patients be unable to bring me to trial on that great day for neglecting them?

2. Have I caused them offense with words, with impatience, with hardness and unkindness, and because of that earned a millstone on my neck?

3. Did my renouncing, quiet, humble self-denial pull them towards the Savior, or did I try to win the people for myself?

4. Have I seriously protected myself from partiality in the treatment of patients?

5. Do I consider, that the soul of mercy is the mercy with the soul to their eternal salvation?

6. As a loyal housekeeper over God's gift, have I given at the right time to each his own spiritual and bodily nourishment in heavenly and earthly medicine?

7. Have I taken the time to lend a willing ear to the needs of the heart and various little wishes of my patients, and not immediately said, "I have no time for that!"?

8. Have I seen the Savior himself in my patients and tried to serve Him in them?

9. Have I given into the wishes and passions of the sick, for example a longing for morphine or going against a diet without orders from the doctor?

10. Have I also not spoken to the patients about my fellow sisters?

11. Have I not accepted any personal gifts from the patients, nor gained personal advantages for myself through their service and work?

12. Have I used every opportunity that the Lord gave me to testify to his redemption, to say a silent prayer or give testimony, in order to win people over for salvation?

VIII.

My Attitude to the Directors, the Doctors and the Brothers

1. Have I happily achieved results for my directors according to their orders?
2. Am I not dependent on certain personalities? Do I avoid making unchristian distinctions between, for example, local preachers and workers for the Kingdom of God?
3. Have I spoken about the directors unfavorably behind their backs?
4. Have I not denied God before my superiors?
5. Have I been meticulously obedient to all medical and diet orders of the doctors?
6. Have I not in any way undermined the authority of the doctors with the patients?
7. Have I admitted any possible mistake in my nursing at the command of the Lord, or have I not always remained by the truth?
8. Is my attitude towards the doctors not too familiar or in any way unchristian?
9. Have I not lost an opportunity to give testimony of my Lord to the doctors?
10. Have I followed the instructions of the Motherhouse with the male nurses?
11. Have I troubled myself to lighten the workload of the brothers in the hospital as far as is possible, and acted in a proper and Christian way towards them?

IX.

My Attitude to the Employees

1. Do I see the common inheritance of eternal life in them?
2. Am I constantly considerate about their bodily and spiritual well-being? Do I attentively care for them and afterwards seen to it that they are saved and become true children of God?
3. Have I raised myself above them?
4. Have I avoided false intimacy with them?
5. Have I always passed on orders with love and peace?
6. Have I not demanded unnecessary personal services from them?

X.

My Attitude to Travel

1. While traveling, have I kept up my inner contact with the Lord, stopped for silence and reading the Bible, and not made myself noticeable either through gossip and boasting of my abilities, or through an affected silence?
2. During unavoidable encounters with men have I maintained the fine line of propriety?
3. Have I shown myself to be a true Deaconess towards my fellow travelers through friendliness, modesty, and helpfulness?
4. By possible encounters with sisters from other Motherhouses, have I shown them love and honor?
5. In journeying together with our sisters of loud nature, have I not objected to conspicuous singing or the like?

XI.

My Behavior on Sick Days

1. Have I faithfully carried out the doctor's orders on my sick days, or have I given myself other medicine without the consent of the doctor or the Motherhouse, and gone my own way?

2. Have I always told the doctors the complete truth, even in reports about pain, weakness, and temperatures?

3. Was it a concern to me to be a blessing for my roommate? Was I happy to serve true inner community with them? Have we used the quiet time for true priestly service?

4. Have I made it easy for the nursing sisters, or was I offensive to them and the other sick sisters?

5. Have I given myself in to the sickness, or have I held myself in childlike belief in the Lord's words: "I am the Lord, your doctor"?[17]

XII.

My Behavior During Holiday and Rest Periods

1. During my work, have I not willfully wasted by strength and needlessly sacrificed my health? Upon the true need for rest, have I prayed faithfully for the help of the Lord? Have I indulged in food, drink, rest, and observation of all orders really and fully as opportunities for recovery?

2. Have I used my resting period faithfully, not only to serve the body, but also used the gifted silence in order to aid my interior person?

3. Have I not used up my travel time with much traveling around by relatives, so that I returned exhausted? Have I allowed myself to be led by the Lord?

---

17. Exod 15:26.

XIII.

Concluding Questions

1. Do I work hard, whether I am at home or somewhere foreign to please my Savior?

2. Do I not forget my own soul out of worry for others, and do I stand in happy, faithful expectation of the coming of our Lord?

3. Does it truly come from the deepest bottoms of my heart, when I pray: "Lord Jesus, you I love, for you I die. Lord Jesus, yours am I, dead and living. Make me blessed, O Jesus!"?[18]

Reflection Questions

1. In what ways was this daily, self-examination practice relevant to the life and ministry of Methodist deaconesses? To the Christian life today? What challenges might arise from engaging these questions?

2. What impact do these 116 questions have on your estimation of the Methodist deaconess movement?

---

18. The opening stanza from the hymn, "Herr Jesus, dir leb' ich."

Iva May Durham (later Vennard), Deaconess, Methodist Episcopal Church

Lucy Rider Meyer, Deaconess, Methodist Episcopal Church

Chapter II

A "THIRTY YEAR WAR" AND MORE

Exposing Complexities in the Methodist Deaconess Movement[1]

Overview

THIS CHAPTER FOCUSES ON three women who helped propel the Methodist deaconess movement in the US, Lucy Rider Meyer, Jane Bancroft Robinson, and Iva Durham Vennard. All three played vital roles, yet only Meyer has been studied substantively by historians. A similar bias privileges social service as the only deaconess labor of significance. This chapter expands the historiography—and thus our understanding of the movement—by demonstrating that evangelism was also a pivotal commitment of Methodist deaconesses. We see this firsthand in the source document, "Experiences of a Deaconess Guitar," penned by Vennard with her guitar as the narrator. Her narration provides a glimpse into what deaconesses encountered daily while ministering to the broken and the lost.

Most were of marriageable age. Some had been schoolteachers; others were nearly illiterate. Few had encountered a metropolis except in their imagination. Yet from rural farms in Iowa, river towns in Ohio,

---

1. This chapter was first published in *Methodist History* 47 (2009) 101–16. Changes to this version eliminated duplication with material included in chapter 1.

and one-street villages in Illinois, to the great urban centers—Chicago, New York City, San Francisco—they flocked, seeking an opportunity to put their Protestant faith into action. In these cities, they knew that needs abounded with unsanitary and overcrowded tenements housing new arrivals from southern and Eastern Europe as well as from rural America.[2] There they could nurse a torn and tattered humanity, school the unlearned child, mentor the expectant mother, interpret for the immigrant, and tell the stories of Jesus to sinners. These women from America's heartlands, who became Methodist deaconesses, felt an unmitigated compulsion to rescue urban America.

In myriad ways, Methodist deaconesses resembled scores of Protestant women during the Progressive Era who, through the Woman's Christian Temperance Union, settlement houses, and Women's Clubs, reached out beyond their homes to ameliorate society's ills. During these decades of heightened optimistic reform, when "religious inspiration, self-improvement, and civic engagement were closely intertwined,"[3] organizations proliferated.[4] Many organizations and movements of the Progressive Era have received plentiful attention by historians in recent years; yet scholarly interest in the Methodist deaconess movement, since its first blush of studies in the late 1970s and early 1980s, has not found a similar niche. In the intervening two decades, the very few studies promulgate the earliest conclusions about the movement without critique.

2. The influx of European immigrants and "urban-bound folk from the countryside" drastically and swiftly altered the population complexion of the United States, "from a primarily rural country in 1890 (64.6 percent of the population) to a mainly urban nation thirty years later (51.4 percent)." Riess, *Touching Base*, 6. See also Buenker, *Gilded Age and Progressive Era*, 300.

3. Putnam, *Bowling Alone*, 391.

4. Some historians refer to the Progressive Era as the "organizational revolution" because of the exponential increase in the number and varieties of organizations, associations, and clubs. Buenker, *Gilded Age and Progressive Era*, 458. See also Putnam, *Bowling Alone*, 383–93. I use the term, Progressive Era, for the straightforward reason expressed by Steven J. Diner, "because historians routinely use this label and readers recognize it more." Diner, *Very Different Age*, 13. Still, as with any term intended to encapsulate an historical time period, it is problematic. Robert Putnam reiterates this point. "Like any historical demarcation, this division is not strict, since developments associated with the Progressive movement had clear antecedents during the earlier period, and developments associated with the Gilded Age persisted into the later period." Putnam, *Bowling Alone*, 367. Because of this, some historians prefer to consider "the period from 1877 through WWI as a single historical era." Buenker, *Gilded Age and Progressive Era*, 1.

Particularly influential in this regard is Mary Agnes Dougherty's dissertation on the first three decades of the Methodist deaconess movement that established two longstanding, interpretative conclusions. The first is that Lucy Rider Meyer is the only deaconess leader of historical interest, presumably because she founded the first Methodist Episcopal Church (MEC) deaconess training school in the US, the Chicago Training School for City, Home and Foreign Missions and the Chicago Deaconess Home (CTS), which set the precedent for the rest. The second conclusion is that the principal deaconess labor was social service. Deaconesses are best understood, in Dougherty's opinion, as early social workers. Subsequent historians adopt these conclusions without testing their validity or methodological presuppositions. As we shall see, in the hands of notable historians, from Rosemary Skinner Keller to Jean Miller Schmidt, the Methodist deaconess movement is misleadingly reduced to one leader—Lucy Rider Meyer—and one labor—social service.

In this chapter, I first unmask the fallacy that perpetuates a myopic focus on Meyer, a misjudgment that leaves the legacies of other deaconess leaders to languish. In particular, I assess the legacy of Jane Bancroft Robinson, who is treated by historians merely as a foil to Meyer on account of their legendary feud, rather than as a principal player in the movement. Robinson's leadership strategy for expanding women's roles in a patriarchal church, viewed in light of Estelle Freedman's concept of "female institution building," a strategy implemented during the Progressive Era, challenges historians' interpretation of Meyer's strategy as more liberative for women and therefore of more historical significance than Robinson's.

Second, I challenge the assumption that deaconesses chiefly provided social service by demonstrating, with primary source evidence, that evangelism was also an essential deaconess labor. Again, I proceed by focusing on another prominent deaconess leader, Iva Durham Vennard, who crossed paths with both Meyer and Robinson. Archival material concerning Vennard provides insight into a deaconess leader and training school founder who believed that the primary deaconess labor was evangelism. She and Robinson had their own feud over whether deaconesses should be evangelists. Similar to Meyer and Robinson's feud, it is in the nexus of the conflict that we are privileged to see complexities emerge among deaconess leaders and deaconess labors.

In light of these two challenges, I demonstrate further that the fullness of women's religious history becomes compromised when movements that were once dynamic and multi-faceted with myriad personalities are insufficiently represented by one leader or one labor. It may even be true that this reductionist tendency contributed to a scholarly malaise about the deaconess movement in the last decades, almost as if its historical importance has already been documented. In contrast, this chapter expands and reinvigorates the historical reconstruction of the Methodist deaconess movement by exploring its conflicts and complexities.

Deaconess Leaders: Lucy Rider Meyer and Jane Bancroft Robinson

Among the earliest and most influential leaders of the Methodist deaconess movement was Lucy Rider Meyer (1849–1922). Raised in a Methodist home, she was converted at age thirteen. Her education was extensive, including a Bachelor of Arts from Oberlin College, studies in Chemistry at Massachusetts Institute of Technology, and, in later life, a medical degree from Woman's Medical College, Northwestern University. Prior to her deaconess work, she was Professor of Chemistry at McKendree College in Illinois and a field secretary for the Illinois State Sunday School Association. Certainly, the most noteworthy years of her life she devoted to the Methodist deaconess movement, particularly through CTS, the school she founded and served for over 30 years as fundraiser, Bible teacher, and principal. Her husband, Josiah Shelley Meyer, worked alongside her as the school's business agent. When the couple retired, forty agencies, including hospitals, orphanages, training schools, and homes for the elderly had been established either directly by CTS or one of its graduates.[5] Along with these accomplishments, Meyer was elected to be the first laywoman seated as a delegate when the MEC General Conference admitted women for the first time in 1904; she was elected a delegate again four years later.

Meyer's importance to the Methodist deaconess movement rightfully captured historians' attention because she played such a pivotal role in its inception and development. However, for more than three decades, she has occupied center stage in every study of the movement beginning with Dougherty, who rarely moves the spotlight to anyone else. The longest chapter in Dougherty's study (chapter 2) chronicles

---

5. Prelinger and Keller, "Function of Female Bonding," 326.

Meyer's life, and the remaining chapters (chapters 3 through 6) investigate the first thirty years of Methodist deaconess work through the lens of CTS and its graduates. Rosemary Skinner Keller continues the trajectory by crediting Meyer as single-handedly instigating the Methodist deaconess movement. "Five years later, Lucy Rider Meyer founded the Chicago Training School for women missionaries and almost immediately originated the deaconess order, one of the most significant forms of home missionary work in the denomination's history."[6] With this statement, Keller essentially erases from history the contributions of other leaders and organizations, such as Jane Bancroft Robinson and the Woman's Home Missionary Society (WHMS). Susan Hill Lindley at least nods generically in the direction of other leaders when she surmises that others besides Meyer had to be involved. "Credit for the success of the deaconess movement in American Methodism must surely also be given to other leaders and supporters, male and female, as well as to the deaconesses themselves."[7] However, she identifies no one by name other than Meyer, with the exception of a one-sentence reference to Jane Bancroft Robinson as Meyer's feuding combatant.[8]

This blinkered perspective on Meyer has deep roots and was diagnosed more than a century ago in a booklet published by the WHMS, the organization Robinson represented. WHMS leaders disagreed with the common assumption circulating even then in Methodist circles that the deaconess movement was due *not* "to many individuals, but to one only, [Lucy Rider Meyer] and consequently that one individual is entitled to direct and shape the Deaconess Work of the Church." They exhorted the Methodist constituency to recognize that the "Deaconess Work of American Methodism owes its rise to *various causes and individuals.*"[9] This critique cannot be dismissed lightly because both the WHMS as well as Robinson exercised a formidable role in developing and promoting the Methodist deaconess movement.

Jane Bancroft Robinson (1847–1932) was the daughter of a Methodist minister. Like Meyer, she was well-educated with a PhD from Syracuse University. She worked at Northwestern University for nine years as

6. Keller, "Creating a Sphere For Women," 251. Keller's focus on Meyer also appears in other articles, such as "Deaconess: 'New Woman,'" 33–40; "Women and the Nature of Ministry," 99–114; and Prelinger and Keller, "Function of Female Bonding," 318–37.

7. Lindley, *'You Have Stept Out of Your Place,'* 132.

8. Lindley, *'You Have Stept Out of Your Place,'* 133.

9. *Early History of Deaconess Work*, 5, 6. Emphasis added.

Dean of the Woman's College and Professor of French. Then, when Bryn Mawr College opened, she became its first Fellow of History. While on an extended study leave in Europe, she encountered Methodist deaconesses in Zurich, Switzerland. As noted in chapter 1, she published a book cataloguing her research on European deaconesses. Christian Golder, a leader of German Methodist deaconess work in the US, had nothing but praise for her book. "Several editions of the book have been published, and it has been the means of enlightening the Church on the important subject of which it treats." He also called her "the Evangelist of the Deaconess Work in the Methodist Church in the United States."[10]

After her return to America in 1888, the WHMS appointed her as General Secretary of their newly formed Deaconess Bureau. In this position, she traveled from city to city giving speeches, opening deaconess homes, and raising funds, devoting twenty years in all to deaconess work. Golder catalogued her accomplishments in these words:

> The Homes at Philadelphia, Baltimore, Buffalo, Pittsburgh, San Francisco, Los Angeles, Washington, Brooklyn, and Denver owe their existence to her efforts, and under her direction the work of the Deaconess Bureau has increased to such an extent that to-day no less than forty-two institutions are connected with the Woman's Home Missionary Society. The aggregate value of the property amounts to over half a million dollars. There are 375 deaconesses, including probationers, in these Homes.[11]

Unfortunately, Robinson and Meyer engaged in a legendary and long-lasting feud. It was likened by a contemporary as to the "'Thirty Years War' which, like its historical prototype of the Middle Ages, ended without victory and little glory to either side, and for a time threatened to wreck the cause for which it was waged."[12] The disagreement erupted over the question of where, or to which Methodist organization, deaconess work belonged. Meyer interpreted the decision of the 1888 General Conference of the MEC, which sanctioned the Office of Deaconess, as placing deaconess work under the authority of the general church. Her organizational model was known as "the Church Plan." Dougherty suggests that

---

10. Golder, *History of the Deaconess Movement*, 327.
11. Golder, *History of the Deaconess Movement*, 326–27.
12. Horton, *High Adventure*, 190.

Meyer preferred this model because "she believed the deaconess movement 'immensely larger' than any society."[13]

Robinson countered that deaconess work belonged to a woman's organization, specifically the WHMS, which she believed initiated the movement. Perhaps she preferred this decentralized organizational plan, as Dougherty conjectures, because it replicated the "European model of deaconess work" in which the principal of each institution supervised their own deaconesses. A second possibility that Dougherty mentions but does not pursue, is that Robinson advocated the WHMS as the organization to administrate deaconess work because it was "an independent woman's society," which was "financially and administratively autonomous of the church."[14] It is this second possibility that I will pursue further in light of Estelle Freedman's concept of "female institution building." From Freedman's perspective, Robinson's strategy of housing deaconess work under the authority of a woman's organization can be interpreted not as diminishing women's sphere of activity, but rather as investing it with power and increased opportunities.

Freedman argues that women reformers' political and social power during the Progressive Era, particularly among well-educated women like Meyer and Robinson, began with, was sustained by, and ultimately triumphed in large measure through the separatist strategy of female institution building.[15] Women reformers utilized this strategy to develop organizations separate from men in order to exert their power and influence in the public sphere. The benefit to women was that this strategy "helped mobilize women and gained political leverage in the larger society" while at the same time maintained "the positive attraction of the female world of close, personal relationships and domestic institutional structures."[16] Kathryn Kish Sklar makes the same case in her article on the Hull House settlement in Chicago. "Strengthened by the support of women's separate institutions, women reformers were able to develop their capacity for political leadership."[17] Studies of other reformers, such

---

13. Dougherty, "Methodist Deaconess," 57.
14. Dougherty, "Methodist Deaconess," 57.
15. Freedman, "Separatism As Strategy," 513.
16. Freedman, "Separatism As Strategy," 513, 517.
17. Sklar, "Hull House in the 1890s," 659.

as Florence Kelley,[18] Julia Lathrop,[19] and Miriam Van Waters,[20] demonstrate that women effectively utilized the strategy of female institution building. They exploited the power base available to them from voluntary organizations to women's care for children. For instance, Robyn Muncy demonstrates the connection between female institution building and political reform in Julia Lathrop's child welfare policy in the early twentieth century. She writes, "Lathrop used the national network of female voluntary organizations which she knew through her work in the settlements . . . The chief [Lathrop] self-consciously wooed these voluntary groups . . . Already a member of the General Federation of Women's Clubs, Lathrop joined many more women's groups after becoming head of the Children's Bureau."[21]

Historians also find that women reformers in religious organizations adopted this same strategy. Evelyn Brooks Higginbotham applies Freedman's thesis to her study of the women's movement in the Black Baptist Church. Higginbotham contends that Black women, by utilizing this separate sphere strategy, gained leadership opportunities, a sense of sisterhood, and denominational influence: "The success of the overall movement depended, in no small measure, upon what Estelle Freedman calls the 'separatist strategy of female institution building.' Moreover, the existence of a female community and its mobilization into a separate organizational base commanded greater authority and respect for women."[22] Keller draws similar conclusions concerning the strategic importance of MEC women's organizations, though she curiously omits any reference in her article to Robinson, who was the deaconess leader to champion this separatist strategy. Instead, Keller focuses on Meyer who rejected it.[23]

Keller's preference for Meyer is not unique. Other historians of the deaconess movement interpret Meyer's strategy of seeking power and opportunities in the men's sphere as more liberative for women. While they

18. See Sklar, *Florence Kelley*, and Sklar, "Two Political Cultures," 36–62.
19. Muncy, *Creating a Female Dominion in American Reform*.
20. Freedman, "Separatism Revisited," 170–88.
21. Muncy, *Creating a Female Dominion in American Reform*, 58. Maureen Flanagan draws similar conclusions about the strategy utilized in this same time period by the Woman's City Club of Chicago as compared to the Men's City Club of Chicago. See Flanagan, "Gender and Urban Political Reform," 1032–50.
22. Higginbotham, *Righteous Discontent*, 79–80.
23. Keller, "Creating a Sphere For Women," 246–60.

attest to the empowerment of the female institution building strategy for some women's groups, they dismiss its application to the deaconess movement.[24] In doing so, they continue to overlook Robinson's contributions. This persistent trend erases the complexities of a movement, replete with vying personalities and strategies. In contrast, a more accurate reconstruction will integrate Robinson's legacy alongside Meyer's as two deaconess leaders who endeavored in their respective ways to expand women's roles and access to leadership in a patriarchal church.

Deaconess Labors: Social Service and Evangelism

The second conclusion from Dougherty's study to be re-evaluated is that deaconesses labored principally in social service. Her emphasis on social service fits her stated agenda, which is to gain recognition for deaconesses as early social workers. She critiques historians of social work for failing to grasp the pivotal role played by religious groups, like the deaconess movement, in the development of the profession. "In separating the history of Christian social service from the evolution of social work as a profession, scholars have exaggerated the differences and obscured the similarities between religious and secular reformers in the Progressive period."[25] Dougherty develops this connection to social work, however, only by minimizing the religious sensibilities of deaconesses. She writes, "Yet, the more committed the movement became to the necessity for social change and the more involved deaconesses became in bringing about that change the more indistinguishable deaconesses became from secular social workers."[26]

Despite her concentration on social service, Dougherty's study includes data that confirm that evangelism was also a common deaconess labor. In her statistics on the career profiles of 509 deaconesses who

---

24. One historian even blamed Robinson's supposedly unsatisfactory strategy on her socio-economic status. "Beside Bancroft Robinson's more elite vision, Rider Meyer's was inclusive and inspirational to women of various classes." Oehler, "Femininity and Religious Anxiety," 70.

25. Dougherty, "Methodist Deaconess," 121.

26. Dougherty, "Methodist Deaconess," 123–24. Following Dougherty's lead, Sarah Sloan Kreutziger repeats these same conclusions. "All women of early professional social work, however, owed a debt to their deaconess sisters . . . for helping to make 'perfecting society' a legitimate concern and subsequent career path for women of the late nineteenth century." Kreutziger, "Going On To Perfection," 236.

were graduated from Meyer's training school, the number of deaconess evangelists (88) nearly equaled that of deaconess nurses (87).[27] The highest number in any category applied to deaconess visitors (381).[28] This last statistic is pertinent for measuring the extent of evangelistic work because the deaconess visitor often evangelized, sharing the gospel as she visited. Meyer herself explained that the deaconess visitor was often also an evangelist, who rejoiced "in little children rescued, souls saved, and the 'sweetness and light' of the gospel penetrating homes and hearts till now in the darkness and shadow of death."[29] Given this profile of a deaconess visitor, we should include, even provisionally, the 381 deaconess visitors along with the eighty-eight deaconess evangelists for a total of 469 deaconesses from CTS engaged in evangelism.

In her interpretation of the data, Dougherty admits that deaconesses often attended to the spiritual as well as the physical needs of a person, so both evangelism and social service were requisite deaconess labors. Precisely this attention to spiritual needs, often through evangelism, provided the point of separation between the deaconess movement and the settlement movement, two movements that in Dougherty's opinion were otherwise quite similar.[30] Nevertheless, despite her statistics and at least the tacit acknowledgment of evangelism as a deaconess labor, she still concludes that deaconesses primarily provided social service, an interpretation that diminishes evangelism and exaggerates social service. More puzzling, however, is the tenor of a later essay in which she lists many deaconess labors without including evangelism: "The first generation of Methodist deaconesses served as pastor's assistants, nurses, traveler's aids, social workers, and educators, roles deemed gender appropriate by church and state."[31] The complete exclusion of evangelism from this list is a noteworthy example of the inaccurate reduction of the deaconess movement's multi-faceted activities.

Once again, subsequent historians follow her lead. Carolyn De Swarte Gifford, in her introduction to a collection of deaconess source

---

27. Dougherty, "Methodist Deaconess," 102.

28. Dougherty, "Methodist Deaconess," 102.

29. Meyer, *Deaconesses*, 71.

30. She concludes, "Convinced that the whole person, body, mind, and spirit had to be considered in any philosophy of social work, deaconesses were pre-disposed to lament the purely secular social settlement's insistence on the elimination of religion." Dougherty, "Methodist Deaconess," 121.

31. Dougherty, *My Calling To Fulfill*, x.

documents, lists the following as their labors: teachers, nurses, caregivers for the poor and children, and "social service professionals" who canvassed neighborhoods "to identify and detail bad living conditions in an area and to project what was needed to correct them."[32] Evangelism did not make the cut. Further, in her description of the practical training that CTS offered, Gifford neglects to mention that evangelism was a curricular option and lists only "nursing, religious education, and home economics."[33] Jean Miller Schmidt, in her history of women in Methodism, reiterates Dougherty's conclusion that social service was the principal deaconess labor: "Trained for and consecrated to the order, they became experts in the field of Christian social service."[34] Schmidt does briefly acknowledge two types of deaconesses—"nurse deaconesses and missionary deaconesses (also referred to as visitors or evangelists)"—although she proceeds to discuss only nurse deaconesses, paying no further attention to missionary deaconesses who labored in evangelism.[35]

When evangelism is repeatedly excluded from lists and descriptions of deaconess labors, historians misrepresent not only the deaconess movement but also Meyer, herself, who maintained an essential commitment to evangelism both educationally and personally. Educationally, she showcased her commitment to evangelism in her training school curriculum, which included elective courses in each department. In the course listing under the Department of Instruction for Evangelism at CTS, there were three elective courses: Individual Evangelism, World Wide Evangelism, and The Psychology of Evangelism.[36] Meyer encouraged students training to become deaconess visitors to take these courses because she considered education in evangelistic work to be a premium. "It is not a light matter to undertake in any degree to be the spiritual guide and help of an immortal soul; and those who are to make this their constant work should be as well prepared as possible, by qualities both natural and acquired."[37]

The curriculum demonstrated what Meyer believed personally about the importance of evangelism. In her article entitled,

32. Gifford, *American Deaconess Movement*, 10.
33. Gifford, *American Deaconess Movement*, 5.
34. See Schmidt, *Grace Sufficient*, 207.
35. Schmidt, *Grace Sufficient*, 202–03.
36. This list of courses comes from an appendix in Isabelle Horton's book on the early years of the Chicago Training School. See Horton, *Builders*, 205.
37. Meyer, *Deaconesses*, 68–69.

"Deaconesses and the Need," she expressed in passionate prose her high regard for evangelism:

> Would you have everybody interested in the evangelistic work? Jesus would. A work for which God the Father spared not his own Son may well claim *the intensest energies of every one of us*, until it is done. But what my art, my literary pursuits, my society? May I not live for them? No, no, no! In a world full of souls with eternal life or death just before them—souls every one of whom has cost the heart's blood of a God to redeem—no one has a right to live for art, or for literature, or for science, or society, or wealth. . . . All these things God intends as means and means alone—not an end—not to live for. We may use them just as long as they . . . can be used directly in furthering God's work . . . To amass money that one may simply have it—O foolish one. 'This night shall thy soul be required of thee.' It is to lie down, after all, in an empty coffin.[38]

Another deaconess leader who also believed that evangelism required "the intensest energies of every one of us" was Iva Durham Vennard (1871–1945). She became a Methodist at the age of twelve during her conversion in a revival meeting. Vennard attended Wellesley College for a year and was poised to continue her education at Swarthmore College when, at a camp meeting, her educational plans were altered by a call to evangelistic work. Opportunities immediately came her way to participate in revival meetings first as a singer, then as a preacher. In her early twenties, she attended a lecture on deaconess work by Lucy Rider Meyer. Evidently, Vennard heard something that resonated in Meyer's talk because she soon enrolled in the Deaconess Home in Buffalo, New York. She was assigned to be a deaconess evangelist under the auspices of the WHMS Deaconess Bureau, which Jane Bancroft Robinson administered. In this capacity, Vennard held evangelistic meetings in churches throughout the state of New York. After several successful years as a deaconess evangelist, she was appointed to be a Deaconess-at-Large, which required her to travel around the country promoting the work of the WHMS Deaconess Bureau. This institutional focus sidelined her evangelistic ministry, but when she protested, Robinson's reply, according to Vennard's biographer, was that "evangelism was not the method of the WHMS."[39] Robinson also declined to pursue Vennard's idea for establishing a course of study to

---

38. Meyer, "Deaconesses and the Need," 9. Emphasis added.
39. Bowie, *Alabaster and Spikenard*, 90.

train deaconesses in evangelism. When they could not reconcile their conflicting opinions on evangelism, Vennard resigned her position with the Deaconess Bureau.

A cryptic editorial note buried at the end of Robinson's annual report for 1899–1900 encapsulates the conflict between the two women. After a column of statistics on Vennard's work for the Deaconess Bureau, including the number of miles traveled, addresses given, and funds raised, this note was appended by Robinson and her sister, Henrietta Bancroft, who was also active in the WHMS Deaconess Bureau: "Miss Durham's service and influence are not to be measured by material standards, as her work as Deaconess-at-Large has aimed at spiritual rather than material results. She has, however, procured substantial money aid for the Society, as future events will disclose."[40] One observation about the editorial note is that its curious wording not only evinces a distinction between the material and spiritual realms but also clearly states a preference for the material. This preference coincides with every one of Robinson's annual reports with their overwhelming display of financial, personnel, property, and institutional statistics.

Another observation is that Vennard's accomplishments in the spiritual realm had to be justified by the final reference to material results, the "substantial money aid for the Society" which she raised. The addition of this editorial note to interpret Vennard's statistics suggests how maladroitly evangelism suited Robinson's conception of deaconess labors. In fact, Robinson did *not* consider evangelism to be a deaconess labor. In her book's penultimate chapter, she outlined three areas of deaconess work—nursing, teaching, and assisting a pastor. Again, evangelism did not make the list. As adamant as Robinson was that evangelism was *not* a deaconess labor, Vennard believed with equal ferocity that evangelism was *the* priority of deaconess work.

After Vennard left the WHMS Deaconess Bureau, she founded Epworth Evangelistic Institute (EEI), a deaconess training school in St. Louis. EEI was characterized, as its middle name implied, by her intention to train students to be evangelists in every deaconess labor. "Real, genuine, soul saving work," she stated, "is the fundamental mission of all deaconess work, and no deaconess measures up to her privilege in service

---

40. Robinson and Bancroft, "Bureau for Deaconess Work," 134.

or fulfills her responsibility toward God who does not aim persistently at the definite regeneration of her people."[41]

Yet, the school's name did not encapsulate all that Vennard believed and taught about deaconess labors because even though evangelism was the priority, she set up her training school to offer students practical experience in a range of social services. Such experience came readily since she located EEI in a notorious tenement district in St. Louis called Kerry Patch. This neighborhood was vividly described by Maria Woodworth-Etter, an evangelist who held a tent revival there for several weeks a decade earlier.

> The only place we could get room enough was 'Kerry Patch,' a place noted for the hoodlum element . . . People have been shot down or robbed or stoned here, any hour of the day. . . . The Christians tried to persuade us not to pitch our tents in 'Kerry Patch' . . . they said there had been several show tents put up where ours stood, and the rough element cut the ropes and tore their tents down. . . . They would shoot off firecrackers, and when we sang, they sang the louder; when we prayed, they clapped their hands and cheered us. Several ministers tried to talk, but they were stoned down or their voices drowned out. It looked like surrender or death.[42]

As we will see in the next chapter, the practical work EEI sponsored in Kerry Patch provided students with experience in settings where needs were great, from the juvenile court to the red-light district. Like Meyer, Vennard also envisioned deaconess labors as a two-fold approach merging evangelism and social service.

Still, there were differences between Vennard and Meyer regarding how much to emphasize evangelism. Vennard believed that evangelism was paramount in everything a deaconess did. She stipulated that *all* deaconesses were to be evangelists no matter what their specific assignment, which meant they evangelized as they visited door to door, nursed the sick, taught sewing, or supervised children. Meyer was less prescriptive in her approach to evangelism, which is evident in its being an elective, not a required course, in the CTS curriculum. She considered it as one category of deaconess work, alongside nursing, teaching, and social service. Still, despite the difference in emphasis, they both considered evangelism to be a significant deaconess labor. Evangelism, as Meyer declared,

---

41. Vennard, "'Help Those Women,'" 8.
42. Woodworth, *Life, Work, and Experience of Maria Beulah Woodworth*, 342–43.

"may well claim the intensest energies of every one of us, until it is done." The implication of this discussion, therefore, calls for an expanded reconstruction of the Methodist deaconess movement that incorporates evangelism alongside social service as significant deaconess labors.

A "Dangerous and Powerful" Woman

Although Vennard may appear at first glance to be the less intimidating among these three women, nevertheless, a group of Methodist men in St. Louis became consumed with ousting her as principal of EEI.[43] The story begins shortly after the school's founding when these prominent clergymen and laymen began to raise multiple objections about the school as well as about her. They criticized her appointment of women faculty to teach courses in theology and the Bible. They objected to women being trained in evangelism because women, in their opinion, were not suited for evangelism, only for religious education. And they lodged the accusation that Vennard trained "women preachers under the guise of deaconess work." For that reason, the Presiding Elder of the St. Louis Annual Conference of the MEC called Vennard a "dangerous and powerful woman."[44]

Their accusations were not entirely unfounded. After all, they had open access to faculty rosters, book lists, and student activities. They could peruse announcements in the "Personals" column of EEI's monthly newsletter, *Inasmuch*, about alums leading revivals, preaching, and serving local churches. For instance, they might have read about Miss Rebecca Bell who "visited Epworth a few days before going South for a three months' revival campaign. Her first engagement is with Rev. Wm. R. Chase's church in New Orleans, La."[45] They might also have seen announcements about the deaconesses who became pastors, such as "Mrs. Cooper, a Deaconess who has been acting as Pastor of the Methodist Episcopal Church of Harrisonville, Mo., by appointment of the Presiding Elder of that District, spent the week after Conference resting at Epworth."[46]

---

43. Bowie, *Alabaster and Spikenard*, 136.
44. Bowie, *Alabaster and Spikenard*, 124.
45. "Personals," 8.
46. "Personals," 8.

Opposition from these men rose to a crisis point in the fall of 1909 when Vennard returned from maternity leave, after the birth of her only child, William, to find sweeping changes at EEI. These men took advantage of her absence to stage a coup. They revised the school charter, removed evangelism courses from the curriculum, and replaced EEI's female faculty with clergymen who taught Bible and theology. Their rationale for these changes, according to Vennard's biographer, was that these women, like Vennard herself, had overstepped women's sphere and moved into the male sphere where they did not belong. "Methodist preachers do not want deaconesses who study theology. We can attend to that ourselves. We want women as helpers who will work with the children, care for the sick, and visit the poor. If our deaconesses are trained in theology they will become critical of the preachers, and that will be the end of the deaconess movement."[47] After Vennard resigned as EEI principal, the minutes of the St. Louis Annual Conference provided an ironic epitaph to her departure: "Epworth Deaconess Institute is getting a firmer grip on the situation in St. Louis."[48]

Vennard's vision for EEI and the Methodist deaconess movement did not focus on forging political inroads for deaconesses or championing publicly the ordination of women (although she did among her students). She was neither theologically nor socially progressive. In that respect, it is no wonder she fell through the historiographical cracks of studies in American women's religious history in general or even the Methodist deaconess movement more specifically. Rather, what her opponents, both male and female, found so disturbing was her unrelenting vision of deaconesses as evangelists. For Jane Bancroft Robinson, she was an anomaly. For Methodist clergymen and laymen in St. Louis, she was a dangerous and powerful woman. For the rest of us, she represents a tragic loss of memory when any such multifaceted movement, like the Methodist deaconess movement, is reduced simply to one leader, one labor.

Reflection Questions

1. How does the focus on Lucy Rider Meyer as the central figure of the Methodist deaconess movement overshadow the contributions

---

47. Bowie, *Alabaster and Spikenard*, 145.
48. *Minutes of the Forty-Third Session of the St. Louis Annual Conference*, 307.

of other leaders, like Jane Bancroft Robinson and Iva Durham Vennard? Which leader do you resonate with most, and why?

2. What were the implications of this internal debate on women's roles in the Methodist church at the time? Where do you see this debate continuing today?

"EXPERIENCES OF A DEACONESS GUITAR"[1]

Iva Durham Vennard

During her years in the Deaconess work under the W.H.M.S., Miss Durham composed a soliloquy supposed to come from her guitar. It was published in the September 16, 1899, issue of *The Epworth Herald*,[2] and was set out in pamphlet form by the W.H.M.S. from New York City.

I suppose in the other days when my strings knew so well the jingle of gay college tunes, that people thought me a very frivolous instrument, and little did they predict a really useful future for me. When I entered this new life I had no idea how thrilling it would all be, but this was the reason of it. A great change had come over "my lady." She found my soul, and for love of her I was glad to become a deaconess guitar. We have good times together, my lady in her black garb,[3] and I. I've been dedicated to the glory of King Jesus, and it is so beautiful to belong to God. Would you like to know about a few of the many, many places where we have been?

One night about nine o'clock we went down to a midnight mission in the very heart of the slums. We had such a pitiful audience there—men with manhood gone, wrecked and lost in vice. A thrilling message was given, then my lady sang the invitation:

    1. This source document is in Bowie, *Alabaster and Spikenard*, 74–77.

    2. The *Epworth Herald* was published from 1890 until 1940 as the official newspaper in the northeastern United States of the Epworth League. The Epworth League, founded in 1889, was the MEC youth organization, which became the largest Protestant youth organization in the US.

    3. The deaconess uniform

If you are tired of the load of your sin,
Let Jesus come into your heart.[4]

How those men wept! The altar was soon filled, and that night the Lion of Judah[5] broke the shackles from sin-cursed souls.

One day one of our nurse deaconesses found a poor woman who was suffering extremely. She was a wretched, friendless outcast, and had no one to care for her but a little girl about eleven years old. She was in an indescribable condition of neglect and almost crazed by the opium she had been using for several weeks. The nurse came home and told us all about the case, and the next day my lady and I went with her to do all we could do to comfort the sufferer. When we entered the sick room the woman was moaning and raving, sometimes praying, sometimes cursing. My lady tried to soothe her, but it was of no avail; then she took me up, and as she softly touched my strings I knew she wanted me to be tender. She sang over and over again:

You've carried your burden, you've carried it long,
O bring it to Jesus, He's loving and strong.[6]

And the poor tired woman was quieted. A few weeks later the penitent Magdalene[7] accepted "the Jesus story," and her sins, though as scarlet, were blotted out.

One Christmas eve we went over to a Christmas tree which our kindergartners had for their troop of dear foreign "babies." The tree was beautifully trimmed, and everywhere among the tinsel were toys peeping out. We had the happiest music that night, all singing with good cheer, and when we sang the sweet old cradle hymn, "Little Lord Jesus asleep in the hay,"[8] all the children joined in. When we came to the distribution of

---

4. The first two lines in the hymn, "If You Are Tired of the Load of Your Sin," authored by Lelia (Mrs. C. H.) Morris (1862–1929).

5. In Rev 5:5, the term, Lion of Judah, is applied to Jesus Christ: "Then one of the elders said to me, 'Do not weep. See, the Lion of the tribe of Judah, the Root of David, has conquered, so that he can open the scroll and its seven seals.'"

6. A hymn written by Ballington Booth (1857–1940), the second child of William and Catherine Booth.

7. Mary Magdalene was a follower of Jesus named in the Gospels as accompanying him on his travels along with other women and the disciples. In Luke 8:2, she is described as someone "from whom seven demons had gone out." Throughout church history, she has often been portrayed as a prostitute, an image to which this document alludes.

8. A line from the Christmas hymn, "Away in a Manger."

gifts the tiny tots were wild with delight. Some little girls clasped to their hearts a doll of their very own for the first time in their lives, and they were supremely content. When everyone had gone I heard one of my sisters say that it was the happiest Christmas eve she had ever known. I suppose it is really true that it is more blessed to give than to receive.[9]

I remember so well a meeting we had one Sunday at a rescue home.[10] Our audience was a strange one—all women who had known the bitterness of the dregs of the cup of sin. We learned the stories of some of them, and they were so full of cruel injustice that we yearned to bring them peace. The message was a gentle one, all radiant with love, and then my lady sang the plaintive old plantation melody, "De Massa ob de Sheepfol."[11] As the girls followed the song which told how "de Massa" loves the lost black sheep, and came Himself to "let down de bahs" for them all to come in, the precious Spirit touched their heavy, hopeless hearts, and at the close of the song, eight sobbing voices asked for prayer. It was a glorious hour, for One was in the midst whose name is Wonderful—the Prince of Peace.[12]

But this life does not always keep us among the submerged classes. Once, while in parish work for a few days in a strange city, we were entertained in the luxurious home of a very wealthy man of the world. On our first evening there our host took us into the spacious and elegant music room where he had often received noted artists. He asked my lady to sing. What a contrast our music must have been! But she took me up and struck one simple chord. The hymn was "Christ is all,"[13] and again that dear consecration hymn:

> I'll go where you want me to go, dear Lord.[14]

---

9. Acts 20:35.

10. A rescue home was a place where prostitutes and unwed mothers could take refuge from the world and hear the gospel. Rescue home founders hoped that women staying in the home would experience a conversion to Jesus Christ. For more on Vennard and rescue work, see Pope-Levison, "Expanding the Historiography of Methodist Settlement Work," 169–90.

11. This song came from a poem, "De Massa ob de Sheepfol," by Sarah Pratt McLean Greene (1856–1935).

12. Isa 9:6.

13. "Christ is all, all in all" is the refrain from the hymn, "I Entered Once a Home of Care," written by William A. Williams (1854–1938).

14. The first refrain line in a hymn by the same title written by Mary Brown (1856–1918).

The proud man was touched. He became an ardent friend of our work, and when my lady left his home he gave her a handsome check and bade her a fervent "Godspeed."

But perhaps I am tiring you by these reminiscences. In parting, let me say there is nothing so sweet as serving others "for the love of Christ and in His name."

Reflection Questions

1. How is music portrayed both as a vehicle of ministry as well as an emotional connection in the various settings—slums, rescue homes, and wealthy homes—described in the soliloquy?

2. What is your opinion about how Vennard ministered to the poor, the rich, and the outcast? Is her approach applicable today?

Scarritt Bible and Training School, Methodist Episcopal Church South

Staff of The Deaconess College, Wesley Deaconess Order

Chapter III

PIONEERS IN AMERICAN WOMEN'S THEOLOGICAL EDUCATION

Methodist Deaconess Training Schools[1]

Overview

THIS CHAPTER TAKES UP the topic of deaconess training schools. While two schools are analyzed in detail—Chicago Training School (CTS) and Epworth Evangelistic Institute (EEI)—the core academic curriculum in every deaconess training school covered the same subjects: Bible, theology, church history, methods of evangelism, and the history of Methodism with a particular focus on women. The other part of the curriculum focused on practical work experience in a wide range of ministry settings. Through an in-depth look at the curriculum, particularly how substantively the academic subjects were covered, this chapter will demonstrate that deaconess training schools provided theological education to women decades before Protestant theological seminaries opened their doors to them. The first source document, "An Examination of Candidates," sets out in detail what aspiring students were expected to know *before* they were accepted into the Deaconess College of the Wesley Deaconess Order (WDO) in the UK. Then, the second source document, "A Student's View

---

1. This chapter was first published in *Methodist Review* 10 (2019) 73–91. Changes to this version eliminated duplication with material included in earlier chapters.

of College Life," details what a typical day was like for those who passed the examination and were enrolled as a student in the college.

From the late nineteenth to the mid-twentieth century, religious training schools, not seminaries, provided theological education for Protestant women. Seminaries lagged far behind in seating women in their classrooms. As Virginia Brereton commented, women "fared better" at training schools "than at most theological seminaries, where either they were not admitted at all or were relegated to subordinate status."[2] Scores of women enrolled in these schools, including deaconess training schools, compared to a few brave women who matriculated at a theological seminary. That very accomplishment took its toll on Anna Howard Shaw, who faced isolation and opposition from the forty-two male students in her class at Boston University School of Theology in 1876. She recalled in her autobiography, aptly subtitled *The Story of a Pioneer*, that the class "was composed of forty-two young men and my unworthy self, and before I had been a member of it an hour I realized that women theologians paid heavily for the privilege of being women."[3]

Gender discrimination at seminaries had financial ramifications as well because women students did not qualify for the room and board remuneration available to men.[4] As a result, Shaw languished in poverty while taking classes. She skipped meals for prolonged periods to save money, a starvation diet which rendered her susceptible to illness. More than a decade later, the situation had not improved for women at the Boston school. According to Benjamin Hartley, "In 1890 the student enrollment list contained only five women, all special students apparently not admitted to a degree program."[5] Not until after the Second World War would women enroll in seminaries in noticeable numbers. In his monumental work on theological education, Glenn Miller ties the increase in the number of women in seminary to the United States government, rather than to a sudden change in course or principle by seminary administrators. According to Miller, "The GI Bill also had an indirect influence that no one, including the government planners, appeared to have anticipated. By funding the education of men with wives and, in some cases, children, the government changed the character of

2. Brereton, *Training God's Army*, 129.
3. Shaw, *Anna Howard Shaw*, 82–83.
4. Zink-Sawyer, *From Preachers To Suffragists*, 113.
5. Hartley, "Salvation and Sociology," 189.

seminary education. . . . The schools came to see themselves as places for both genders."[6]

However, for more than fifty years before the 1944 passage of the GI Bill, women had full access to theological education in deaconess training schools. In their classrooms, they studied the Bible, book by book, with corresponding maps and geographical diagrams, became conversant with ancient Jewish and Christian authors, mastered theological movements in successive generations of church history, and learned about theological doctrines from creation to glorification. They also became experts in Methodist history and doctrine through assiduous study of the discipline, catechism, and James Porter's *Compendium of Methodism*, which covered "The History and Present Conditions of Its Various Branches in All Countries, with a Defence of its Doctrinal, Governmental, and Prudential Peculiarities." Due to the robust curriculum in core theological subjects, I will argue in this chapter that deaconess training schools provided theological education for women decades before seminaries admitted them as students. I then conclude with the observation that the holistic curriculum of deaconess training schools, integrating theological and practical dimensions, presaged future developments in theological education.

Women's Education in Late-Nineteenth Century America

The institution building of deaconess training schools from the mid-1880s coincided with a meteoric rise across the US in the number of women students enrolling in secondary educational institutions.[7] This increase happened despite Edward Clarke's medical warning of the impending danger to women's wombs and childbearing potential of too much education, as cataloged in his highly influential book, *Sex in Education*, published in 1873. Clarke stated that a woman's energy, needed primarily for childbearing, would be depleted because "'a regular, uninterrupted, and sustained course of work' diverted 'blood from the reproductive apparatus to the head.'"[8] This argument coincides, suggests Ann Douglas Wood,

---

6. Miller, *Piety and Profession*, 656.

7. Portions of this section are reprinted and adapted from the author's *Building the Old Time Religion: Women Evangelists in the Progressive Era* with permission from NYU Press © 2014.

8. Clarke, *Sex in Education*, 125–26; quoted in Sklar, *Florence Kelley*, 52–53.

with "an underlying logic running through popular books by physicians on women's diseases to the effect that ladies get sick *because* they are unfeminine—in other words, sexually aggressive, intellectually ambitious, and defective in proper womanly submission and selflessness."[9]

Nonetheless, women came to school in such numbers that statistics on the disproportionate gender enrollment evoked widespread concern about the feminization of high schools and attracted the US Commissioner of Education's attention when, in 1888, male enrollment in public high schools only reached 25 percent in the ten largest cities. This trend continued into the next decade when female high school graduates outnumbered males by a two-to-one ratio.[10] Mary Agnes Dougherty cites statistics demonstrating that many deaconesses benefitted from these educational opportunities and had already completed a high school education before enrolling in a deaconess training school.[11]

In a comprehensive study of religious training schools, Brereton set out their general description:

> an institution—sometimes denominational, sometimes nondenominational—operating at roughly a high school level and training men and women as evangelists, missionaries, religious teachers, musicians, pastors, and other workers for the conservative Protestant evangelical churches. To this end the schools sent their students out to supplement their classroom experience with actual religious work and offered subjects such as the history of missions, Sunday school pedagogy, methods of evangelism, and, above all, Bible study.[12]

Nathan Hatch depicts the significance of religious training schools for thousands of working-class Protestants in these words: "Like early Methodism, these movements opened educational and leadership opportunities to common people. The movements initiated a massive, if largely unnoticed, educational effort by founding at least two-hundred-fifty Bible schools in the twentieth century. Seldom barring anyone who possessed a rudimentary education, these schools replenished churches with leaders who bypassed normal professional certification."[13]

9. Wood, "'Fashionable Diseases,'" 8.
10. Rury, *Education and Women's Work*, 4, 19.
11. Dougherty, *My Calling to Fulfill*, 98n6.
12. Brereton, *Training God's Army*, vii.
13. Hatch, *Democratization of American Christianity*, 216.

Unlike theological seminaries, training schools offered a shorthand curriculum, promising "brevity, practicality, and efficiency."[14] "What was wanted by these young enthusiasts was a practical course of study in the scriptures—one that would not force a student to wait around for years to do undergraduate work, then attend seminary before entering the ranks of the ministry."[15] Advocates of training schools lobbied against seminaries, claiming that they could only educate so many students with the heavily academic curriculum, they could not manage the countless influx of students wanting to be trained, and they did not offer training in practical work. An additional argument in favor of training schools was their willingness, even eagerness, to enroll women, especially in the early years. Thus, religious training schools stepped into the gap between a seminary education and no education at all, to provide a modicum of education and training before students embarked on their religious work.

An early supporter of the idea of deaconesses in Methodism, Susan Fry, had already identified the need for such women to be trained before heading into full-time religious work. In 1872, she published her rationale for thorough training. She began with a brief historical survey of Roman Catholic women's communities devoted to service, then she made an impassioned plea for Protestant women to do the same but only *after* completing a thorough training. "Looking at the sisterhoods, we can not fail to see that their success lies not in celibacy, but in system; not in monarchism, but in organization; not so much in blind devotion as in *thorough training*. When shall the question cease to be asked, 'Why can not Protestant women do what these Roman Catholic women do?'"[16] More than twenty years later, Maria Layng Gibson, Principal of Scarritt Bible and Training School in Kansas City, Missouri, described the institution's purpose similarly as a place of "thorough systematic training for Christian service." Continuing, Gibson declared, "The need for an increased number of trained workers in the Church is manifest, and the mission of this institution is to meet this need and to develop the unused power of Christian women."[17] Such schools provided the classrooms, curriculum, and teachers for training thousands of women for their deaconess labors as nurses, teachers, evangelists, pastors, visitors, and missionaries.

14. Brereton, *Training God's Army*, 62.
15. Brown, "Comparative Analysis of Bible College Quality," 53, 55.
16. Fry, "Ancient and Modern Sisterhoods," 245.
17. Bigham, "Scarritt Bible and Training School," 262.

Chicago Training School (CTS) and Epworth Evangelistic Institute (EEI)

As noted in the previous chapter, CTS, founded by Meyer, was the first Methodist deaconess training school launched in the US. Meyer's dream for a school took root as she worked for several years for the Illinois State Sunday School Association. She traveled to churches, church conventions, and Sunday school gatherings throughout the state and found herself dumbfounded by people's biblical illiteracy. "I became greatly impressed," she confided, "with the astonishing, and to me alarming ignorance of the Bible on the part of our Church people, Sunday-school teachers, and Christian workers. My own knowledge of the word of God was superficial enough, but when I saw people looking for Jude in the Old Testament, or for one of the minor prophets in the New, I realized the great need of more thorough and comprehensive Bible study on the part of those who were, or might become religious teachers."[18]

A similar resolve to establish a deaconess training school ignited in twenty-six-year-old Iva Durham Vennard. Supported by a trio of Methodist bishops, including James Thoburn, she opened EEI in St. Louis in 1902 and marketed it as "A School of practice for Deaconesses, Evangelists and Missionaries" whose design was "to give the impulse of direct soul-winning to every department of Christian service."[19]

Curriculum

The curriculum at deaconess training schools, like CTS and EEI, followed the bishops' course of study instituted for deaconesses. This pattern of an established course of study approved by bishops replicated the earliest provision for theological education in the Methodist church in the US as set out in the 1816 *Discipline*. As Gerald McCulloh explains, "For the first time, a formal action was approved which was to provide a curriculum and system of supervision for the study and intellectual qualifications of the preacher."[20] The 1816 report commended

---

18. Meyer, *Deaconesses*, 90.

19. *Minutes of the Thirty-Ninth Session of the St. Louis Annual Conference*, back page.

20. McCulloh, *Ministerial Education*, 12. Dale Patterson introduces the course of study with these words: "Methodism in nineteenth century America took a unique approach toward ministerial education. Adapting the apprentice system to its ministerial education needs, early Methodists developed an educational approach, in

the following: "That it be the duty of the bishop or bishops, or a committee which they may appoint in each annual conference, to point out a course of reading and study proper to be pursued by candidates for the ministry."[21] This course of study, according to Kenneth Rowe, constituted "an important first step toward formal theological training for the ministry of the Methodist Episcopal Church."[22]

Not only did the bishops' course of study for deaconesses carry on the practice of a set curriculum for theological education, but also the curriculum itself nearly duplicated the areas of study—biblical studies, church history, logic, doctrine, ethics, psychology, biography, preparation and delivery of sermons, Christian education, church government, and administration—required for ministerial candidates.[23] The deaconess course of study included all but two of these subject areas—sermon preparation and administration.

The deaconess course of study, as did that for ministerial candidates, focused on theological disciplines. The attention to Bible study alone was exhaustive. Along with a book-by-book study of the English Bible, students would learn biblical history and geography of the ancient world that included maps and diagrams of principal cities and localities. At CTS, for at least an hour every morning and five days a week, students learned both the content and context of all 66 books of the Bible. They also took instruction on how to develop Bible lessons that included maps, charts, and simple drawings intended to reinforce the teachings. Such accoutrements, as Meyer knew well from her own experience with the Sunday School Association, would prove invaluable as they taught the Bible in churches and industrial schools.

During both years of the required curriculum, students read about the life of Christ. In the first year, the assigned text, *The Life of Jesus Christ* by James Stalker, presented a basic rendition of Jesus's life and ministry, including a chapter on the background of ancient Judaism. In the second year, the reading on the life of Christ intensified with Cunningham Geikie's *The Life and Words of Christ*. This thick, encyclopedic

---

lieu of seminary, which was based on a reading of selected texts and a battery of examinations. This process was called the course of study. The graduate of the course became an ordained minister within the denomination." Patterson, "Ministerial Mind of American Methodism," 1.

21. Methodist Episcopal Church, *Journals of General Conference*, 1:151.
22. Rowe, "New Light on Early Methodist Theological Education," 59.
23. McCulloh, *Ministerial Education*, 12.

tome referenced ancient authors like Josephus and Papius as well as leading contemporary biblical scholars from Johann Gottfried Eichorn and Ernest Renan to Constantin von Tischendorf. The corresponding bibliographic notes include Latin, Greek, and Hebrew citations. Further, both Stalker's and Geikie's books introduced, albeit briefly, the basics of gospel criticism, particularly the dating of the fourth gospel. What these readings demonstrate is that CTS students became familiar not only with biblical content but also with issues of biblical authority and higher criticism, which were front and center in ecclesial conversations and conflict in US Protestantism.[24]

By the turn of the twentieth century, many seminaries in the US had already adopted this interpretive method. Meyer followed suit and enthusiastically enrolled in courses taught by Shailer Mathews, a well-known advocate of higher criticism on faculty at the University of Chicago Divinity School.[25] She drank deeply of Mathews's teaching on the scientific examination of the biblical text and eagerly passed it on to CTS students and faculty. Following her lead, most CTS instructors enrolled in classes at the University of Chicago Divinity School.[26] Even when the impending demise of her school might have been delayed had she relinquished her favorable opinion of higher criticism, thus quieting critics who found her too liberal, Meyer remained adamant. "I can never consent that the historic method of Bible teaching shall be given up. It is reasonable and sensible. I could no more go back to the old way than I could put myself into the little calico dresses I used to wear when I was ten years old."[27]

Biblical languages were not required at deaconess training schools; however, the CTS curriculum offered multiple elective courses in New Testament Greek that would give "the student a sufficient working knowledge of the principles of the Greek language to enable her to read the New Testament in the original."[28] There was a similar interest in pursuing studies in Greek at the New England Training School for Deaconesses. A 1909 issue of the school's journal announced, "A number

---

24. See Holifield, *God's Ambassadors*, 169–172 and Pope-Levison, *Building the Old Time Religion*, 21–22, 123–26.

25. See Mathews, *New Faith for Old*. For his contribution to the culture and curriculum of the University of Chicago Divinity School, see The University of Chicago Library, "Shailer Mathews (1863–1941)."

26. Horton, *Builders*, 213–14. See also Dougherty, "Methodist Deaconess," 180.

27. Horton, *High Adventure*, 323.

28. Horton, *Builders*, 202.

of students, anxious to study Greek, have formed themselves in a class. Rev. Mr. Walker willingly consented to give them instruction and they are making fine progress."[29]

Church history was a core curricular component taught at deaconess training schools. According to the course description for "Studies in Church History," CTS students would encounter doctrinal controversies in the early church, scholasticism, humanism, the great schism between the Roman Catholic and Orthodox churches, Calvinism, Arminianism, the papacy in the nineteenth century, and more.[30] The required two-volume textbook, John Fletcher Hurst's *History of the Christian Church*, comprised over 900 pages in the second volume alone, covering church history in minute detail from Bishop Robert Grosseteste (ca. 1170–1253), an English theologian, philosopher, and bishop, to a plan for church union in the US at the dawning of the twentieth century.

The curriculum also provided a strong emphasis on women in Methodism, including the history of deaconesses. Required books for this subject included *Women of Methodism* by Abel Stevens, *Women and Temperance* by Frances E. Willard, and *Deaconesses in Europe, and Their Lessons for America* by Jane Bancroft Robinson. Hartley underscores the central curricular focus on women through this observation: "The emphasis on women in ministry in the Training School's curriculum is the greatest area of difference between Boston University's School of Theology and the [New England] Training School during this time. Boston University offered no classes with an emphasis on women during the 1889–1890 academic year."[31]

The curriculum at EEI also promoted women's issues. In the required reading from *Binney's Theological Compend*, the authors advanced biblical support for women's preaching. For instance, in the book's final section, "Woman's Sphere in the Church," they dismissed the separate sphere argument that relegated women to household domesticity. Women's sphere, they argued, must not be "limited to the duties of the family or household, since she is often by nature and grace pre-eminently adapted for a wider service."[32] Continuing on, the authors also tackled 1 Cor 14:33b–35, a passage commonly interpreted as Paul's prohibition of

---

29. Hartley, "Salvation and Sociology," 192.
30. Horton, *Builders*, 208.
31. Hartley, "Salvation and Sociology," 187.
32. Binney and Steele, *Binney's Theological Compend Improved*, 192.

women from religious leadership.[33] In their exegesis, they denounced a universal application of the text.

> To say that his [Paul's] prohibition applies alike to all times and conditions of society, is to say that the prudential regulations of a degraded heathen people, eighteen hundred years ago, are universally binding, and that Christianity in this respect has wrought no change in the world it came to reform. Paul surely had a different estimate of woman service. Rom. Xvi, 1–7, 12–15. His first public discourse in Europe was at a meeting of women, and his first convert and host was a woman. Acts xvi, 9–15.[34]

In a sweeping statement, the authors sanctioned not only women engaged in public prophesying, preaching, and teaching but also women serving in positions of "the higher ministerial duties, as appears from the rank next after apostles."[35] Considering the emphasis given to women's issues in the core curriculum, an argument could be proffered that deaconess training schools pioneered women's studies in theological education.

Practical Work

Along with academic courses, the other core curricular component was practical work. Practical work balanced classroom learning with experience in real-life settings, where students gained hands-on proficiency, as in an internship. To prepare for their practical work experience, students signed up for courses that equipped them with up-to-date information and constructive methods. As Dana Robert notes, "The [CTS] catalogue for 1902–1903 showed that in addition to well-developed departments of Bible, Missions, Medicine, and Nursing, courses were offered in psychology, ethics, sociology, and educational methods."[36] These courses prepared them for the burgeoning field of social work.[37]

---

33. "[F]or God is a God not of disorder but of peace. As in all the churches of the saints, women should be silent in the churches. For they are not permitted to speak, but should be subordinate, as the law also says. If there is anything they desire to know, let them ask their husbands at home. For it is shameful for a woman to speak in church."

34. Binney and Steele, *Binney's Theological Compend Improved*, 193.

35. Binney and Steele, *Binney's Theological Compend Improved*, 192.

36. Robert, *American Women in Mission*, 156.

37. Rowe et al., *Methodist Experience In America*, 315. Proponents of the Social Gospel, such as Walter Rauschenbusch, Richard Ely, Francis Peabody, and Harry Ward,

After taking courses in the morning, students went off-campus to gain firsthand experience in practical work during the afternoons. To provide numerous sites for practical work, most training schools originated in high-density, urban locations.[38] Students at CTS, during their visitation rounds in overcrowded, vermin-infested Chicago tenements, came in contact with people living in desperate conditions. With a population increase of 800,000 between 1870 and 1890, the city's infrastructure could not keep up. The result was the proliferation of social problems. "Epidemics traveled like wildfire through these human warehouses, piling up staggeringly high infant mortality rates, and making tuberculosis an accepted corollary of urban life. Those who were poor, stayed poor, crushed by casualized labor, periodic unemployment, and the cyclical depressions of an industrializing economy."[39] During their visits, students did what they could to help in tangible ways, like cleaning, light cooking, and childcare, and they offered prayer and a Bible reading. Students also served in Chicago churches, relief agencies, and city missions.

Students at EEI gained practical work experience in evangelism and social service at many places throughout St. Louis, such as city missions, the jail and juvenile court, Bethesda Institutions, American Bible Society, city hospitals, workhouse, rescue missions, Old Ladies' Home, and Jefferson Barracks. They also ran a Travelers' Aid ministry to care for runaway children and unchaperoned girls, staffed the Epworth Emergency Home, which sheltered girls considered incorrigible by the juvenile court, and some lived in Epworth Settlement, a settlement house offering programs for the community, such as a Sunday School, Kindergarten, Sewing School, Kitchengarten,[40] Girls and Boys Club, a Library, and a Thrift Fund.

The two parts of the curriculum—theological education and practical work—came together when training school students carried their Bible on their visitation rounds. Bible in hand, they tended the sick, impoverished, addicted, and dying. In one year alone, 1887–1888, CTS students paid more than 5,000 visits to residences and incorporated

---

authored several books assigned in these courses. Rowe et al., *Methodist Experience In America*, 315. For an in-depth analysis of the Methodist deaconess movement's intersection with the Social Gospel movement, see Blue, *St. Mark's and the Social Gospel*.

38. Russell Richey observes that "Methodism deliberately 'located' its theological schools in urban settings"; the same was true for many deaconess training schools. Richey, *Formation for Ministry*, 6.

39. McCarthy, *Noblesse Oblige*, 29.

40. A small parcel of land in an urban area where vegetables can be grown.

Bible readings and prayer in close to 600 of them. In addition, they taught over 19,000 Bible lessons in Sunday Schools and more than 8,000 in Industrial Schools, all in a single year.[41]

The Legacy of Deaconess Training Schools on Theological Education

This chapter advances the argument that these schools provided theological education for laywomen in the Bible, church history, theology, and more, the same courses that still constitute the framework for theological education today. This is not to say that the deaconess course of study replicated the seminary curriculum. It did not. Training schools offered a briefer curriculum in theological education, two years instead of four, and maintained a significant emphasis on practical work. As Methodist Episcopal Church (MEC) deaconess, Isabelle Horton, quipped about CTS, it "is not a feminized theological seminary."[42] Nevertheless, the Methodist church maintained the stance that laywomen training to be deaconesses were required to complete a robust theological education before heading into full-time religious work.

Like their earlier counterparts, who completed their training and went on to serve as nurses, evangelists, social workers, educators, pastors, pastor's assistants, and missionaries, current United Methodist Church (UMC) deaconesses in the US maintain this curricular tradition in which theological education and practical work strengthen the effectiveness of each other. As deaconess Kandi Mount explains, "We have a sterling example before us of Lucy Rider Meyer. She incorporated Biblical knowledge for use as practical knowledge. I, too, find that a fine way to work and to live." Working in eight different cities in Arkansas affords Mount, a hospital chaplain, plenty of time to pray and reflect on scripture while driving. She begins her prayers for the day by quoting Ps 19:14: "Let the words of my mouth, and the meditation of my heart, be acceptable in thy sight, O Lord, my strength and my redeemer." Her reliance on scripture to evoke an awareness of God's presence steels her for the work ahead: "I am completely open to the process that God will be supplying all that is needed for his children that day. Before asking my patients to trust, I trust. There is a

---

41. Horton, *High Adventure*, 139.
42. Horton, *Builders*, 157.

solemnity in releasing my spirit to allow this 'free fall' into oneness with the Holy Spirit. . . . Thank you God for your tenderness."[43]

Bible study informs and infuses the practical work for which deaconesses are renowned. Deaconess and Research Chemotherapy registered nurse, Juliet Hahn Choi, quotes scripture to help patients focus in a way "that allows them to receive their treatment as best they can with faith, trust in God. They seek peace, comfort, and refuge at a time when fear of death is so real." Mount expresses similar sentiments about the importance of talking about scripture with patients.

> Many terminal or actively dying patients vocalize fears that they will not reach heaven, even though they have earnestly asked for forgiveness. The scripture that seems to resonate with these patients spiritually is Romans 8:38-39: 'For I am persuaded, that neither death, nor life, nor angels, nor principalities, nor powers, nor things present, nor things to come, nor height, nor depth, nor any other creature, shall be able to separate us from the love of God, which is in Christ Jesus our Lord.' I then ask these questions: 'Do you have any idea how much Christ adores you? Can the blood of the cross show you the power and commitment of God's love for you? Whether you choose to accept it or not, you are His child.'

Deaconesses continue, more than 140 years after CTS began, to combine theological education with, as Mount so deftly puts it, "bringing hope and peace to the wounded, sick, and dying, physically or spiritually, in this world, that's pretty much all of us at one time or another."[44]

The holistic curriculum of the training school, integrating theological and practical dimensions, presaged future developments in theological education. Its legacy lives on in the curricular emphasis on practical training, on service learning, on the integration of theory and practice, knowledge and method. Glenn Miller confirms this to be true. He answers his own question—"Did the women's training schools have an impact on the larger world of Protestant education at the turn of the [20th] century?"—with a resounding, Yes! He explains further, "The new practical fields were essential to this understanding of theological education, as was some type of theological clinic or field experience . . . the training schools made significant contributions to their development and,

43. The author is grateful to Kandi Mount for the email correspondence.

44. The author is grateful to Kandi Mount and Juliet Hahn Choi for their email correspondence.

hence, to theological education as a whole."[45] A case in point was the 1899 declaration by William Rainey Harper of the University of Chicago, who claimed that the theological seminary curriculum leaned too heavily into academics which, in turn, generated scholarly pastors. Instead, Harper envisioned connecting academics and practical work by assigning seminarians to participate in "'theological clinics' in urban settings, like the slums of Chicago."[46] Brooks Holifield contends that Harper's paradigm for theological education, which closely resembled the training school curriculum, would "reshape Protestant training for ministry."[47]

Russell Richey gives the opposite answer to Miller's question. Richey finds no evidence that deaconess training schools had any influence on theological education. Under the subheading, "Overlooked Model: Deaconesses," he asks two questions: "Did the men get it? Did Methodist men take guidance from their women?" No, they did not, according to Richey. "If the men who led the seminaries looked to deaconess education for a model of how to integrate the myriad strains of theological education, they have not left very clear footnotes of that indebtedness."[48] Further, he suggests that if Methodist men had indeed learned from the curricular implementation of the deaconess training schools, then theological seminaries would have solved "the integrative challenges" several decades earlier.[49] In the final analysis, however, both Richey and Miller lift up the holistic curriculum of the deaconess training schools not only as a relic from the past but also as an essential ingredient for the formation and training of contemporary religious leaders.

Reflection Questions

1. How did societal attitudes toward women's education and roles during the late nineteenth century shape the development of and

45. Miller, *Piety and Profession*, 222–23. Ben Hartley demonstrates "cross-fertilization" between the New England Deaconess Training School and Boston University School of Theology particularly in the seminary's development of missionary courses and city missionary work. Hartley, "Salvation and Sociology," 187.

46. Harper, "Shall the Theological Curriculum Be Modified," 56–59, 61–63; quoted in Holifield, *God's Ambassadors*, 174. Conrad Cherry explains Harper's vision succinctly in this statement: "Harper insisted that the training of ministers should be every bit as practical as the training of attorneys and physicians." Cherry, *Hurrying Toward Zion*, 6.

47. Holifield, *God's Ambassadors*, 174.

48. Richey, *Formation for Ministry*, 64.

49. Richey, *Formation for Ministry*, 64.

curriculum for deaconess training schools? What challenges did these attitudes present, and how did the schools address them?

2. How did Methodist deaconess training schools offer a theological education that differed from traditional seminaries? What advantages did the training school approach provide for women who became deaconesses? Where do you see continued evidence of this approach today?

3. What resonances do you find connecting past and present Methodist deaconesses?

"AN EXAMINATION OF CANDIDATES"[1]

THE CANDIDATES CAME [TO the Deaconess College][2] on Friday evening, November 29th, and received the kindest of welcomes from the students, who remembered their own recent candidature, and did their very best to ease the situation of their successors. On Saturday morning, two examination papers, occupying an hour and a half each, were written. So many people write and ask what the examination is like, that we print the papers below to shew them. Only we give them this warning that the next papers may be entirely different. For we don't want our candidates to prepare diligently some work which we may give marks to. Our object is to give an opportunity to each one to shew her range of knowledge, her powers of observation, and her ability to write down what she knows in a methodical and intelligent way. If we thought one of our papers could be "got up," or crammed for, we would try and replace it with another as unlike it as could be invented. However the present papers served their purpose this year.

On Saturday afternoon the medical examination was soon over, with very satisfactory results, and the candidates were free to explore the place or cultivate the acquaintance of the students for the rest of the day. On Sunday afternoon a very happy testimony meeting was held, attended by the students, and (by their own special request) the servants, as well as some of the lady members of the Committee who live in Ilkley and

---

1. *Flying Leaves* 72 (1908) 185–86. Used with permission by the Library of the Wesley Historical Society.

2. The Deaconess College at Ilkley in the Yorkshires was the training school for the Wesley Deaconess Order in the UK. The college opened in the fall of 1902 with 17 students and closed over 60 years later in 1968.

the neighbourhood. The Committee met on Monday morning at eleven o'clock. After seeing the candidates, hearing them and asking them questions, an adjournment for lunch was made at one o'clock. The Committee resumed its work at half-past two, without the presence of the candidates being further required, and in an hour had decided every case. The candidates left the College in the course of the afternoon, and were told the decisions of the Committee by letters posted to them the same evening. And so ended a day of many prayers and anxieties, but, we trust, a day of the guidance of God, when all might sing together:

> By Thine unerring Spirit led,
>   We shall not in the desert stay;
> We shall not full direction need,
>   Nor miss our providential way;
> As far from danger as from fear,
> While love, Almighty love, is near.[3]

Paper I.

1. Tell the story of the Temptation in the Garden of Eden as correctly as you can.
2. Tell what you know of one of the following:—Abraham, Jacob, Joseph, Moses.
3. Tell correctly one of the stories of David's life.
4. Write down five or six verses of any Psalm you know by heart (except the XXIII.).
5. Write down one of the Parables of Christ as nearly as possible in His own words.
6. What are the words that Christ spoke upon the Cross?
7. What do you know of either the Apostle Thomas or Andrew?
8. Give some account of the contents of one of the following:—John i., Acts ii., Romans viii., I Cor. xv., James i.
9. Give the meaning of two of the following:—Repentance, Justification, Regeneration, Salvation.

---

3. The second verse of Charles Wesley's hymn, "Captain of Israel's Host and Guide."

10. What blessings may we hope for at the Lord's Supper?
11. What does "The Kingdom of God" mean?
12. How do we know that there is a God?
13. What is the meaning of Providence?
14. What is the good of Prayer?

Paper II.

1. Give any information you can about the town or village you know best.
2. Name three of the great Railway Companies of England, and in each case mention six towns they serve.
3. Give the names of three towns in Canada, three towns in Australia, and three towns in South Africa. Tell what you know of one of them.
4. Give the names of four towns in France, Germany, and Italy, and give some information about one in each country.
5. Write down the names of either twenty English wild plants, ten English freshwater fish, ten English wild birds, or six English wild animals.
6. What are the duties of three of the following:—a Policeman, Guardian of the Poor, Member of the Town Council, Magistrate, Sanitary Inspector, or School Attendance Officer.
7. Name the author of each of the following works:—Canterbury Tales, The Tempest, The Fairie Queen, Paradise Regained, The Holy War, The Lady of the Lake, Excelsior.
8. State what you know of one of the following:—The Norman Conquest, Wars of Roses, Spanish Armada.
9. Give a brief account of either Henry VIII., Queen Elizabeth, Charles I., or William III.
10. Give the titles of four of the works of two of the following:—Charles Dickens, Thackeray, Ruskin, George Eliot.
11. If 3 guineas had to be divided between six women and six boys, the women to get twice as much as the boys, how much would each get?

12. For a Mothers' Meeting tea for forty-eight persons, the following provisions are ordered: 1 lb. tea at 1/8 per lb., 6 lbs. sugar at 2 ½ d. per lb., 2 lbs. butter at ½ per lb., 12 lbs. cake at 6d. per lb., 6 loaves at 3d. each, 3 quarts milk at 3d. per quart. The Chapelkeeper is paid 2/6. How much per head must be charged in order to meet the expenses, without making a profit?

Reflection Questions

1. How does the examination process described in the source document reflect the values and educational priorities of the Methodist deaconess movement?
2. In what ways do the exam questions in Paper I and Paper II assess both the candidates' religious understanding as well as their general knowledge?
3. How well would you do on these questions?

"A STUDENT'S VIEW OF COLLEGE LIFE"[1]

6:20 A.M.—THE STUDENTS GROAN as the rising bell breaks the morning stillness, and Jap, the college dog, howls dismally as though in sympathy with the hardship of "getting up." Sometimes the bell, loud and insistent though it is, fails to arouse a particularly sleepy-headed individual. The kindly efforts of her neighbours in the next cubicle, however, prove effectual, and by seven o'clock all are assembled in the common-room—to be late for roll-call is a distinction coveted by none.

Our Home Sister marks the roll, and a student then announces the motto text for the day, and a verse of a favourite hymn is sung. Various domestic duties then await us. One student with a fantastic turban-like arrangement covering her hair, is seen sweeping the staircase, while another vigorously polishes "taps" [faucets]. Others are setting the tables for breakfast, and punctually at 7:45 we descend to the pleasant dining-hall.

As we gather round the tables bright with plants and flowers, the heart of one student is palpitating strangely. It is her turn to start grace—a severe affliction for one to whom an ear for music has been denied. Our meals are often lively. Discussion on a variety of topics frequently makes us forget the business on hand, and the signal to rise is greeted with a start of dismay as one surveys the portion still unconsumed upon the plate.

Breakfast over, we take our places in the prayer-room, where officers and students in turn officiate. Here strength for the day is sought and

---

1. *Flying Leaves* 109 (May 1911) 72–73. Used with permission by the Library of the Wesley Historical Society.

obtained. The work of our Sisters in England and abroad is constantly remembered, nor are the dear home friends forgotten.

Ten o'clock sees every student at her appointed desk in the library, and Bible study occupies the morning hours. Light is thrown upon the Old Book, making it glow with new meaning and reality. Perhaps we do not see all we have gained in those hours—the future will reveal the help received.

After dinner, a pleasant walk on the moors makes us fresh for the afternoon's work—yes, even for "English Local Government."

At five we are ready for the cup [of tea] that cheers, and the hour's recess which follows.

The evening is spent chiefly in private study, and then the library shelves are raided. They literally groan with good things, making intellectual mouths water.

At nine we gather in the common room for family prayer, and a strange peace steals over our spirits as the Warden[2] prays. It may be we have not kept all the morning resolutions, but at least we have tried. Supper over and "washing up" accomplished, we are free to retire to our own domain, and at ten o'clock the silence bell rings. Half an hour later the voice of the dormitory monitress is heard "lights out, please," and another day is over.

One very important day is District Day. Shortly before one o'clock, every Wednesday we wend our way, a blue-cloaked band,[3] to the station. The afternoon is spent in Bradford,[4] and the surrounding villages. Meetings are conducted, and sick people visited, thus affording a foretaste of the work awaiting us in the future.

And so the days glide past—all too quickly for some of us. We are a very happy household, and College is a splendid place for rubbing angles and corners off. The gentle hints and playful reminders are not resented, believing as we do, the old adage, "Faithful are the wounds of a friend."[5] In the days to come we shall look back with grateful happy memories of the old College days, and the friendships formed then. And above all, our College life means to us a vision of higher heights, and deeper depths of

---

2. The Warden was head of the WDO. The Rev. William Bradfield, a Wesleyan Methodist minister, was the second WDO Warden, serving from 1907–1920.
3. Students at the college wore light blue uniforms.
4. A town thirteen miles from the college.
5. Prov 27:6.

holiness, and an increased hope and determination to "live pure, speak true, right wrong, follow the Christ."[6]

Reflection Questions

1. How does the structure and daily routine at the college reflect the deaconess movement's values and priorities?
2. What role do religious practices play in the daily life of students? How might these practices influence their future work, as suggested in the description of what students do during District Day?

---

6. This line comes from Alfred Lord Tennyson's *Gareth and Lynette*, originally published in 1872.

The Seven Deaconesses in the First Training School for
Colored Deaconesses in the United States

Early Deaconesses in Costume
Mary Jefferson, Ellen Hibbard, Isabelle Reeves
1889

Early Deaconesses in Costume, Methodist Episcopal Church

Chapter IV

"HER DISTINCTIVE DRESS"

Displaying the Ambiguity of the Methodist Deaconess Movement

Overview

AMONG THE MOST CONTESTED aspects of the deaconess movement—and certainly the most visible by its being on bodily display—was the uniform, also called the distinctive dress. This chapter tackles this vexing issue by setting the deaconess dress in the fashion context of the late nineteenth century as well as alongside two other religious groups whose women were active in public ministry, the Salvation Army and Roman Catholic nuns. The chapter concludes that the deaconess dress was not distinctive enough from any of the others to convince critics of its necessity; it remained as ambiguous as the movement itself. Still, the uniform emblematized the deaconess's commitment to living simply, foregoing luxuries, and doing without for the sake of the poor and outcast. These themes show up in Lucy Rider Meyer's hymn, "Give All You Can." She beat a similar drum in the source document, "Autobiography of a Bonnet," in which the bonnet, as the narrator, describes several days in the life and ministry of the deaconess who wears it. This literary device mimics Vennard's guitar in the source document found in chapter 2. In the document from the Martha-Maria Deaconess Organization in Nuremberg, Germany, "Regeln für Martha-Maria" we have a unique look into specific regulations governing every aspect of the deaconess, from pocket money to clothing allotment, from vacation days to each day's regimented schedule.

In the fall of 1888, an unusual fashion show took place in a nondescript, five-story, red brick building at the corner of Dearborn and Ohio Streets in Chicago. The building housed the Chicago Training School (CTS), founded three years earlier by Lucy Rider Meyer. At the time of this event, Meyer was embroiled in significant challenges, such as convincing church leaders to sanction the deaconess order, strengthening the school with minimal funding, and assuaging parental fears about their daughter leaving home to travel to the metropolis. Yet on this day, she faced a different trial because she was modeling prototypes for the "distinctive dress" to be worn by her deaconesses.[1]

What design should it be? What color? A wide range—black, brown, gray, green, and blue—was under consideration. These decisions, according to Meyer, became "a matter seemingly very trivial, but occupying much time, and causing much thought in its settlement." She went on to describe the arduous process:

> Committees were appointed, and grave boards sat on the [color] question. I called the members of the Home about me, and many were the discussions we held over the matter. We verified the old saying, that it was exceedingly difficult to please every one. Finally I submitted, as gracefully as possible, to making myself a dummy for the time being, and two dresses at least were made and fitted to me, that I might be looked over and commented upon by the Deaconesses and the family in general. It seems very funny in looking back upon it, but it was exceedingly trying as an actual occurrence.[2]

Her protégé, biographer, and Methodist Episcopal Church (MEC) deaconess, Isabelle Horton, described the impact of the "troublesome question" on Meyer. She was "nearly worn out with the worry of it all, and trying on the various styles." Then, despite the time and energy invested in the decision, when Meyer first wore the dress in public to attend a

---

1. The phrase, "distinctive dress," appeared in many writings and speeches given by deaconess ambassadors, like Jane Bancroft Robinson. See Robinson, *Deaconesses in Europe*, 249–50.

2. Meyer, *Deaconesses*, 192–93.

Sunday service at Grace MEC several blocks away from the school, "there was plenty of criticism of course, more or less caustic."[3]

The backdrop for this fashion show was a time of women's heightened involvement in public religious activity. Many women from a variety of religious organizations were out and about on their errands of mercy during the late nineteenth century, and each wore a distinctive dress to distinguish their group from others. The hope was that dress would become each group's distinctive sign so that a Methodist deaconess in uniform would be easily distinguished from a Salvation Army female officer or a Roman Catholic nun. To complicate the situation further, many middle to upper class women, clothed in fashionable dress, also showed up to volunteer at a city's soup kitchen. The central question not only for Meyer, but also for the international deaconess movement was, How to distinguish the deaconess distinctive dress from that worn by other women doing the very same activities?

To pursue this question, this chapter will trace one by one the competing dress designs. Part one explores how the design of the deaconess dress aimed to be feminine but not fashionable. Part two considers how the deaconess dress was constructed to fit into any context, whether among the rich or poor. In this regard, it was to look very different from the working-class costume worn by Salvation Army "slum sisters" in their ministry among the poor.[4] Part three documents how the plain style of the deaconess dress was tailored to separate its appearance from the habit worn by a Roman Catholic nun. The conclusion drawn from these three parts, however, is that the aspiration to design a distinctive deaconess dress was never achieved. The dress, like the deaconess movement itself, appeared ambiguous. The word, ambiguous, pops up in several studies assessing the deaconess movement. Cynthia Jürisson, for instance, refers to being a deaconess as an "ambiguous vocation" with an imprecise status and authority.[5] Sean Gill uses the same word in his discussion of deaconesses in the UK. "Crucial *ambiguities* remained concerning the nature of the deaconesses' ministry and its relationship with the ordained priesthood, and these were to hamper its effectiveness and hinder recruitment

---

3. Horton, *High Adventure*, 153.

4. For more on slum sisters, see Abell, *Urban Impact on American Protestantism*, 126–28; Le Zotte, "'Be Odd,'" 258–61; McKinley, *Marching to Glory*, 55–56; Taiz, *Hallelujah Lads and Lasses*, 41–43, 128–30; Winston, *Red-Hot and Righteous*, 67–76, 143–46; and Wisbey, *Soldiers Without Swords*, 101–2.

5. Jürisson, "Deaconess Movement," 830.

far into the next century."[6] Like the movement itself, the dress and the women wearing it remained clothed in ambiguity.

Dress as Sign

Meyer referred to the dress that she fretted and fussed over as a "distinctive *sign*."[7] Her choice of the word, sign, was prescient given that the sign-ification of dress continues to inform current scholarship.[8] As Joanne Eicher writes, "Dress functions as a silent communication system that provides basic information about age, gender, marital status, occupation, religious affiliation, and ethnic background for everyday, special occasions and events . . . Much information about identity is communicated through sensory cues provided by dress without the observer asking questions."[9] Certainly gender is a significant cue to be communicated by dress.[10] This was true for the deaconess dress because it had to display enough femininity for these religious workers to be recognized immediately as women. At the same time, as we will see below, a fine line remained to be negotiated between a dress that signified femininity without appearing too fashionable, thus clashing with the deaconess commitment to thrift and simplicity.

Further, when dress signifies a religious group, it performs the function of solidifying the group's identity and belief system. Dress intensifies the group's cohesion both internally and externally. Internally, the "act of dressing one's body is itself a lived religious practice."[11] When "coupled to religious beliefs, dress itself becomes a sacred item. . . . To feel, smell, hear and move with the total ensemble is to give life to religious dress, and in turn, dress can give life to, even transform, its wearer."[12] The simple act of putting on the dress, therefore, readied the deaconess to engage in her

6. Gill, *Women and the Church of England*, 166–67. Italics added.

7. Meyer, *Deaconesses*, 192. Italics added.

8. See Evenson and Trayte, "Dress and the Negotiation of Relationships," 95; Joseph, *Uniforms and Nonuniforms*, 49, and Rubinstein, *Dress Codes*, 6–15.

9. Eicher, "Clothing, Costume and Dress," 151-52.

10. Gertrud Lehnert explains, "The way people dress is among the most significant ways of doing gender. *Doing gender* means the conscious or unconscious staging of gendered selves in everyday life." Lehnert, "Gender," 8:452.

11. Ammerman, *Studying Lived Religion*, 66. See also McDannell, *Material Christianity*, 2.

12. Hume, *Religious Life of Dress*, 1.

public religious duties. Externally, dress communicates the religious group's values to the public, and it sets those who wear it apart from others not similarly dressed.[13] "Religions rely on material means such as dress," states David Morgan, "to fabricate shared identity, to construct a social body, which may be defined as the shared presentation of self to the group to mirror likeness and to nonmembers to signal difference." He cites "dressing uniformly" as one of the ways religious groups—such as deaconesses—would differentiate members from nonmembers.[14] This was Meyer's goal to accomplish during her stress-inducing fashion show.

Feminine Versus Fashionable

During the age of "conspicuous consumption" in the late nineteenth century, fashion became a more affordable commodity within the economic reach of more women.[15] Even the working-class "could purchase discretionary items. Mass production meant that clothes, souvenirs, newspapers, and more were affordable to almost everyone."[16] Young female factory workers, for instance, spent their meager wages on "uncomfortable and impractical french-heel shoes, inexpensive knockoffs of costly models."[17] In contrast, to signal femininity to the public gaze yet without attracting criticism for its fashion consciousness or cost, the distinctive deaconess dress was to look plain and unadorned to signify a sacrificial lifestyle. It was also to be the antidote to standing in front of a closet of dress choices and worrying over which one to wear. As Meyer explained, "It will relieve our minds entirely of the demoralizing, distressing, devotion-destroying worry of 'What shall I wear?' and 'How

---

13. Leigh Eric Schmidt makes this point in his analysis of sartorial issues among Protestant religious groups in early America. "Clothes, to play upon an anthropological trope, were good to think with. They helped people express ideas about hierarchy, equality, gender, clerical authority, community, ritual, purity, repentance, redemption, sin, pride, shame, and last things. They offered a powerful channel of communication through which people—whether literate or illiterate, lay or clerical—conveyed various messages to one another." Schmidt, "'Church-Going People,'" 50. See also Arthur, *Religion, Dress, and the Body*, 2; Brekus, *Strangers and Pilgrims*, 87; and Dwyer-McNulty, *Common Threads*, 7.

14. Morgan, *Thing About Religion*, 72.

15. See Le Zotte's discussion of Thorstein Veblen's phrase, "conspicuous consumption," as it applies to dress during the Gilded Age. Le Zotte, "'Be Odd,'" 245.

16. Steinbach, "Victorian Era."

17. Le Zotte, "'Be Odd,'" 255.

shall it be made?'" She continued, even punctuating her statement with a hymn verse, "Why, one might almost join the deaconess ranks to be rid of all this, for good and all giving us 'A mind at leisure from itself/To soothe and sympathize.'"[18]

The deaconess dress, following an A-line pattern, connected a straight, close-fitting skirt cinched at the waist—to provide a feminine contour—with a plain bodice decorated only by a vertical line of small buttons. The material used for the dress and buttons was a dark color of serge, a durable twill cloth with a pronounced diagonal rib on the front and back.[19] Over the dress, deaconesses wore an outer cloak. Wesley Deaconess Order (WDO) leaders, for instance, chose a light, rainproof cloak constructed of fine-threaded worsted yarn. This yarn, known as heptonette, took its name from the Hepton Brothers, the tailors who made the garment in their Yorkshire factory, not far from the WDO Deaconess College in Ilkley.

For a head covering, deaconesses wore "sensible, old-fashioned" bonnets with "large round crowns, and close-fitting 'cottage' fronts neatly sheltering their benignant faces,—just such bonnets as we recall our mothers to have worn more than a quarter of a century ago."[20] The WDO bonnet included a veil to which straps were attached that tied under the chin. Put together, the dress, cloak, and bonnet added up to a "neat, quiet and lady-like" look, combining femininity, simplicity and practicality.[21]

The deaconess hairstyle also came under scrutiny. The two-word phrase Meyer's committee agreed upon was "hair plain," which simply meant "no artificial means."[22] In other words, the hairstyle was to be modest, not crimped, frizzed or piled high. Not all deaconesses complied easily, however, as in the case of WDO Sister May Keeling, who was disciplined for her "personal appearance." The only clue that her hair was the culprit appears in this sentence of handwritten notes taken during a 1906 meeting: "The Committee is glad to find that Sister May Keeling has modified the mode of dressing her hair." Evidently, Keeling remained true to the

---

18. Meyer, *Deaconesses*, 237. The phrase comes from the second verse of the hymn, "Father, I Know That All My Life," written by Anna Laetitia Waring in the mid-1850s.

19. One Methodist deaconess dress not constructed in a dark color fabric was the blue-gray dress trimmed in white worn by AME deaconesses. Grant, *Deaconess Manual*, 27.

20. Mead, "European Deaconesses," 561.

21. Graham, *Saved to Serve*, 371.

22. Meyer, *Deaconesses*, 193.

deaconess pledge to "conform heartily to all matters of dress and personal appearance" because in 1917, nine years after being disciplined, she received a badge for twelve years of active service as a deaconess.[23]

In contrast, fashionable dress was by its very nature to be noticed by its bountiful use of strong and bright colors, lavish jewelry, and prominent hats. With the Industrial Age in full swing, the use of synthetic dyes—made from aniline developed from coal tar—created brilliant hues. The crowning result? "Women's clothes were as colourful as a parrot's plumage," and among them came shades of "deep red, peacock blue, bright apple green, royal blue, purple, mandarin, sea green."[24] In addition, the bodice of the fashionable dress sported lots of trimmings—buttons, fringes, braids, puffs, and ribbons—constructed in rich materials, like silk, satin, brocade, and velvet.

Along with the splendored dress, women keeping up with fashions wore jewelry, and lots of it, according to Josiah Allen's wife (the writer, Marietta Holley). In her customary colloquial language, she described the scene of a jewelry-laden woman visiting the swanky Saratoga Springs resort: "Why, one woman had so many diamonds on that she had a detective follerin' her all round wherever she went. She wuz a blaze of splendor and so wuz lots of 'em, though like the stars, they differed from each other in glory."[25]

To top it all off, hats especially "tickled the female imagination." They grew larger in size and adornment into the early 1900s, often measuring three feet tall and two feet wide, while sporting "dangerous pins, and stiff, sharp, pointed feathers or heaps of flowers." Women found ways to attach all manner of things onto their hats, such as "pinnacles, pokes, turrets, inverted baskets—peach or otherwise—and fabrications."[26] Underneath the hat was a maze of complicated coiffure with braids, chignons, and loops of a woman's own carefully arranged hair or false hair.

Nonetheless, despite visible differences between fashionable dress and the deaconess dress, Meyer still had an easier time with the design than she would have in previous decades due to the *au courant* plainer style of the late nineteenth century. Women's fashion even a decade earlier was more outlandish and oversized. Take the bustle. By the early 1880s, it had increased to titanic proportions with the crinolette

23. "Minutes of the First Meeting of the General Committee," no page.
24. Black and Garland, *History of Fashion*, 290.
25. Holley, *Samantha At Saratoga*, 480. For more on Holley, see ch. 5.
26. Joselit, *Perfect Fit*, 111, 121.

superstructure.[27] By the time of Meyer's fashion show, however, the bustle era had ended. Fashionable women donned instead a simpler A-line skirt, smooth and fitted around the hips and slimmer in the front with gathers or pleats in the back. The overall style and cut more easily transferred to the deaconess dress.[28] Nevertheless, Meyer correctly assessed that dress design decisions were not trivial. While the dress had to clothe deaconesses with femininity, it could not appear too fashionable. The fancy bits, bright colors, and costly bells and whistles affixed to fashionable dresses were non-existent on the deaconess dress. And to the delight of clergymen, who railed against women wearing big hats that blocked the view of people sitting behind them in the pew, deaconess bonnets were simple in style and size.[29]

Deaconess Uniform Versus Slum Sister Costume

"Deaconesses arise, and put your bonnets on/Strong in the uniform supplied by Doctor Stephenson."[30] This song, a favorite of students at the WDO Deaconess College, used the word, uniform, to refer to their dress. And that is exactly what it was—a standardized dress provided by the college intended to build cohesion among the students.[31] When worn in public, it also broadcast their religious purpose, what Nathan Joseph would later refer to as "witnessing by wearing the uniform."[32] WDO Sister Elizabeth Barraclough corroborated its religious witness in these vaunted words: "The wearing of God's uniform, if one may be allowed thus reverently to speak concerning our distinctive dress, is to be a solemn privilege and responsibility. It proclaims far more than we sometimes think to the people all round about us . . . it is unobtrusively announcing the fact that we have risen up to do the King's business and

---

27. For more on the crinolette, see Breward, *Culture of Fashion*, 157–61.

28. See Waugh, *Cut of Women's Clothes*, 228. Legath makes this point visually by setting side by side two photographs, one of a Methodist laywoman in fashionable clothing and one of a deaconess in her distinctive dress. The similarity in dress styles is clearly visible. Legath, *Sanctified Sisters*, 85–86.

29. Joselit, *Perfect Fit*, 121–25.

30. Graham, *Saved to Serve*, 373.

31. Joseph, *Uniforms and Nonuniforms*, 2–3, 66–69. See also Ewing, *Women in Uniform*, 12.

32. Joseph, *Uniforms and Nonuniforms*, 51.

are ready for service. Our very uniform is an introduction as one of His servants commissioned on His errands of love and mercy."[33]

Wearing a uniform, even one not designed in a military-style like the Salvation Army, nonetheless evoked a barrage of army metaphors. "What the uniform is to soldiers in the United States army," exhorted Meyer, "our costume is to us. Bid us God-speed as we go forth in it, dear friends, and pray with us that we may fight a good fight for God and the church and precious souls."[34] Bishop James Thoburn likened deaconesses in uniform to a divine army: "It seems to me, when I look forward and think about the great army of consecrated workers that God will raise up, as if I could hear the tread of angels' feet on all the streets of our great cities. I believe that God is about to raise up an army of women workers."[35]

Certainly, the army metaphors did align with the Salvation Army military uniform, ratified in 1880; however, not all women in its ranks wore it. Women in the Salvation Army Slum Brigade, known as slum sisters, dressed instead in a working-class costume, like Emma Bown and Martha Johnson. Before they moved into the Lower East Side neighborhood of New York City in 1889 to "set up housekeeping," they sewed their costumes. "We purchased enough calico to make dresses for ourselves and an apron each. We bought little brown sailor hats and trimmed them very plainly with black and green. These we purposed to wear instead of the regular uniform, which we laid aside entirely until at some future day it would seem appropriate to wear it again."[36] Known to their neighbors simply as Em and Mat, they knocked on doors and offered to clean apartments, prepared food for working parents and the sick, and cared for children, invalids, and the elderly; they also initiated religious conversations and prayed with those they visited.

The strategy of slum sisters was to ease into the area by imitating their neighbors and purposively avoiding religious dress. They believed their costume enhanced their religious purpose by not causing offense.

33. Barraclough, "Privilege and Responsibility of Our Vocation," 100.

34. Meyer, *Deaconesses*, 237. Early rhetoric about nurse's uniforms also utilized the army metaphor. See Steele, "Dressing for Work," 76. Gayle Fischer also identifies army related words, like soldiers, forces, battle, armor, and the phrase, "fighting the battles of the Lord," in connection with dress reform efforts in the Oneida Community, Seventh-Day Adventists, and other mid-nineteenth-century religious communities. Fischer, "Dressing to Please God," 73.

35. Wheeler, *Deaconesses Ancient and Modern*, 295.

36. Booth, "Salvation Army Work in the Slums," 3; quoted in Winston, *Red-Hot and Righteous*, 69.

One slum sister explained that if she wore the Salvation Army military uniform around her neighborhood, the police would have to be called to disperse the crowd.[37] "Changing their dress," observes Diane Winston, "was strategically important when Salvationists wanted to work among people resistant to the uniform's religious and cultural signification."[38]

Deaconesses adopted the opposite strategy, even though they too worked mostly among the poor. By wearing their uniform, they chose *not* to efface their identity as religious workers. Still, while religiosity was on display, they believed that the dress concealed other personal information, like social class, wealth, or education. Meyer made the point cogently by applying Paul's statement in 1 Cor 9:22: "To the weak I became weak, to win the weak. I have become all things to all people so that by all possible means I might save some" to deaconesses: "Our serge dresses and plain bonnets show us willing to 'become all things to all *women,* that we may win some.'"[39] Thus, in contrast to the slum sister costume, the deaconess uniform was "cross-class."[40]

Yet, this conclusion about the opposing strategies of a costume versus a uniform is complicated by an overlap in terminology because deaconess leaders used the two words interchangeably, as synonyms. Vacillation between the two words showed up in the 1889 pamphlet, *Notes Concerning Management of Deaconess Home*. The section on deaconess dress was labeled with the word *costume*. Five words later *uniform* was used instead. Later, in a section titled "Local Management,"

---

37. "Halleluiah Lassie," 69; quoted in Le Zotte, "'Be Odd,'" 259.

38. Winston, *Red-Hot and Righteous*, 91.

39. Meyer, *Deaconesses*, 236. See also Legath, *Sanctified Sisters*, 92, and Winston, *Red Hot and Righteous*, 87–88.

40. I apply Jennifer Le Zotte's term, "cross-class," to the deaconess uniform. See Le Zotte, "'Be Odd,'" 245, 258, 262. For an illustration of how Iva Durham Vennard, dressed in her deaconess uniform, made use of this cross-class movement when she led a religious service in a rescue home, then sang hymns in the living room of a wealthy man, see the source document, "Experiences of a Deaconess Guitar," in chapter 2. Proponents hoping to launch the Methodist deaconess movement in Canada seized on this cross-class dimension. In a lobbying effort with the church's legislative committee, they positioned deaconesses as "the bridge over the vast gulf between yourselves and the very poor." Thomas, "Servants of the Church," 374. Winston states that the Salvation Army military uniform allowed for the same cross-class movement. "Army lassies traveled freely from the dregs of the Bowery to the heights of Fifth Avenue because they were immediately identifiable as religious workers." Winston, "Living in the Material World," 18.

the word *costume* reappeared, then the nomenclature changed back to *uniform* in the very next sentence.[41]

Meyer also switched back and forth between *costume* and *uniform* in speeches and writings. In her 1893 mission conference speech, she began by referring to deaconesses as "costumed women." She used the word *costume* throughout her speech with one exception when she switched—without hesitation or explanation—to the word *uniform* as if they were synonymous.[42] Similarly, in her book on deaconesses, she utilized both words in an extended appendix, titled "Why Deaconesses Wear A Costume." Initially, she alternated between the two words, then at midpoint, she switched to *uniform* and never used *costume* again. Even more telling is the sentence in which she included both words: "What the uniform is to soldiers in the United States army, our costume is to us."[43] This lack of precision in terminology for differing dress strategies, a costume versus a uniform, further elucidates the ambiguity of the deaconess dress.

Plain Dress Versus Nun's Habit

"Whenever I see the typical bonnet on one of our deaconess's head at a train station somewhere, a great joy floods my heart; I know I am not alone. There is help close by," exclaimed MEC Bishop Ernst Sommer while in Frankfurt, Germany. He continued, "And so I always greet the bonnet. Some sisters have said to me: 'I'm surprised you know me,' and I unfortunately haven't always been honest in saying: 'I'm sorry, but I don't know you, I was just greeting the bonnet.'"[44]

When greeting the bonnet, the bishop might unknowingly have crossed paths with a woman belonging to another Protestant group instead of a Methodist deaconess. The Quakers, for instance, wore a similar bonnet as part of their plain dress outfit. Plain dress, observes Pamela Klassen, is simply a style with no "unnecessary ornament" that is "made from solid, drab fabric, usually in a uniform and figure-obscuring style, and with a plain bonnet, usually white or black, worn

---

41. "Deaconess Conference Sets Rules," 1–4; quoted in Richey, *Methodist Experience in America: A Sourcebook*, 409–10.

42. Meyer, "Deaconesses and Their Work," 182–98.

43. Meyer, *Deaconesses*, 237.

44. Jahreiss, *Schwestern erzählen*, 12–13; quoted in Bloedt, "Pioneering Deaconess Movement in Germany," 55.

close to the head."⁴⁵ In other words, the deaconess bonnet was not so unique that the bishop could identify in passing who wore it.

The same was true when distinguishing deaconess dress from the habit worn by a Roman Catholic nun. Meyer seemed particularly discomfited by the habit worn by the Sisters of Charity, founded in 1809 in Maryland by Elizabeth Ann Seton, because it so closely resembled the deaconess dress. Sally Dwyer-McNulty describes the Sisters of Charity's habit as "a more 'modern' habit. . . . she [Seton] chose the 'widow's weeds' of early-nineteenth-century Italian society, with a simple black dress, cape, and bonnet, and a white collar and a rosary."⁴⁶ In other words, this habit's design did not allow for an easy contrast between the deaconess dress and the "stock image" of nuns in their "black, flowing habit and veil."⁴⁷ To the casual observer, then, the Sisters of Charity habit and the deaconess dress would look identical.

On the one hand, this proved beneficial because their similar dress design lent to both groups a verisimilitude of protection. Meyer herself commented that deaconesses should have the same safeguard "which is so well known to be extended to the Romish Sisters of Charity."⁴⁸ Similarly, Jane Bancroft Robinson, when telling a story about a deadly attack in Paris in February 1848, in which forty-two men were killed, emphasized bodily safety with her choice of the word, "unmolested." She explained that "deaconesses went about unmolested, bought food and medicine, hunted friends and relatives for the sick, and through all that period of excitement and strife kept up their ministrations of mercy."⁴⁹

The same root word, molestation, appeared in a report given to WDO founder, Thomas Bowman Stephenson, by a deaconess recalling her experience during the Franco-German War. Her testimony convinced him to put aside his objections to a distinctive dress. "She told me that for days and nights together it had been her duty to travel in trains crowded with men in which she was the only woman, and that it would have been simply impossible for her to pass through that region at that

---

45. Klassen, "Robes of Womanhood," 45–46.

46. Dwyer-McNulty, *Common Threads*, 79.

47. Legath, *Sanctified Sisters*, 86.

48. Meyer, *Deaconesses*, 192. Legath includes a comment from a Roman Catholic author in the early twentieth century who declared that nuns were "protected marvellously by their religious garb." Scott, *Convent Life*, 86; quoted in Legath, *Sanctified Sisters*, 86.

49. Robinson, *Deaconesses in Europe*, 132.

time, and under those conditions, without insult and molestation but for the protection of her uniform."[50] To emphasize its protective quality, the deaconess dress was compared to "a coat of mail," which is a piece of armor offering protection in battle.[51] Many rank-and-file deaconesses expressed appreciation for such fortification; one even claimed confidently that "nobody will hurt us deaconesses."[52]

On the other hand, the deaconess dress that approximated their Roman Catholic counterparts only exacerbated critics charging that the movement was "too Romish."[53] After all, deaconesses, like nuns, were single women without a family or children of their own. Although there was no lifetime vow to remain single as for nuns, still, if a deaconess married, she had to leave the order. Further, the sisterhood nomenclature for deaconesses and nuns overlapped. Stephenson, for instance, titled his book about the WDO's development, *Concerning Sisterhood*. He was influenced in that regard by his Methodist minister colleague, Hugh Price Hughes, who set up an organization for women's religious work in West London, known as "Sisters of the People."[54] Hughes's influence extended farther afield to Australia, where Methodist minister W. G. Taylor also adopted the term *Sister* for women, like Laura Francis, who lived and worked full-time at the Sydney Central Methodist Mission. He reasoned that this word "had warmth and friendship in it whereas the alternatives, 'Bible woman,' 'lady evangelist,' or 'deaconess' were all 'too stiff and unhomelike.' It would be folly to reject a good word just because the Catholics had chosen it."[55] The negative reaction to the term *Sisters* was swift and strong. A letter printed in the regional newspaper, *Maitland Mercury*, charged Methodism with heading "Romewards"; this was "the edge of the wedge"; it was "doing evil that good may come." The letter writer continues, "The next

---

50. Stephenson, *Concerning Sisterhoods*, 70–71.

51. Meyer, *Deaconesses*, 237. See also Legath, *Sanctified Sisters*, 87.

52. Meyer, *Deaconess Stories*, 125. An article in *Flying Leaves*, the WDO magazine, told a different tale about a dangerous encounter in which a deaconess was physically harmed. The author, who requested her name be withheld, emphasized that the dress "does not always bring immunity from danger is my bitter experience." "In Perils Oft," 201.

53. Meyer, *Deaconesses*, 192.

54. For more on Hughes's work as narrated by those who visited it, see Meyer, *Deaconesses*, 43; Robinson, *Deaconesses in Europe*, 163–165; and Wheeler, *Deaconesses Ancient and Modern*, 229–23.

55. Wright, *Mantle of Christ*, 56.

step would be 'auricular confession,' prayers for the dead, and purgatorial fines (a 'goldmine' for the Methodist clergy)."[56]

The deep concern over the deaconess movement's being "too Romish" was never resolved, as explained in chapter 1, and the similarity in dress between Methodist deaconesses and Roman Catholic nuns added fuel to the conflict. Neither the public nor church leaders and members easily recognized the difference in dress. Deaconesses continued to be mistaken for nuns, as this anecdote illustrates: "One of our [deaconess] workers was once called upon to conduct the funeral services of a child in a Romish Bohemian district. With much trembling she was making her way through a crowd of sullen, black-browed men, when one of them said to her, 'Are you a Sister?' 'Yes, a Protestant sister.'"[57]

Conclusion

Meyer understood that dress conveyed essential information to the public about the Methodist deaconess movement, which is exactly why she fussed and fumed over its design when she had myriad other matters to address. More was at stake, she knew, than hue, texture, or adornment. At its core, the dress was intended to distinguish deaconesses from other women engaging in public religious activities in the late nineteenth century. It had to reveal the feminine form yet be devoid of the stylish bits and fancy colors of fashionable clothing. It had to provide access to all classes, rich and poor alike, in distinction from the Salvation Army slum sisters' costume. And its plain dress style had to look different enough from the habit of a Roman Catholic nun. In essence, the distinctive dress had to display what deaconesses were *not*. They were *not* fashionable women. They were *not* nuns. They were *not* costumed slum sisters. Yet, precisely in this regard, her dress design was not successful, since a deaconess wearing the distinctive dress was largely indistinguishable from a variety of other women dressed for religious work. What deaconesses were, therefore, remained clothed—literally—in ambiguity.

There were many attempts to forestall the movement's demise which included altering or even eliminating the deaconess dress. Dress discussions surfaced shortly after the First World War. This emergence

---

56. Wright, *Mantle of Christ*, 56.

57. Meyer, *Deaconesses*, 237. For more on the impact of this criticism of deaconesses being too Catholic, see chapter 1.

was "a sign of the times and the growing status of women which had developed during the war years when many women had taken over men's jobs while they were away fighting."[58] Not long afterward, Methodist deaconesses in the US abandoned the distinctive dress altogether. However, if the expectation was that this decision would close the book on the dress discussion, it did not.

A stubborn nostalgia for a return to a distinctive dress emerged every so often throughout the twentieth century. As late as 1973, a "sketch of a jewel-neck, A-line jumper with a straight-sleeved blouse" in navy blue was proposed for Methodist deaconesses in the US.[59] In the UK, the WDO maintained a distinctive dress into the 1970s with ongoing modifications to each part of the ensemble, including the dress length, badge, and hat. One leader explained that the dress changes took into account that "the work in which the deaconesses were engaged was much more varied and very different from what it used to be and this was reflected by alterations in the uniform."[60] This telling observation about the dress displays the intractable ambiguity at the heart of a movement stuck in no man's land.

Reflection Questions

1. How did the design of the Methodist deaconess dress attempt to balance femininity and practicality? Why was this balance significant for the movement's identity?

2. In what ways did the ambiguity of the deaconess dress reflect broader uncertainties about the role and perception of deaconesses within the church and society?

3. How do these tensions surrounding the deaconess dress inform contemporary discussions about identity and symbolism in religious attire?

---

58. Graham, *Saved to Serve*, 379.
59. Dougherty, *My Calling To Fulfill*, 28.
60. Graham, *Saved to Serve*, 389.

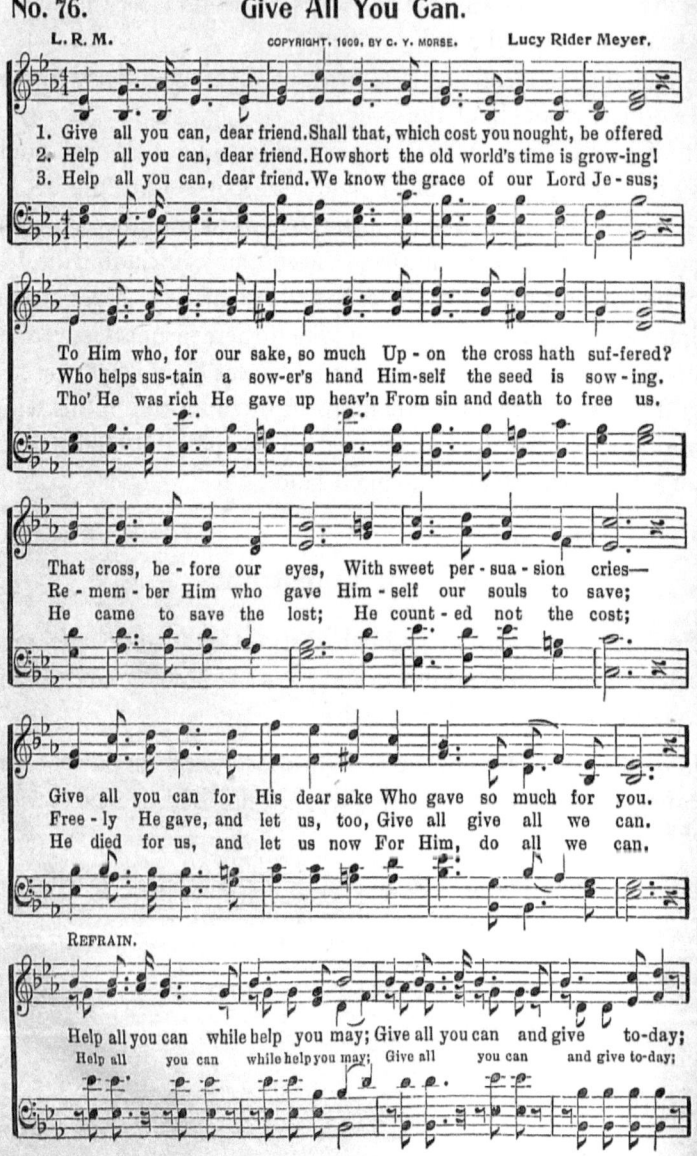

"AUTOBIOGRAPHY OF A BONNET"

Lucy Rider Meyer[1]

You didn't know bonnets could talk? Well, I am glad to contribute a little toward your general information. But perhaps the fault has been yours, not ours, that you have not discovered sooner that we could talk. Confess, now, did you ever try to enter into a conversation with a bonnet? Well then, how can you blame us for being somewhat reticent?

Yes, I'll tell you my story, that's what I started out to do. But on one condition—that you believe what I say. For really, I am going to tell you the truth. "About my being able to talk?" Well, I won't insist upon that. If what I've said above does not convince you, probably nothing will; and I must leave the matter to your own judgment. But I mean you must believe the incidents of the work of my owner that I am going to give; for they are all true. I pledge you the word of a—bonnet, for it.

How well I remember two years ago when I was first made. Not in an ordinary milliner's shop, no indeed, but in the private room of a sweet lady whose black dress and snowy collar and cuffs quite won my heart the moment I saw them. She was a deaconess. I adopted her at once, for I knew instinctively that she was making me for herself. She had a black bonnet frame that she cut and pieced and fitted, and this soft

---

1. *Highways and Hedges* 64 (1893) 78–80. Used with permission from the Library of the Wesley Historical Society. This article exemplifies the international connection of the Methodist deaconess movement. After its publication in CTS's *Message and Deaconess World*, Thomas Bowman Stephenson reprinted it in the WDO's journal, *Highways and Hedges*.

black stuff she coaxed and gathered into folds—no flowers or feathers nor lace—nothing else at all. And all the time she worked she had such a sweet serious smile on her face. Once I heard her say under her breath, "For Jesus' sake!" and again, "If 'who sweeps a floor' may do it for God, surely one who makes a bonnet may. Isn't that so, quaint old George Herbert?"[2] But there was nobody in the room, so I made up my mind it must be some poetry or other she was quoting.

Well, she finished me, pinned two soft white ties to my sides, tucked me away in a bureau drawer and went down to dinner. That very afternoon I started out with her in my work. It made a great impression upon my mind, being my first experience in life. I wish I could make it seem as real to you as it was to me. My Deaconess had a mother's meeting that afternoon at three o'clock, and she started out very early to make a few calls on some poor women in her district whom she hoped to bring to the meeting. Up flights of rickety stairs we went, and into rooms whose odours would have repelled any one who stopped to notice them, down little, dark, back alleys, and into houses behind houses of whose existence you, perhaps, have never dreamed. I remember that in one of these lived a man and his wife and two children. The oldest a little child of three years, was sick, and the man was confined to his bed with a crushed foot. How they lived nobody knew. My Deaconess put her hand on the sick child's head and listened to their broken story of its fever and delirium. "What does the little one eat?" she asked. "Not much of anything. Sometimes she drinks some coffee," was the reply. "Oh, but you should give her milk," said the deaconess, "milk and hot water and sugar. Coffee will make her head worse, I fear." But father and mother declared that she did not like milk, would not drink it even if it was sweetened. Then as the deaconess look perplexed, the mother bethought herself, "O but *she likes beer!*" as if that solved the entire difficulty. I could feel the form of my deaconess tremble with indignation, but it was not much she could do or say. The mother could not leave the children to go to the meeting, so we could only have a few words of prayer, and leave the little sufferer, whose ghastly face made me fear she would not be alive at our next visit.

In another room that afternoon we found father, mother, and five or six children, all practising music and dancing for some of the impromptu

---

2. This phrase comes from the fifth stanza in George Herbert's poem, "The Elixir": "A servant with this clause/Makes drudgery divine:/Who sweeps a room as for Thy laws,/Makes that and th' action fine." Herbert (1593–1633) was a poet and Church of England priest.

street performances by which they evidently made their living. A little two-year-old child was sent out into the middle of the room to dance for us, and its chubby baby feet lifted prettily to the music of its mother accordion, would have been a winsome sight but for the knowledge we had—my Deaconess and I—that the child was being trained to dance in saloons, the lowest and vilest places, to earn money for its degraded parents. In another home that we visited—it was only two little rooms—lived the family of a professional beggar, whose wife lay paralyzed and dying in a little, dark room, unspeakably dirty and forbidding. There was no physical want here, but O, such awful spiritual destitution!

Not all of the homes we visited were like these, however; in some my Deaconess was joyfully greeted, she having been there many times before. In some there were clean floors and clean faces, and women and children gladly ceased their work or play to listen to a few verses from the Bible and join in words of prayer. Four women that day went with us and joined the two or three living in the house where the meeting was held. I can't tell you much about the meeting. You never attended one like it. My Deaconess did most of the talking, and all the audible praying, but I remember how one poor mother's tears dropped down over the baby she held in her arms—her husband was a drunkard,—and how another, a cripple, said it was the first word of prayer she had heard for fourteen years.

Well, that was one of many times. My Deaconess and I went out regularly every day but Monday to such work as this, so I had the best of opportunities to see the sad world in which she worked. Then when we came home at night, tired and dusty—she tired, and both of us dusty—it was very pleasant for me to hang on the hall hat-rack with half a dozen of my sister bonnets, listening to the pleasant clatter of dishes and murmur of voices coming up from the dining-room where the deaconess family were at supper. After this came evening prayers, where the cases of special need found during the day were reported for counsel, encouragement and prayer. I shall not try to describe these evening reunions, I am afraid you might think me irreverent.

But the work of my Deaconess was not always sad and trying. Sometimes we had very pleasant occasions; Epworth League,[3] and King's Daughter's meetings.[4] It frequently fell to my owner to tell about

---

3. See 73n2.

4. Margaret Bottome founded this ecumenical, women's service organization in her New York City home in 1886. The organization continues today as the International Order of The King's Daughters and Sons (IOKDS).

our work at these gatherings. How proud I used to be of her then. She never tried to shirk her duty, though I have heard her say in private many a time, that she would rather do almost anything else than talk in public. But she used to stand up quietly before the people with her lovely, shining face and tell the story right out of her heart. It used to go to their hearts, too; I have seen ladies wiping their eyes many a time when she told them about the work. I always felt too in a modest way, that *I* had some share in her success. At any rate, people always looked at me, and more than once they asked my owner (with an apology) how much I cost. At which she would always reply, with mathematical accuracy, "One dollar and seven cents, including the ties, but I made it myself." I need hardly add that after such occasions my Deaconess would return to the Home richer in love and sympathy, and oftentimes richer in material gifts, than when she went away. I used to fancy that the difference between the price of non-deaconess and deaconess bonnets was made the standard of the gifts sometimes.

Yes, I was "made over" once, and this was how it happened. I don't mind a little rain, even if repeated a good many times, but that October day the rain fell in floods. My Deaconess had no umbrella with her, and before she reached the Home I was soaked through and through. I dried off in a fairly good shape to be sure, and she wore me a month afterward: but she never seemed quite pleased at my appearance, so I was not greatly surprised to find myself one day all ripped to pieces and lying in fragments on her table. She procured a new frame, washed and ironed my cloth cover, and then exhibited me with great pride to the family "as just as good as new." That was four months ago, and I think I am good for some time yet.

I go to lectures once in a while when we can spare an evening from our meetings, and more rarely to a concert or like entertainment down town. Don't I feel out of place among my gay sisters? Not a bit of it. My place is on the head of my Deaconess, and I know my place too well to wish for any other. It is true I am looked at in those places rather curiously, but I don't mind that, I think it is a part of my mission. Do I ever envy the gay bonnets I meet occasionally, with their feathers and flowers finery? Well, I blush to confess it, but there was a time once when such thoughts would come to me—you know what empty headed creatures we are. But I don't feel so now. Indeed I don' [sic] think of myself any more at all. We are so interested in our work day by day, and are kept so busy doing it—my Deaconess and I—that we never think of ourselves at all. But sometimes when I go to a concert or even to church, and see all the gay bonnets, I do have some queer thoughts revolving in my crown—shall I tell you about them? Why, I caught myself making mathematical calculations once right in church! That was wrong, I confess, but let me tell you how it happened. You see my Deaconess had just come from a home of dreadful poverty where a little baby had died, and the mother was so sick! They couldn't have any funeral. The city had just sent a rough coffin by a rougher man, but they had not money to buy anything—no little white shroud nor even a single flower! And the man with the coffin would not wait, but picked up the baby and put it in so roughly! Then the little sister screamed out, "O mamma, he bumped the baby's head!" Do you wonder my Deaconess cried? And the nurse sister who was there helping—you know some of the deaconesses are trained nurses—just took off her own white apron and wrapped it over the coarse pillow and around the little form in the coffin. Then after the man had carried it out, and my Deaconess had had a little prayer with the broken-hearted mother, she left the nurse to take care of her and came to the church. And as she sat there so quietly—it was before service began—thinking how she wanted to help that sick mother and oh, so many others, and how little she could do because she had no money, why, before I knew it I found myself wondering what the feathers and ornaments on those bonnets cost! Yes, I reckoned it up. I know pretty well what such things cost, even if I don't wear them myself. And if you'll believe it, it was hundreds of dollars, not for the bonnets with all their velvet and silks and ribbons, but just for the feather and flowers and jewels—the *extra* things on them! I know covetousness is an awful sin but I am afraid I did covet. I wished—Oh, how I *did* wish, that my Deaconess had the price of every one of those extra things, to help her poor folks with. And then, while the minister preached his sermon, I went to sleep and had a dream—it isn't wicked for bonnets to go to sleep in church, is it? I dreamed that all the rich folks in the world made up their minds that they would never wear feathers and flowers and jewels on their bonnets any more at all, but would give the whole price of them to the deaconesses to use in their work. O, I never can tell you how happy I was while I was dreaming that dream! My very frame quivered with joy, and my ties trembled all over. I saw the bread—whole wagon-loads of it—that was bought with part of the money! And the poor widows whose rent was due—some of it was used to keep them from being turned out into the streets. And it bought milk for poor starving babies, and shoes and warm things so that children could come to Sunday-school and hear about Jesus. And the angels up in heaven—for I saw them too in my dream—they rejoiced and sang so exultingly, "On earth, peace,"[5] that I wondered if Christmas was coming again so soon! For it was only February.

Suddenly my Deaconess rose, with the rest of the congregation, for the doxology[6] was being sung. I awoke with a start. The angels were gone, and I was still in the midst of the feathers and flowers. But that dream has always lingered in my mind. It was so beautiful that I can't help believing it will come true some day. For it seems to me—bonnets have brains in them sometimes you know—it does seem to me, though I'm only a foolish creature, that mustn't judge my superiors, that when folks really and truly love their neighbours as themselves, they will not spend money on the extra things for themselves, while their neighbours starve, body and soul, for what that same money would so quickly buy.

Reflection Questions

1. How does the bonnet serve as a symbol of the deaconess mission? What does it reveal about the values and challenges of being a deaconess?

2. How might the bonnet's reflection on wealth and poverty have been a critique of ecclesial and societal priorities when it was written? What about in our day?

---

5. Luke 2:14.

6. A doxology is a statement of praise glorifying God that can be spoken or sung. In many Christian services, the congregation stands during the singing of the doxology, which would explain why the bonnet "awoke with a start."

RULES FOR THE DEACONESSES OF THE MARTHA-MARIA ORGANIZATION FOR GENERAL NURSING CARE IN NUREMBERG[1]

§1

A Deaconess is, in the exception of cases of sickness and unforeseen events, entitled to four weeks of vacation every two years. Apart from that every sister receives the necessary rest.

§2

The reports that are issued by the direction of a hospital to the names of the sisters, from which the sisters receive their education, must be seen as the property of the Organization, and may not become handouts without the special permission of the chairman.

Sisters who have been dismissed or who have resigned will receive the certificate from the chairman, that and how long they were active in the Organization, but their testimonials, since they stand in a relationship of service to the Organization, are much more as members and daughters of the same.

---

1. I am grateful to Anna Lowery, with additional help from Reiner Kanzleiter, for the German translation of this document: "Regeln für die Diakonissen des Martha-Maria-Vereins für allgemeine Krankenpflege zu Nürnberg." Used with permission from the Martha-Maria Deaconess Organization Archives.

§3

If the resignation or dismissal of a sister is successful, then it is left to the administration of the Organization, whether and what reimbursement should be given to the same.

If a pre-trial or trial sister leaves before the end of the third year, then she must reimburse the established costs of her education to the Organization, she loses all demands upon the Organization and is only given that which she had already brought with her.

§4

The pocket money that the sisters come to monthly is:

For sisters on probation, 1st year:		Mk (Marks). 2, –
- " -	2nd year:	Mk. 2,50
- " -	3rd year:	Mk. 3, –
For ordained sisters		Mk. 4, –
For head sisters		Mk. 4, –
For those, who enter after education is completed		
	in the 1st year:	Mk. 2,50
	in the 2nd year:	Mk. 3,–
	in the 3rd year:	Mk. 3,–
	after finishing probation time:	Mk. 4,–

On behalf of the holiday month the pocket money is increased up to 10,– Mk. (Handwritten correction: by 5 Mk.)

If one sister stays away for more than three months to care for her sick parents, she should receive her pocket money for the three months and for the later time. In comparison, the parents, if they are in need of it, receive a part of their support from the Organization, so far as their means permit it.

If a consecrated sister has to take her holiday in a special rest or health resort, then she receives the regular pocket money for the first month, for the other months only 1 mark, just as she is gone for the holiday in this way. Trial sisters receive their pocket money in such cases.

If a consecrated sister is secured, then she receives for the first month the regular pocket money, for the later time 1 mark per month.

Trial sisters receive in such cases only the regular pocket money in the first month.

§5

Consecrated sisters receive a grey dress every three years, calico dresses as needed. The senior sisters receive a grey dress every two years and calico dresses as needed, so that the consecrated sisters as a rule have two grey and two to three calico dresses, the senior sisters three grey and one calico dress. The grey dresses should be replaced at Christmas, the calico dresses in the course of the year.

At their consecration, probationary sisters receive as a rule:

> one black dress,
> one calico dress,
> one summer coat,
> new collars and new caps.

For their birthdays, the consecrated sisters, if necessary, two new aprons; the probationary sisters, in necessary cases, in the first year, otherwise in the second and in the third year. For those concerned, it is considered an intercession on this day. If she is present, then she will sing a fitting song. If not, the senior sister delivers in writing or in person the good wishes for the sisters.

The collars should be un-sewn by 7 cm wide at the front, the material should be linen.

As a rule, coats are replaced every four years, underclothes and footwear as needed. After the run of four years, estimated from their entrance, the sister receives six new shirts. Dresses and coats should always have the same buttons.

The article of clothing, umbrellas et cetera should be bought at the following prices: rain umbrellas 3–6 marks, sun shades 3–5 marks, corset 4–5 marks, petticoats 3–5 marks, winter undershirts 2–3 marks, summer undershirts 1.50–2 marks.

Shirts should be made from cotton material or half linen, winter trousers from fustian[2] or flannel, summer stockings from cotton, winter stockings from wool—both dark-colored. The sisters should make their own gloves.

---

2. Heavy cloth woven from cotton.

Boots and slippers should have low heels.

Shirts, nightgowns, and trousers must be made following simple, uniform patterns. Winter trousers may be equipped with a simple cross seam. The points on shirts and nightgowns may not be over 1.5 cm., and on the trousers not more than 2. cm. wide.

It is up to the senior sister to give away old clothes.

§6

The sisters are asked to memorize and maintain the Christian orders, which are found in Colossians 3:12–17.[3]

§7

The sisters are put under the order of the Martha-Maria Organization with respect to the concerned administration.

They have to apply themselves to being good natured and to have good will towards the other, to abstain from all slander and in general be helpful to each other in the improvement of blessedness. James 4:11,[4] Matthew 18:15–18.[5] Domestic affairs may not be discussed outside of the House.

---

3. "12 Therefore, as God's chosen ones, holy and beloved, clothe yourselves with compassion, kindness, humility, meekness, and patience. 13 Bear with one another and, if anyone has a complaint against another, forgive each other; just as the Lord has forgiven you, so you also must forgive. 14 Above all, clothe yourselves with love, which binds everything together in perfect harmony. 15 And let the peace of Christ rule in your hearts, to which indeed you were called in one body. And be thankful. 16 Let the word of Christ dwell in you richly; teach and admonish one another in all wisdom; and with gratitude in your hearts sing psalms, hymns, and spiritual songs to God. 17 And whatever you do, in word or deed, do everything in the name of the Lord Jesus, giving thanks to God the Father through him."

4. "Do not speak evil against one another, brothers and sisters. Whoever speaks evil against another or judges another speaks evil against the law and judges the law, but if you judge the law, you are not a doer of the law but a judge."

5. 15 "If your brother or sister sins against you, go and point out the fault when the two of you are alone. If you are listened to, you have regained that one. 16 But if you are not listened to, take one or two others along with you, so that every word may be confirmed by the evidence of two or three witnesses. 17 If that person refuses to listen to them, tell it to the church, and if the offender refuses to listen even to the church, let such a one be to you as a gentile and a tax collector. 18 Truly I tell you, whatever you bind on earth will be bound in heaven, and whatever you loose on earth will be loosed in heaven."

If a sister has cause for complaint, then she should turn to the chairman or the senior sister.

If a sister wishes to go out, then she has to ask for permission and say where she is going. She should be at home middays at 12:00 and evenings at 7:00.

Every sister has to see to order and cleanliness for herself and in the House. If the private care is over, then the sister is to order her clothing before all others (that is, to disinfect, if she were caring for contagious sick people), so that she can undertake nursing at any time.

The dresses et cetera must be laid in a designated place. If anything is missing from the articles of clothing et cetera, then the sister is to report it to the senior sister.

§8

In summer as well as in winter, the sisters get up at 5:30. Sisters who have returned to the House for rest or tired from private care are allowed to rest for longer.

Dressing and making the beds has to happen as quietly as possible. No sister is allowed to leave her room unwashed and uncombed. None refrain from strengthening themselves for the day's work through prayer and reading the Word of God.

In their outer appearance the sister should observe decency and good custom without exception, 1 Timothy 2:9.[6] Hence, they are always to be decently clothed from the established morning hour until bed time.

At 9:00 the sisters receive their breakfast.

At 12:30 they eat lunch, which they close with a short prayer. "You now eat or drink, or whatever you do, do it all to God's honor." 1 Corinthians 10:31.

At 2:30 the sisters take coffee. Gather the remaining lumps, so that nothing dies. Job 6:12.[7]

---

6. "[A]lso that the women should dress themselves in moderate clothing with reverence and self-control, not with their hair braided or with gold, pearls, or expensive clothes"

7. "Is my strength the strength of stones, or is my flesh bronze?"

§9

The trial sister's lessons are from 3:00–5:00 on the designated days. On every Wednesday an hour of Bible, prayer or learning.

Every sister is strongly recommended to withdraw during the afternoon for half an hour for prayer and for consideration of the Word of God.

The silence belongs to the character of the sisters. All of the work in the House is only to be performed in silence, the doors are to be closed quietly. Everything superfluous and loud talking in the corridors and stairwell is to be avoided.

§10

Every day, each sister should take some time for herself to move around a little in peace.

§11

At 9:30 the sisters retire to rest. At 10:00 the lights in the sisters' rooms must be out. Fire and light is to be used carefully and economically.

§12

The sisters are not allowed to accept gifts for themselves. Should they be offered gifts, they should make the giver of gifts aware of the Organization's provision for the elderly. If they [the giver] refuse to donate the gift to the provision for the elderly, then they are only right to accept the gift after they have received permission from the senior sister or the chairman.

Acting contrary to this involves a loss of this demand for the provision for the elderly. Generally, it is expected that the sisters are concerned for the execution of the Organization's order.

Nuremberg, July 1890

Reflection Questions

1. What role does discipline and structure play in the daily lives of deaconesses? How might such a regimented lifestyle both contribute to and challenge their mission?

2. What might the values inherent in this source document of simplicity, modesty, and communal living mean for religious and/or service-oriented organizations today?

"'I don't want 'em—'ope I never see 'em again,' said the drunken father."

Chapter V

"MOTHERING NOT GOVERNING"

Maternalism in Late Nineteenth-Century
Methodist Women's Organizations[1]

Overview

THIS CHAPTER ASSESSES THE maternalism ideology of the Methodist deaconess movement that shows up in the oft-repeated sentiment that rather than being mothers themselves, they chose to be mothers to humanity's orphans. Maternalism helped the movement find acceptance in the church because it aligned with the prescribed sphere of women's nurturing, tending children, and mothering. What maternalism did not promote was women's governing in the church. Support for maternalism is particularly perplexing coming from Lucy Rider Meyer, a progressive female leader in Methodism, who nonetheless embedded maternalism in photos, church newsletters, a novel, and published prayers. More than a politically expedient stance, this chapter demonstrates that Meyer embedded maternalism in everything she produced for public consumption about the deaconess movement. Maternalism even saturates her prayer, the first source document in the chapter, in which she asks God to bless women's "special work"—a phrase repeated twice—and their "gentle ministries." In the second source document, "Report of the Tory Street Mission," we read about the wide-ranging, unceasing, grinding work

---

1. This chapter was originally published in *Methodist History*, 55 (2016–2017) 32–46. Changes to this version eliminated duplication with material included in earlier chapters.

undertaken by New Zealand deaconess, Isabel Sinclair, the "peripatetic" international traveler introduced in the book's opening paragraphs.

A young woman named Joy, the protagonist in the late nineteenth-century novel *Joy the Deaconess*, declined a marriage proposal from a handsome, successful doctor with whom she had worked closely for many years in a local hospital. When pressed about how she could make such a decision, Joy replied, "Cousin Emma, I'm not so foolish as not to know that it is the right and proper thing for most girls to marry. And if there were no sorrow and sin and trouble in the world, perhaps God would put the desire to marry into the hearts of all of us. But think of the orphans, and those who need special care from some one, which they would never get if all women were absorbed by family cares. It seems as if God wanted some of us to be the mothers of humanity's orphans."[2]

Why did Joy make what many at the time would consider an imprudent decision? *Because Joy was a deaconess*. She was motivated by maternalism, not of mothering her own nuclear family but a much wider family in need. The phrase our intrepid protagonist adopted, "mothers of humanity's orphans," encapsulated the maternalistic ideology of the Methodist deaconess movement, as well as the Woman's Home Missionary Society (WHMS) of the Methodist Episcopal Church (MEC). Maternalism also permeated Methodist women's writing in denominational journals, such as Lucy Rider Meyer's article on deaconess work, "The Mother in the Church." Even more telling about its saturation, maternalism showed up in popular literature authored by Methodist women, like *Joy the Deaconess*, written by deaconess leader and educator, Elizabeth Holding. It is these publications, largely forgotten and untapped by contemporary historians, that ground the thesis of this chapter.

Based on popular writings authored or compiled by Lucy Rider Meyer, Elizabeth Holding, Jennie Fowler Willing, and other female Methodist leaders in the US, I argue that maternalism was not simply a compromise to mollify a male church hierarchy but an ideology that these women embraced and perpetuated among a wide swath of the faithful. In other words, the maternalistic ideology disseminated by women in the WHMS and the deaconess movement restricted women—by their own rhetoric and strategy—to "mothering not governing." I adopt this phrase from Carolyn De Swarte Gifford, who coined it to summarize

---

2. Holding, *Joy the Deaconess*, 92.

MEC General Conference decisions in the 1880s concerning women's rights and responsibilities in the church. Gifford rehearses, for instance, the complexity of the 1888 General Conference decision that sanctioned the Office of Deaconess while simultaneously denying laity rights to women. She uses that decision, alongside others from General Conferences throughout the 1880s, to argue that official church decisions made by clergymen and laymen "intended to delineate clearly the boundaries of woman's sphere within the church, relegating her to mothering not governing, allowing her to be a pastor's helper but not a pastor."[3]

I concur with Gifford. However, what I will demonstrate in this chapter moves a step beyond Gifford and other scholars who have overlooked these more widely disseminated resources published by Methodist women. For instance, the novel written by Holding that features Joy the deaconess expressed as strongly as denominational documents—and certainly for a much wider audience—a maternalistic ideology. The same was true in Meyer's novel, *Mary North*, where maternalism was as rampant as in her article with the explicit title, "Mother in the Church." It is these popular resources that demonstrate how pervasive maternalism was and how unchallenged it remained, even by Meyer and other prominent female Methodists who wielded the influence to extinguish it, certainly within their organizations.

Before we go further, it is important to define maternalism, the pivotal term in this chapter. Unfortunately, this is not an easy task. Authors of an essay on maternalism, which surveys the vast amount of literature published since the 1990s, concede that the meaning of the term "has not become clearer over time. To the contrary, the term has been defined in a variety of competing ways from the outset, and the confusion surrounding it has only multiplied in recent years."[4] Rather than sort through the morass of definitions and corresponding contexts, I will utilize one of the earliest definitions, because it fits well the context and character of late nineteenth-century Methodist women's organizations. Seth Koven and Sonya Michel define as maternalist those "ideologies that exalted women's capacity to mother and extended to society as a whole the values they attached to that role: care, nurturance, and morality." These ideologies, they claim, functioned simultaneously in the

---

3. Gifford, *American Deaconess Movement*, 4. See also Schmidt, *Grace Sufficient*, 202.

4. Plant and van der Klein, "Introduction," 5.

private sphere of domesticity as well as in the public sphere.[5] Elizabeth Clapp reiterates this understanding of maternalism. "The concept of maternalism accepted, even idealized, women's traditional role as wife and mother but at the same time insisted that women had a duty to extend their female skills and concerns beyond their own homes."[6]

Koven, Michel, and Clapp describe precisely the maternalistic ideology that WHMS members, for instance, asserted as their mission. Most were mothers themselves, and they endeavored through the WHMS to extend maternalism into the homes of the poor and needy. The conundrum, however, that maternalism exacerbated, according to Michel, is "its acceptance of the existing gender order, although strategically necessary, also hindered the expansion of women's roles and rights."[7] In other words, as Linda Gordon attests, women's subordination remains intact with maternalism.[8]

Maternalism in the Woman's Home Missionary Society

The WHMS emerged in 1880 as an organization dedicated to the evangelization and uplift of women, children, and homes across the nation. At its first annual meeting, every speaker spotlighted the home—and mothers in particular—as simultaneously the reason for people's degradation and the gateway for their redemption. The central question was, How could homes be reached and brought to shine as Christian exemplars? The answer: by WHMS members instructing poor, unfortunate women how to be mothers who would create homes displaying Christian virtues. As WHMS Corresponding Secretary Elizabeth Rust explained, the organization replicated here at home the work of the Woman's Foreign Missionary Society in foreign fields, "women working in the homes of women."[9] By pursuing this strategy—from one mother

---

5. Koven and Michel, "Womanly Duties," 1079.
6. Clapp, *Mothers of All Children*, 3.
7. Michel, "Maternalism and Beyond," 27.
8. Gordon, "Gender, State and Society," 146–48.
9. Rust, "Letters from Friends," 44. The WHMS advertised itself not in competition to the WFMS, founded over a decade earlier, but rather as its counterpart. The WHMS focused on mission at home, particularly for "the neglected condition of the population of our own country," while the WFMS focused on mission to women in foreign lands. Rust, "Woman's Home Missionary Society," 653.

to another, from one home to another—WHMS leaders set out a maternalist strategy that women, as surrogate mothers of the underprivileged, were to evangelize across three concentric circles—the nuclear family, the home, and eventually the nation.

Maternalism showed up on many pages of the *Souvenir Exhibit*, a photographic catalog of every WHMS industrial home and mission, compiled in celebration of the organization's twentieth anniversary. In the caption, for instance, for the Thayer Industrial Home in Atlanta, Georgia, an educational institution for young, Black women, like deaconess Anna E. Hall, maternalist rhetoric was prevalent: "It is impossible to place too high an estimate upon the value of training that develops into a cultured, modest Christian womanhood the young women of a race who are later to become the teachers, wives, mothers, and leaders . . . of their people." Expressing similar sentiments, the caption under the Palen Mission in Savannah, Georgia read: "hundreds of young women, trained in hand, head, and heart, are carrying the lessons they have learned to others. . . . Some have married and are good home-makers."[10]

Most WHMS members were mothers, like the nation's First Lady, Lucy Webb Hayes, a mother of five children who served as the first president of the organization. Her staunch Christian faith earned official praise from the 1880 MEC General Conference, which passed a resolution "expressing high appreciation of the personal worth and noble example of the President and his wife and commended to all the women of America the heroic conduct of Mrs. Hayes in regard to temperance and especially the beautiful simplicity of her Christian life."[11] In one of her many speeches, Hayes reinforced the centrality of maternalism in this brief phrase, "Elevate woman, and you lift up the home; exalt the home and you lift up the nation."[12] This quote encapsulates the concentric circles of family, home, and nation.

Even WHMS members who were not mothers themselves nonetheless embraced maternalism. Take Jennie Fowler Willing. She helped from the ground up to organize the WHMS, served as Vice President and Secretary of the Bureau of Spanish Work, and contributed frequently to its magazine, *Woman's Home Missions*. She was married with no children, yet maternalistic rhetoric saturated her voluminous writings. She often linked motherhood with power as in her article, "The Mother's Power in

10. *Exhibit of the Industrial Homes*, 6, 14.
11. Meeker, *Six Decades of Service*, 8.
12. Deen, "Lucy Webb Hayes," 247.

Evangelism:" "Among the mightiest of undiscovered forces the mother's power for good ranks all."[13] In other words, maternalism applied as well to women like herself without children. Women use their power, their strength to mother the world.

This maternal work for the "world's bettering" was centered in the home, as she explained in her essay, simply titled, "The Home": "None can ever hope to wield the power for good that God has put into the mother's hand. She shapes the life."[14] Similarly, in a speech given at the WHMS fifth annual meeting, she declared, "Home-making is the special work of our Society. No service can be more important. All people are, and will be forever, what their homes make them. The home is the work-shop where is wrought out the character and destiny of the individual, the nation, the civilization, the race."[15] With repeated sentiments like these, Willing grounded even more deeply the WHMS's purpose and strategy in maternalism.

Maternalism in the Methodist Deaconess Movement

Lucy Rider Meyer's "Mother in the Church"

Like the WHMS, the Methodist deaconess movement also embraced a maternalist ideology. Meyer took the lead in this effort in church publications geared to a clergy audience. She established a direct connection between deaconess work and maternalism in her pivotal article, "The Mother in the Church," published in *Methodist Review* in 1901. *Methodist Review* targeted a ministerial audience; in the same volume as Meyer's, there were two articles penned by MEC bishops—Bishop John Heyl Vincent's "The Class Meeting in Methodism" and Bishop James Thoburn's "Our Missionary Polity."

Meyer opened the article with the image of the church as the "household of faith," following Paul's usage in Gal 6:10.[16] In the

---

13. Willing, "Mother's Power in Evangelism," 220.

14. Willing, "Home," 20.

15. *Fifth Annual Report of the Woman's Home Missionary Society*, 27. She expressed identical sentiments in another publication that same year, "Let the home where she does her best work, have her strongest thought, her main strength, her most devout prayer." Willing, *Potential Woman*, 182.

16. "So then, whenever we have an opportunity, let us work for the good of all, and especially for those of the family of faith."

household of faith—the church—the pastor is the father, and the laity are the brothers and sisters. After these declarations, she queried, "But—where is the mother?" Her answer: The deaconess movement.[17] "The real origin of the [deaconess] work in America was in the mother instinct of woman herself, and in that wider conception of woman's 'family duties' that compels her to include in her loving care the great needy world family as well as the blessed little domestic circle."[18] Two questions frame her article, both of which showcase maternalism. As she began with the question—Where is the mother?—so she ended with a question that unmistakably portrayed the deaconess movement with maternalist rhetoric: "Who can realize what it will mean to Protestantism when the Mother [now with a capital 'M'] shall have been fully established again in her place in the Household of Faith?"[19]

One might conjecture that Meyer chose for political reasons to position the deaconess movement as the Mother in the Church in this journal geared to clergy, particularly since they continued to object to deaconesses. Perhaps, also for political reasons, Meyer purposively left church hierarchy intact in her article with pastors (men) as the father in the church to allay any fear of deaconesses usurping the pastoral role.[20] This would make sense given the vagaries of clergy support for women's work in the church. After all, only a decade earlier, by a vote of General Conference, local preacher's licenses previously issued to women were revoked. Then, delegates at the 1888 MEC General Conference voted to deny laity rights to women even while they approved the Office of Deaconess. Hence, the atmosphere for women's rights and responsibilities in the church remained charged. While one might conjecture that Meyer's political savvy prompted her to utilize Mother in the Church rhetoric for

---

17. It would be natural to surmise that she considered women to be the mother in the church. She does in fact raise that possibility but rejects it in this statement: "Nor can it be successfully maintained that woman's helpful but necessarily limited activity in unofficial lines supplies the need of the mother in the Church." Meyer, "The Mother in the Church," 716. Her reasoning remains enigmatic: "For, if so, then the converse would hold, that because of the assistance of our stewards, trustees, class leaders, and Sunday school superintendents, who are usually men, we do not need the pastor." Meyer, "Mother in the Church," 717. In yet another statement, Meyer answered the question—Where is the mother?—in a more direct fashion: "The deaconess movement puts the mother into the Church." Horton, *Burden of the City*, 146.

18. Meyer, "Mother in the Church," 730.
19. Meyer, "Mother in the Church," 732.
20. Meyer, "Mother in the Church," 716.

the *Methodist Review* audience, this option is contradicted by two of her publications for a popular, non-clergy audience in which a maternalistic ideology remains on display.

Lucy Rider Meyer's *Deaconess Stories* and *Mary North*

Consider the staging of photos in *Deaconess Stories*, published in 1900, the year before the *Methodist Review* article. Many portray deaconesses in a motherly pose with children. In two photos with a parent at least partially visible, the deaconess remains front and center. One of the photos shows the father halfway out the door while the deaconess, facing the camera, holds a baby, and two other children huddle near her skirts. The caption underneath reads: "'I don't want 'em—hope I never see 'em again,' said the drunken father."[21] In the other photo with a parent present, the mother, lying on her sick bed, is nearly hidden from view; again, it is the deaconess who stands upright and tall while folding laundry and keeping watch on the three children.[22]

Maternalism also permeates Meyer's little-known novel, *Mary North*, published in 1903, two years after the *Methodist Review* article. The book narrates the twists and turns faced by protagonist Mary North, who eventually, on the brink of death in a Chicago tenement, recovers thanks to the maternal care of a Methodist deaconess. The story opens with Mary and her widowed mother living on their own in a small New England village. Tragedy strikes when Mary's mother dies leaving her motherless at a young age. Tragedy soon strikes again when a ruthless rogue skillfully and relentlessly takes advantage of Mary's innocence and implores her to marry him. "I cannot go alone—it will kill me," he begs. "I plead with you. I need you for my little nurse. I have no mother—no one to care for me." His appeals hit home with Mary, who knows what it is to be motherless. Even after she recognizes his deceit, she responds maternally: "She would devote her whole life to him. She would pray. She would *compel* his salvation. Mary had never come so near to truly loving this man before, but it was the love of a mother—a savior."[23] She soon realizes, however, that he is an abusive alcoholic.

---

21. Meyer, *Deaconess Stories*, 49b.
22. Meyer, *Deaconess Stories*, 16a.
23. Meyer, *Mary North*, 146.

In desperation, Mary escapes to Chicago, where she tries unsuccessfully to support herself as a shop assistant in a large department store. Again, her penchant for mothering the helpless results in her being fired when she tries to protect her coworker, Vinnie, from a manager's sexual advances. Mary's economic situation becomes desperate when she cannot find another job, and after weeks of starvation and homelessness, she collapses on a Chicago street, not far from the deaconess home. There, she is mothered back to health by a deaconess nurse, Sister Elizabeth, who "begged that the 'case' might be given to her, and had watched over the stranger day and night, ministering to her as no mother, untrained, ever cared for a child."[24] When she is back on her feet, she makes plans to open a boarding house in Chicago to train young girls like herself, "a motherless lambie," in domestic skills for better employment opportunities. In the end, she opens the "School for Trained Helpers" as an extension of Meyer's Chicago Training School (CTS).[25]

Maternalism provides the thematic infrastructure for this novel. Several leading characters are motherless—Mary, the man who betrayed her, and Vinnie, her coworker in the department store. In turn, several leading characters, including Mary, act as a mother to another. It is curious, though, that her first two attempts at mothering fail; the man who betrayed her never did turn from his abuse of her, and Vinnie drank carbolic acid to end her life. Mary only succeeds as a mother after receiving maternal care from a deaconess, Sister Elizabeth. This time, on her third attempt, Mary succeeds and begins an institution to provide a practical means for young women in the city to survive and prevent further victimization from men who prey on the innocent; now she mothers the motherless. However, it is Sister Elizabeth who stars in the novel as the mother *par excellence*. She fits the maternalist profile as voiced by Methodist deaconesses themselves. "I never married, never had children of the flesh," stated one deaconess, "but God has given me many spiritual children."[26]

---

24. Meyer, *Mary North*, 275.
25. Meyer, *Mary North*, 317.
26. James, "Tributes from Deaconesses and Missionaries," 308. Dougherty confirms the maternalistic approach of deaconess work. "As single women free from the domestic claim, deaconesses could direct their maternal instincts into mothering the masses of men, women and children abused by the socioeconomic system." Dougherty, *My Calling to Fulfill*, ix.

Elizabeth Holding's *Joy the Deaconess*

Maternalism permeates even more Elizabeth Holding's novel, *Joy the Deaconess*, published in 1893, a decade before Meyer's. Holding was a protégé of Meyer's. They first met when Holding studied Chemistry under Meyer at McKendree College. Later, when Holding returned home on furlough from mission work in Chile, Meyer offered her a position at CTS. After several years on Meyer's staff, Holding went to Scarritt Bible and Training School to teach the Bible when the institution opened in 1892 in Kansas City, Missouri.

Like Mary North in Meyer's novel, Joy is an orphan, and both protagonists exhibit maternal instincts from a young age, particularly for the poor and mistreated. This inclination leads Joy in her early twenties to train to become a nurse and work in the local hospital. When she hears Meyer speak at a Sunday morning service on the deaconess movement, she invites her home to dinner to hear more. Their lunchtime conversation convinces Joy to enroll in CTS.

In Part II, after Joy completes the deaconess course, she becomes Superintendent of a deaconess home and hospital. At this juncture, the deaconess home moves front and center as the space where family, home life, and spiritual guidance coalesce for the deaconesses. As Colleen McDannell explains, "Family religion," when family members came together to pray, sing hymns, and read the Bible, "created a sacred time when the change and chaos of the profane world dissolved into the order and meaning of the eternal."[27] The scene describes the aim of the deaconess home, to be a sacred space, set apart from the world, to which deaconesses returned after a long day of visiting in overcrowded tenements or nursing the infirmed. They gathered to eat, discuss the day's events, share each other's burdens, and worship together, as Meyer described in her ideal depiction: "The deaconess home: its model is the family life, with the Superintendent taking the place of mother . . . As Miss [Isabella] Thoburn beautifully says, 'The happiest place in the world is that where father and mother gather their children into a family circle, but the next happiest place is one like ours, where women to whom no other home has been allotted, may live and work and pray and rejoice together.'"[28] In the deaconess home, the women live together as a family, and the Superintendent fills the mother role.

27. McDannell, *Christian Home in Victorian America*, 104.
28. Meyer, *Deaconesses*, 70.

Holding recreates in her novel a portrait of deaconesses as a family settled in their home with Joy as the Superintendent and mother figure. Several deaconesses even grew up as orphans, which makes this home the only one they have ever known. As Annie, a deaconess, remarks, "I never had a home before, Mrs. Huntley. I found a verse in the Bible the other day, and I thought of myself and the Deaconess Home. 'He setteth the solitary in families.'[29] Isn't that beautiful?"[30] Another deaconess, Mamie, requests that her wedding take place in the home, "the place that seemed more like home to her than any place else."[31] When Mamie announces her decision to marry, someone asks Joy, "Is this the first break in the family?"[32] Joy responds that "she felt very much as if her eldest daughter was being married."[33] She even buys Mamie her wedding gown of white cashmere. Joy, who willingly gave up being a mother to a family of her own, considers the "blessed deaconess work" as her lasting heritage. The novel ends with Joy's final words: "It is the joy of my life."

Maternalism Compared in *Mary North* and *Joy the Deaconess*

The theology of both Holding's and Meyer's novels conforms to McDannell's portrayal of "maternal Protestantism," which she summarizes in these statements: "God's loving mercy and kindness surpassed [God's] fearsome characteristics. Intuition, emotion, and sentiment were the prerequisites for salvation. Salvation was demonstrated not by a violent submission to the will of God, but through acting out, in daily life, Christian virtues. Self-sacrifice, love, and interior devotion . . . The mediation of the clergy and the institution of the church took second place."[34] These features fill the two novels. First, the presence of clergy and the institutional church is minimal. The only clergyman to appear in either novel does so under pretense in the fake wedding ceremony of Mary North and her betrayer, who hires a con man to dress up like a minister and read vows from a prayer book for a $100 extortion payment. In *Joy the Deaconess*,

29. Ps 68:6.
30. Holding, *Joy the Deaconess*, 150.
31. Holding, *Joy the Deaconess*, 199.
32. Holding, *Joy the Deaconess*, 203.
33. Holding, *Joy the Deaconess*, 200.
34. McDannell, *Christian Home in Victorian America*, 128.

the only preacher introduced is none other than Meyer, who delivers the Sunday sermon in Joy's local church.

Second, in *Mary North*, there is a theological conflict between God's wrath (a more masculine dimension) versus God's mercy and kindness (a more maternal dimension). Mary's mother tells her that God is good, yet what comforts the child when she cries and worries that she will never be converted and will go to hell is her mother's presence. "Then the sobbing would grow quieter, and holding fast to her mother's hand the child would fall asleep, with the heterodox but comforting conviction that some way or other mother's hand would keep her from going to perdition, even if she should die before she wakened."[35] However, when her mother's hand is not there to console her, Mary does not know what to make of a God who allows suffering. In her darkest hour, as she flees from her betrayer on a train ride from Boston to Chicago, she engages in a lengthy internal debate about her perception of God.

> It was a hideous blunder—a sin too great to be forgiven. Yes, a sin—she would not spare herself. . . . She saw only the mistake, the sin. It loomed up enormous, colossal, through the distorting mists of her shame and sorrow. Earth was ashes before her, and Heaven was brass above her. She had always prayed before—prayed about everything. Now, the thought of God was an added agony.
>
> If she had been a man and not a girl, a girl, too, into the very fiber of whose life had been woven the profound belief that God is good—if she had been a man and ten years older, she would have fiercely arraigned God for bringing this trouble upon her. She would have told Him to His face that He had been a poor guide, a false father to her. She would have asked Him how, even if she had done wrong in not speaking, He could permit the one little error of an ignorant girl to bring upon her such awful, eternal ruin! She would have demanded to know where His promised love and care were, that He had let her blindly fall into this lowest hell. . . . God was angry with her, but righteously so. The fault was all her own—she would not now commit the supreme sacrilege of trying to throw the responsibility of it off on Him. No, suffer as she might, God was good. Mother said that with her dying breath. . . . She clung desperately to her childhood traditions and prayed in an agony to be delivered from this last temptation.[36]

35. Meyer, *Mary North*, 20–21.
36. Meyer, *Mary North*, 131.

On the one hand, Mary blames God for "the mistake" and wrestles internally with the thought that God is "a poor guide, a false father," that God is responsible for "bringing this trouble upon her," that God is "angry with her" and withholds "promised love and care" and allows her "blindly [to] fall into this lowest hell." On the other hand, given her age, gender, and religious upbringing, she attempts to block out those thoughts about a God who masochistically delights in her downfall, and she blames herself instead. "Yes, a sin—she would not spare herself." Her mother's final words, "God is good," become her mantra, but she turns it on herself with this implication—if God is good, then I am not.

This theological debate over God's nature returns to the fore as she recovers in the deaconess home. Once again, the view of God as good, loving, and kind triumphs in the end and comforts her as it did when, as a child, she held onto her mother's hand. However, she must shed the view of God as wrathful and punitive to be healed physically and spiritually. It is the mother love of a deaconess, Sister Elizabeth, that sparks the transformation. She tells Mary a story of a lost lamb who runs away, but the father, "who knew every lamb by name," searches for it, rescues it, and brings it back home.[37] The father, exhibiting great love, does not punish the lamb but "gathered the little crying creature tenderly up in his arms and carried it home." Sister Elizabeth then calls Mary her "little lost lamb" and promises to bring her home. Meyer, as the narrator, comments that Mary does not come around primarily because of argument or assertion; rather, she responds to the maternal love of "this pure beautiful woman who knew all the dreadful things of her past, did not loathe her, did not shrink from her, but actually loved and trusted her."[38] It is Sister Elizabeth who helps Mary theologically to see herself not as a sinner but as the sinned against, to view God not as one who brings wrath and enmity but as one who forgives and nurtures. Consistent with maternal Protestantism, as narrated by McDannell, Sister Elizabeth, not a clergyman, acts as the theological interpreter for Mary.

Maternalism and Separate Spheres

By constructing their religious work as maternalism, leaders in the WHMS and the deaconess movement maintained rather than

37. Luke 15:1–7.
38. Meyer, *Mary North*, 280.

dismantled separate spheres for men and women, for clergymen and deaconesses. Ann Taves offers this succinct summary of separate spheres: "The standard rendition depicts the ideology of separate spheres as a dichotomized view of male and female nature and function wherein men, economics, and politics were associated with the public sphere and women, children, religion, and morality with the private sphere."[39] WHMS women operated in the domestic sphere with the uplift of poor women and children and the creation of pious and orderly homes, and deaconesses, in conformity to their consecration vow: "minister to the poor, visit the sick, pray with the dying, care for the orphan, seek the wandering, comfort the sorrowing, save the sinning."[40]

Understandably, clergymen applauded this delineation because, as Gifford declared, deaconesses mothered; they did not govern. In an annual report at the 1900 WHMS annual meeting, the Rev. Dr. A. H. Ames, Superintendent of the Lucy Webb Hayes National Training School in Washington, D.C., set deaconesses apart from clergymen in this statement: "Preachers and deaconesses represent the two ministries of the Christian Church: the ministry of the Word and the ministry of work; the expounding and enforcing the message which God has ordained for the quickening and perfecting of souls, and the making that Word real in the removal or mitigation of sorrow, poverty, and pain."[41] The purpose of deaconess training, Ames continued, was to preserve these separate spheres. "The education of a deaconess must be conformed to our idea of the proper scope and sphere of her mission. True education is that which fits one best for the duties which are to be performed."[42]

Separate spheres can also be defined in a more literal sense as a physical space apart from men which women claim and develop as their own. This understanding of separate spheres has gained traction with contemporary historians. For instance, as we saw in chapter 2, Estelle Freedman argues that the separate female sphere, what she calls "female institution building," proved beneficial because it promoted the development of women's political and social power during the Progressive Era. Rosemary Skinner Keller applies Freedman's thesis to women's organizations in the MEC, like the WHMS and the deaconess movement. She interprets the formation of a separate sphere for women's religious

39. Taves, "Women and Gender in American Religion(s)," 263.
40. Meyer, *Deaconesses*, 232.
41. Ames, "Lucy Webb Hayes National Training-School," 137.
42. Ames, "Lucy Webb Hayes National Training-School," 137.

activities as an essential step to developing a powerful organization of their own, training themselves for broader positions of leadership, and strengthening sisterhood among church women.[43] Even though she claims that one day, "women and men together [would] eliminate a separate sphere for women in church and society," how or when that would happen is not specified.[44]

In another article, Keller delves specifically into Meyer's maternalism, what Keller calls "motherly leadership," and presents it as a "style of soft feminism, an effort to extend the home into the public sphere." By slowly and carefully introducing young women from rural areas to the wiles of the big city, providing protection and maternal care along the way, deaconess leaders like Meyer "gently moved them [deaconesses] into leadership and control of their own public organizations and private lives." With such rhetoric, Keller spins "motherly leadership" into an expansive strategy. At the same time, she recognizes that this strategy "may seem conservative and protective to readers a century later." She explains, however, that Meyer's "motivation was to liberate young women of the late nineteenth century. The 'new woman of Protestantism,' the single woman who could have a life and a vocation of her own, was created through the leadership and community building of Lucy Rider Meyer and the deaconess family of the Chicago Training School."[45] Again, as stated above, this strategy left deaconesses in the mothering role for an indeterminate length of time.

Josiah Allen's Wife on Separate Spheres

A prominent, proto-feminist, literary humorist, and reformer of the day, Marietta Holley, did not find expansion for women's roles in the maternalist ideology. Holley's writings under the pen name, Josiah Allen's wife, were a "household word" in American popular culture from 1870–1920.[46] *The New York Times* claims that "she was as widely read as Mark Twain and even achieved a considerable audience in foreign countries."[47] Holley took on with acerbic wit the prominent issues of her day, like temperance

43. Keller, "Creating a Sphere For Women," 247.
44. Keller, "Creating a Sphere for Women," 260.
45. Keller, "Leadership and Community Building," 47.
46. Williams, "Crackerbox Philosopher as Feminist," 16.
47. Gjelsness, "Centenary of Samantha," quoted in Tholin, "Samantha and Her Sisters," 204.

and Jim Crow laws, to name a few, but she focused particularly on "wimmen's rites," as she called them in her colloquial language. Over 40 years and 20 published books, she advocated for women's suffrage, "equal pay for equal labor, a mother's equal right to her children, and the right to speak out in public without being considered 'unwomanly,'" and inclusive language.[48] Especially relevant for this study, she also fought for "adjustments in the separate spheres ideology" so that women would be liberated for participation in the public sphere.[49]

To that end, Holley threaded through her books a critique of organized religion's restriction of women to a separate sphere of duties. In *Samantha Among the Brethren*, published in 1892, she turned the spotlight directly on it. This book, into which a biographer of Holley claims she poured her "angry response," arose from a particular event relating to "wimmen's rites," in the MEC.[50] As noted previously, in 1888, by a long-winded discussion and vote at the MEC General Conference, women duly elected by their annual conference were not admitted as lay delegates. Holley, a member of the MEC, took on, through her beloved character, Josiah Allen's wife, this decision.

In the book's preface, Holley analyzed the semantic debate concerning the word, laymen. What exactly did it mean and whom did it include? Josiah Allen, the hapless husband, explained that laymen did not always include women; only sometimes it did. He likened it to the way the Declaration of Independence uses the word, "man" or "men." "Now that word 'men,' in that Declaration, means men some of the time, and some of the time men and wimmen both. It means both sexes when it relates to punishment, taxin' property, obeyin' the laws strictly, etc., etc., and it goes right on the very next minute and means men only, as to wit, namely, voting, takin' charge of public matters, makin' laws, etc."[51]

Further, the General Conference vote to create the Office of Deaconess came under Holley's scrutiny. In this scene, as is generally the case in her novels, women were busy getting things done. "Wall, we wuz all engaged in the very heat of the warfare, as you may say, a-scrubbin' the floors, and a-scourin' the benches by the door of the old meetin' house, and a-blackin' the 2 stoves that stood jest inside of the door. We wuz workin' jest as hard as wimmen ever worked." Here they were

48. Curry, *Marietta Holley*, 21.
49. Curry, *Marietta Holley*, ix.
50. Winter, *Marietta Holley*, 110.
51. Holley, *Samantha Among the Brethren*, 256.

cleaning the church when Josiah and several other male deacons barged in to announce that women, specifically unmarried women, could be deacons. The men believed without hesitation that this news would please the women. Josiah Allen's wife put her characteristically witty spin on it. "Josiah wanted me to know immegietly that I, too, could have had the privilege if I had been a more single woman, of becomin' a deaconess, and have had the chance of workin' all my hull life for the meetin' house, with a man to direct my movements and take charge on me, and tell me what to do, from day to day and from hour to hour."[52] In other words, what was good about this news?

A woman in the crowd, Miss Sypher, pursued the matter and asked if she, like the male deacons, could pass around the bread and wine during communion and the offering plate during the service. The answer—No! "These hard and arjuous dutys belong to the male deaconship. That is their own one pertickiler work, that wimmen can't infringe upon. Their hull strength is spent in these duties, wimmen deacons have other fields of labor, such as relievin' the wants of the sick and sufferin', sittin' up nights with small-pox patients, takin' care of the sufferin' poor, etc., etc." She did not take no for an answer. "But," sez Miss Sypher . . . "wouldn't it be real sweet, Deacon, if you and I could work together as deacons and tend the sick, relieve the sufferers—work for the good of the church together—go about doin' good?" The answer—again, No! That is "wimmen's work," he told her. And then he uttered the phrase that explained all: "We will let it go on in the same old way. Let wimmen have the privilege of workin' hard, jest as she always has. Let her work all the time, day and night, and let men go on in the same sure old way of superentendin' her movements, guardin' her weaker footsteps, and bossin' her round generally."[53] Thus, Marietta Holley, with a seasoned wit likened to Mark Twain, let the reader know that, in her opinion, despite the news about the Office of Deaconess for women, "the same old way" would prevail. After all, as Deacon Sypher remarks, this is "wimmen's work." Mothering not governing.

In conclusion, I find Holley's realism to be appropriate because the MEC hierarchy propagated gendered separate spheres to keep roles and responsibilities for men and women "the same old way." Further, as this chapter demonstrates, Methodist women's organizations did not

---

52. Holley, *Samantha Among the Brethren*, 263–64.
53. Holley, *Samantha Among the Brethren*, 263–67.

challenge it either. Considering then this reality of separate spheres perpetuated by male and female leaders alike, I contend that Keller draws overly optimistic conclusions concerning the impact of these women's organizations for supporting women's rights and leadership opportunities in the church. Instead, the maternalist ideology rampant in these organizations and their writings—authored by women and read by women—enlisted women for mothering, not governing.

Reflection Questions

1. How did the novels *Joy the Deaconess* and *Mary North* reinforce the maternalistic values of deaconesses and leaders in Methodist women's organizations?

2. What were the political reasons Meyer might have had for positioning deaconesses within the church as mothers rather than challenging the male-dominated structure? Do you see this same strategy operative in the church today? If so, where?

3. Do you think the approach of mothering not governing contributed to the decline of the deaconess movement?

"LITTLE PRAYERS"[1]

Lucy Rider Meyer

LORD, BLESS THOSE WOMEN that labor in the gospel. We thank Thee that women's hands are being consecrated to Thy special work; that their gentle ministries are being felt in so many homes of the needy and by so many beds of the sick. Lord, bless the deaconess and the home missionary and the foreign missionary, and greatly multiply their number. So many of Thy handmaidens are providentially free from the dear duties of the sweet domestic family—oh, may the thoughts of such turn naturally to the great world family pitifully calling for help, to the friendless and the orphan and the aged, to the sick and desolate and lonely. And so may woman's special work be greatly blessed of Thee, and become a still mightier agency in lifting the sad world nearer the throne. Phil. 4:3.[2]

---

1. Meyer, *Some Little Prayers*, 32.
2. "Yes, and I ask you also, my loyal companion, help these women, for they have struggled beside me in the work of the gospel, together with Clement and the rest of my co-workers, whose names are in the book of life."

"REPORT OF THE TORY STREET MISSION"[1]

Sister Isabel Sinclair

June 30, 1908

The good work of the Tory Street Mission has been carried on through another year very much on the old lines, and with the same warm appreciation by the people, also with the same blessing from our Heavenly Father. With regard to the work in general, its value was never more appreciated, its necessity was never greater than at the present time. To brighten the homes of the people, to solace the poor in their poverty, the sick in their suffering and the dying in their last experiences, is the sacred ministry to which we have been set apart. And surely there is a vast amount of such work that needs to be done. No attempt is made to use this organisation for sectarian purposes: its basis is a desire to serve the needy, whatever may be their relation to the churches of the cities. If the people are blessed and helped to live a brighter and purer life, if in any way sad hearts are cheered and brought under the gracious influence of the Gospel of Christ, our aim is accomplished. To all who like our Lord and master have compassion on the multitude because they are distressed and scattered abroad as sheep having no shepherd,[2] we make

---

1. This excerpt comes from Chambers, *Not Self–But Others*, 18–19. Used with permission from Wesley Historical Society (New Zealand). The Tory Street Mission, under the auspices of Taranaki Street Methodist Church, was located in Wellington, New Zealand.

2. Matt 9:36.

our earnest appeal. I could give you many instances of blessing accompanying the work, but everyone will see that save in a few cases, details cannot be put into print. Most of the results of the work of a Deaconess can never be scheduled, or even reported in public addresses. George Eliot said: "The only true secret of assisting the poor is to make them agents in bettering their own conditions."[3] And so this is the motto of our work—helping them to help themselves. In all our work the mothers' meeting takes first place. It is steadily increasing, and the attendance every Wednesday afternoon is very good. There are over 70 names on the register, and many of these have scarcely been absent in two or three years. The Saving Club is a great attraction, and a great boon, especially to those whose husbands are among the casual workmen.[4] Also the left-off clothing for which we most heartily thank our lady friends. Miss Kate Denton is one of our best helpers in the work: she cares for and amuses the little children during the course of the meeting.

The Tuesday evening class meeting is well attended, and is a source of great helpfulness to our young Christian men and women, at which Miss Matson kindly assists. The Thursday evening concerts, so willingly and cheerfully arranged by most of the musical circles of the city, are much appreciated by the people of the district, Mr. Kober has kindly undertaken charge of the Band of Hope,[5] with an occasional lantern lecture,[6] which has been attractive and interesting to the children. The Free and Easy meetings on Saturday evening are well sustained, and prove a shelter and hiding place to many intemperate men. Here Mr. McCluskey and

---

3. George Eliot was the pen name of Mary Ann Evans (1819–1880), a leading writer during the Victorian era. She wrote seven novels, including *Adam Bede*, *Middlemarch*, *Silas Marner*, and *Mill on the Floss*.

4. A Saving Club provided a way for individuals, who might struggle on their own to save money, to pool small amounts of money with others in order to purchase an item they could not afford on their own or to pay for an unexpected expense.

5. The Band of Hope was a nineteenth-century temperance organization for working-class children. Children from the age of six could enroll, and they took a pledge of abstinence from alcohol.

6. The precursor of a slide projector, the magic lantern, as it was called at the height of its popularity in the 1800s, "consisted of a box containing an oil lamp which illuminated painted glass slides through a lens. The images on the slides were projected onto a screen or a wall and were magnified to appear much larger. By the 1800s, magic lantern slide shows had become wildly popular forms of entertainment. Projectionists would travel from town to town, hosting shows for eager audiences. Themes of the shows varied widely, but military feats, cartoons, fairy tales, and bible stories were among the most common." Rosenberg Library Museum. "Magic Lanterns."

Miss Dowman have been ably assisted. Free suppers are given, to which Mr. Turvey supplies the tea and Mr. H. Hunger the refreshments.

The Sunday School continues to do good work, under the guidance of Miss Kate Jamieson and Miss Fuller.

The services on Sunday are increasing in number, and I rejoice to say that here we see the resurrection power of God transforming the lives of men and women into followers and ambassadors for Jesus Christ. At these services the orchestra, under the leadership of Miss Coventry and Mr. Otho Wilton, are performing a strong and powerful force of attraction, and a means of bringing the people to our services.

The Hospital and other institutions are diligently visited.

We feel very much encouraged and helped by the widespread sympathy and interest which continues to grow around our work year by year. We are much indebted to our faithful collectors, who give so much of their time cheerfully to that part of our work. Many gracious and generous gifts have been given to us during the past year—namely, a garden party by Mr. and Mrs. Justice Cooper, in aid of the building extension: an "At Home" by Mrs. W. E. Redstone, in aid of Christmas gifts, the mothers' meeting picnic, by Hon. and Mrs. T. W. Hislop. Mrs. Glasson and her Bible Class provided a Christmas tree for over 100 children: also a number of new garments for the winter; St. Andrew's Church Young Women's Bible Class, a social for the Sunday School Scholars: Miss K. Denton and Miss Fuller, a large birthday party: the ladies of Newton, an afternoon tea to the mothers' meeting: Miss Oreti Chisholm and Kathleen Tonks, a sale of work and raised 11 -: the C.E. Society, -14: two cases of fruit by Messrs Crabtree, coal by Mr. Thompson, and the late Miss Wilkinson; a pulpit Bible by the Rev. P. W. Fairclough: a sewing machine by Mrs. Millington, fruit and vegetables from the Thorndon Harvest Festival. Also gifts of clothing and cash.

On behalf of my workers, I most heartily thank all who have in any way helped us in our work. We are encouraged by your confidence, sympathy and support. Above all, we recognise the good hand of God in this work, and thankfully acknowledge that to Him all praise is due. Moreover, it is our cherished hope that there are still greater things to be achieved by your increased help and interest, and all may have a share in this great work by contributing what they can toward it.

To the giver shall be given:
If thou would'st walk in light,
Make other spirits bright;
Who, seeking for himself alone ever entered heaven?
In blessing we are blest.
In labour find our rest:
If we bend not to the world work, heart, and hand, and brain.
We have lived our life in vain.

Reflection Questions

1. Sister Isabel states that the mission's focus is to serve the poor and those in need without pushing specific denominational beliefs. She writes, "No attempt is made to use this organisation for sectarian purposes." Do you agree or disagree with her statement? What is the rationale for your response?

2. Her report highlights events hosted for the community, including concerts, free meals, and educational programs. How do you imagine these activities enhance the mission's effectiveness, or detract from it? What lessons can churches draw from this report in terms of engaging their communities in outreach efforts?

*Mr. and Mrs. Meyer
at the time of the founding of the School
1885*

Sister Dora Stephenson, Deaconess, Wesley Deaconess Order

Chapter VI

MALE ADVOCATES IN THE EARLY DECADES OF THE INTERNATIONAL METHODIST DEACONESS MOVEMENT[1]

Overview

THIS CHAPTER TURNS THE focus to the men who supported the deaconess movement and helped it to flourish. The various contributions of male advocates are set out, from founders to benefactors, from clergymen to authors. These male advocates, as we have seen with women leaders, like Lucy Rider Meyer and Jane Bancroft Robinson, were not monolithic; they disagreed with each other. Bishop James Thoburn and Rev. Christian Golder, for instance, were staunch deaconess advocates, yet their vision for the scope of the work diverged widely. Thoburn's was more expansive, as he explains in the first source document: "We ought to take a broad view... and teach all our people to be prepared to hear the Master's voice at any time or in any place, summoning them forth to new duties and new responsibilities." Golder's was more restrictive because he maintained an immovable distinction between the sexes and their concomitant sphere of work, which he believed was God's design. To cite a line from the source document he authored, "The order of creation has placed upon woman,

---

1. This chapter was originally published as "Male Advocates in the Early Decades of the Transatlantic Methodist Deaconess Movement" in *Methodist History* 59 (2021) 215–27. This expanded version includes new material about male advocates from Methodism in other countries as well as from more Methodist churches in the US.

on account of her natural endowments, certain restrictions which can not be removed without injury to her highest interests."

Male adversaries of the Methodist deaconess movement were plentiful and vocal. When the vote to sanction the Office of Deaconess came before the General Conference of the Methodist Episcopal Church South (MECS), in 1901, Rev. J. B. McGehee spoke for many of his clergy colleagues when he declared that a favorable vote would be the first step in an inexorable advancement toward women's ordination: "I am opposed to establishing a female hennery in the Church for hatching out female preachers."[2] Even though the presiding bishop ruled McGehee's language out of order, nonetheless his words remain permanently recorded in the conference minutes. Another minister, Rev. William Nast Brodbeck, promised a nearly identical threat. "One thing is certain, the deaconess is not a substitute for a pastor, and it will mean the destruction of the order for her to take up pastoral lines of work."[3]

Even though McGehee, Brodbeck, and other male adversaries endeavored to block the movement, they were ultimately eclipsed by male advocates who, as this chapter will argue, helped to ensure its emergence and expansion. Susan Hill Lindley nods briefly in a sentence to the critical contribution made by male advocates in support of deaconesses: "Credit for the success of the deaconess movement in American Methodism must surely also be given to other leaders and supporters, male and female, as well as to the deaconesses themselves."[4] Lindley did not explore further men's contributions beyond this one comment, and neither have subsequent historians of the movement, except for Laceye Warner's dissertation that features the founder of the Wesley Deaconess Order (WDO), Thomas Bowman Stephenson, alongside Lucy Rider Meyer and compares their respective deaconess work.[5]

To redress this lacuna, this chapter will trace the contributions of male advocates—founders, benefactors, bishops, clergy, authors, and husbands—in the early decades of the international Methodist deaconess movement. These men utilized their power to lobby and cast affirmative votes for denominational approval, they penned detailed studies about deaconesses to provide historical precedent for the movement,

2. McDowell, *Social Gospel in the South*, 63.
3. Keller, "Deaconess: 'New Woman,'" 38.
4. Lindley, *'You Have Stept Out of Your Place,'* 132.
5. Warner, "Methodist Episcopal and Wesleyan Methodist Deaconesses."

and they donated buildings and capital to start and maintain deaconess work in their city. Despite their advocacy, however, there was not universal agreement about the rationale for their support. Some, like Methodist Episcopal Church (MEC) Bishop James Thoburn, considered the deaconess movement as a stepping stone on the way to wider opportunities for women's ministry in the church. Others, like Rev. Christian Golder of the German Methodist Church in the US, promoted it as a safer alternative to the woman's rights movement. In the conclusion, we will explore further these differences and their adherence—or not—to traditional gender roles.

Founders

Deaconess work in the MEC Annual Conference of Germany-Switzerland got off the ground due to the efforts of four clergymen—Carl Weiss, Heinrich Mann, Friedrich Eilers, and Jürgen Wischhusen. After a proposal at the 1874 annual conference about starting a deaconess work was vigorously debated and then rejected, these clergymen met immediately to discuss alternative options. They decided to form an "independent Deaconess Society on their own which they named *Bethanienverein*."[6] The first Motherhouse opened in Frankfurt am Main in 1876. This branch of German Methodist deaconess work spread to a host of European cities, including St. Gallen and Zurich in Switzerland, Vienna in Austria, Budapest in Hungary, and Rotterdam in the Netherlands.[7]

In the UK, before Stephenson founded the WDO, he had already started the National Children's Home two decades earlier in Lambeth, a poverty-stricken London neighborhood. Through his work with this first institution, he recognized the need for women who were trained and fully dedicated to caring for and educating the children under the home's protection and supervision. To investigate whether a deaconess order would be appropriate for this venture, he spent time at Kaiserswerth, the deaconess Motherhouse in Dusseldorf, Germany, which became the model and inspiration for deaconess work internationally.[8] Stephenson became enamored of Kaiserswerth and endeavored to

---

6. Bloedt, "Pioneering Deaconess Movement in Germany," 51.
7. Bloedt, "Pioneering Deaconess Movement in Germany," 52.
8. For more on Kaiserswerth, see ch. 1.

emulate it in myriad ways in the WDO.[9] He even became convinced to mandate a deaconess uniform due to the testimony by a Kaiserswerth deaconess about the protection it afforded her as she moved about nursing the wounded during the Franco-German War.

In 1890, with one Sister-in-Charge and one probationer, Stephenson opened Mewburn House, the first WDO deaconess training home. The same year, he published *Concerning Sisterhoods*, in which he laid out his carefully constructed plans for a deaconess order. The number of deaconesses increased steadily so that just over a decade after it began, by 1902, the WDO received full approval from the Wesleyan Methodist Conference. Stephenson's final accomplishment was to open the Wesley Deaconess College in Ilkley, a town in the Yorkshires. When he retired in 1907, the WDO had grown to a sizeable number of 173 deaconesses.[10]

Bishops

A handful of bishops labored in the vanguard to secure their respective church's approval for the establishment of the Office of Deaconess and to oversee its implementation. Bishop Eugene Russell Hendrix was on the cusp of deaconess work in the Methodist Episcopal Church South (MECS) when on April 19, 1903, he consecrated the denomination's first five deaconesses—Mattie M. Wright, Amy Rice, Annie Heath, Elizabeth R. Davis, and Anabel Weigel.

Elsewhere in US Methodism, a trio of Methodist Episcopal Church (MEC) bishops, James N. FitzGerald, William Oldham, and James Thoburn, not only lent their ecclesial power and influence to the movement in general but also helped to launch Iva Durham Vennard's training school with evangelism at its center. Vennard first met Thoburn in 1901 at Camp Sychar in Mt. Vernon, Ohio. During the camp meeting, they discussed the evangelistic outreach possibilities of deaconesses, and she presented him with her design of a deaconess training school with evangelism at the center. Vennard's biographer records that Thoburn responded, "This is an answer to the prayers of my sister Isabella in India. She has been

---

9. For instance, the WDO service for the recognition of deaconesses was copied, with only slight modifications, from Kaiswerswerth's version. "Recognition Service," 178. In addition, *Flying Leaves*, the title of the WDO's monthly journal, was simply the English translation of Kaiserswerth's journal, *Fliegende Blätter*. Bradfield, *Life of the Reverend Thomas Bowman Stephenson*, 407.

10. Graham, *Saved to Serve*, 243.

asking God to save the deaconess order, and to make it a soul-winning agency."[11] Thoburn urged Vennard to proceed with her school plans and promised to write a letter of support to his episcopal colleagues. Within a short time, she received a letter from Bishop FitzGerald, Secretary of the Board of Bishops, with authorization to start the training school and the suggestion of St. Louis as its location. With this bastion of episcopal support, Vennard founded Epworth Evangelistic Institute.[12]

Amidst the trio of bishops, Thoburn was the most indefatigable and influential. His zeal for training and deploying deaconesses as evangelists, even as ministers, emerged from his experience in India, specifically his recognition that "women should be empowered to administer the sacraments to the secluded high caste women of the zenanas, to whose presence no man could be admitted."[13] To learn more about deaconesses, he and Isabella visited several institutions, including Kaiserswerth and Mildmay in England, while traveling from India to the US. He continued touring deaconess work stateside and visited the Chicago Training School (CTS) several times in 1887.

The following year, Thoburn brought to the 1888 MEC General Conference a resolution from the Bengal Conference in India to establish an Office of Deaconess. According to Meyer, the resolution passed largely due to his relentless advocacy and political wrangling.[14] Still, the resolution fell short of his original intent, which was to ordain deaconesses to serve in India. In a comment in Thoburn's obituary on this failure, his episcopal colleague, William F. Oldham, made the following remark: "He [Thoburn] tried to secure their ordination that they might exercise a fuller ministry among the shut-ins of India. It is laughable

11. Bowie, *Alabaster*, 91. Thoburn's reference to his sister, Isabella, is significant. She was the first unmarried woman missionary sent overseas by the Woman's Foreign Missionary Society of the MEC when she left for India in 1869; she also was one of the first MEC deaconesses to be consecrated.

12. For more on this school, see chapter 2.

13. Horton, *Builders*, 87. As Thoburn explained, "it is by no means improbable that Indian Phoebes [Rom 16:1] will yet administer the ordinances of the Church to the secluded women of the zenanas. I have baptized frightened village women under circumstances which made me wish that some Phoebe might be employed to take my place; and as for the inmates of the zenanas, it is simply impossible for a man to gain access to them, and, even if he could be admitted to them, his services would be very unsatisfactory. . . . as in ancient times, we shall see the church in the house revived, and Christian women sent to minister to those who are inaccessible to the ordinary minister of the public congregation." Thoburn, *My Missionary Apprenticeship*, 255–56.

14. Meyer, "Mother in the Church," 728.

to recall that a General Conference sought to censure him for allowing the tips of his fingers to rest on the heads of some of them when being 'consecrated.' It might be mistaken for ordination! And, now, to see that even this is coming!"[15]

Clergymen

Clergymen advocated for deaconesses in several ways. The first was through their dedicated support of the training schools. As mentioned in chapter 1, Rev. Walter Riley started a training school in his Cincinnati parsonage, since there were none for Black women. He and his wife taught two classes, and "several resident clergymen and physicians lent them a helping hand free of charge."[16] The school only remained open from 1900 to 1904, before it closed due to lack of funding.

Clergymen also taught courses and gave guest lectures at the training schools, particularly in Bible, theology, and Methodist polity. The United Methodist Church in the UK, for instance, enlisted clergy to teach in several subject areas, as listed in these Minutes, dated September 8, 1908:

> Concerning the Tutorial Arrangements the Committee agreed to the following
>
> Theology 1. That the Rev. C. Ogden be asked to continue his lectures on Christian Theology
>
> Bible Study 2. That Dr. A. Jones of the Mallinson Ro Church be requested to assist in the tutorial work at Bowron House and that the selection of books be left to him and the Secretary . . .
>
> Our Polity 8. That the Rev. Smith be asked to instruct the students in the Polity of the United Methodist Church[17]

In an earlier list of instructors, from 1904–1905, Rev. Samuel Chadwick, a Wesleyan Methodist minister, was named as the instructor for three biblical courses: Interpretation of the Four Gospels, Epistle to the Hebrews, and the Prophecies of Amos and Habakkuk.[18] At the same time,

---

15. Oldham, "Thoburn–Mystic, Seer, Prophet, Missionary," 189–90.
16. Golder, *History of the Deaconess Movement*, 411.
17. *Deaconess Institute Minute Book 1906–1917.*
18. *Wesley Deaconess Order, 1904–1905.*

Chadwick also taught Bible and theology at Cliff College, a Methodist lay training center in Derbyshire.

At CTS, Chicago clergymen taught upper-level classes, particularly for the Department of Theology, Apologetics, and Interpretation. Rev. Dr. Louis Lesemann, pastor of Trinity MEC, who would become the school's second principal after Meyer's retirement, taught "Biblical Interpretation." Another course, "The Office of the Holy Spirit," was taught by Rev. Dr. M. M. Parkhurst, a Methodist minister, CTS trustee, and popular biblical expositor, who "from the beginning has faithfully every year given valuable courses of lectures at the School."[19]

Clergymen also supported deaconesses by inviting them to preach in their church, like Rev. Dr. William F. Oldham, who went on to become an MEC bishop. Oldham asked Vennard, then a deaconess evangelist, to hold a revival in 1900 for his well-heeled congregation in Columbus, Ohio. When she offered an altar call, at first, no one moved. "In the tenseness of the moment, Dr. Oldham stepped to her side and said, 'Friends, this courageous young woman has been God's messenger to us. She had declared the truth, and I, for one, am coming to this altar of prayer.' Tension was immediately released. Many others came forward with tears and prayers."[20] Twelve years later, in a speech at the National Holiness Association convention, he recalled that moment:

> There stood that slip of a college girl pleading with that group of aristocrats and millionaires who made up my Sunday morning congregation. As she exhorted them, I was increasingly amazed at her courage. No one could get away from the sincerity of her appeal. The utter devotion of her soul and the nobility of her spirit shown in her earnest, expressive face. I could not let such a moment pass without a response. I stood by her side while my people came. . . . Thank God, that noble woman is now training other workers.[21]

Inviting deaconesses to preach and hold revivals in local churches helped immensely to promote the cause. This scenario was memorialized in the novel *Joy the Deaconess*, introduced in chapter 5. When Joy, the protagonist, hears Meyer speak about deaconess work during a Sunday morning service, she invites her home to hear more.[22] Their lunchtime

19. Horton, *Builders*, 43.
20. Bowie, *Alabaster and Spikenard*, 83.
21. Bowie, *Alabaster and Spikenard*, 198–99.
22. Holding, *Joy the Deaconess*, 119.

conversation convinces Joy to enroll in CTS. In real life, it happened this way for Vennard, who first heard about deaconesses when Meyer preached at her Methodist church in Normal, Illinois. Not long after, Vennard enrolled in the deaconess training school in Buffalo.

Yet one more avenue of support from clergymen came from Rev. Reverdy Ransom. As noted in chapter 1, he initiated a Board of Deaconesses in 1894 in St. John's African Methodist Episcopal Church (AME) in Cleveland, Ohio, then he repeated it several years later in his Chicago AME church. He expressed in his autobiography that these initiatives helped to establish an Office of Deaconess in the AME Church by vote of the 1900 General Conference.[23]

Authors

Male advocates wrote books that lent gravitas to the deaconess movement at a critical time in its emergence and initial growth. In these books, published between 1889 and 1903, the authors endeavored to ameliorate objections as well as to ground the movement biblically and historically, from the early church to the contemporary context.

The first book, *Deaconesses Ancient and Modern*, published in 1889, was written by Henry Wheeler, a Methodist Episcopal Church (MEC) minister in Pennsylvania and a member of the Ocean Grove Camp Meeting Association. He was an apologist for the "advancement of woman's work in the Church."[24] In the book's Preface, he set out his agenda: "As the Church is baptized with the Holy Ghost she goes back to the spirit of primitive Christianity, recognizes the ministry of woman, and sends her forth with blessing and authority."[25] The book commences with several chapters covering women in the Bible, from Old Testament prophetesses to women in the Epistles. Then, the focus turns specifically to deaconesses, beginning with the apostolic church and ending with the contemporary church. Wheeler's advocacy shows up in his admonition that deaconesses are consecrated and set apart to be the hands, feet, and face of Christ to the poor and destitute crowding into urban areas. The deaconess, he

---

23. In his autobiography, Ransom expressed disappointment that Bishop Abraham Grant did not give him credit for the deaconess order but instead presented it as his own idea. Ransom, *Pilgrimage of Harriet Ransom's Son*, 69.

24. Wheeler, *Deaconesses Ancient and Modern*, 4.

25. Wheeler, *Deaconesses Ancient and Modern*, 3–4.

declared, "can be the almoner of the Church's liberality to the destitute. She will, [do this] more than any other officer of the Church."[26]

The second book, *The Deaconess and Her Vocation*, published in 1893, was a collection of Bishop Thoburn's sermons and addresses. His stated hope for the volume was to clear away "objections and difficulties" and to promote "the general interests of this most important cause."[27] He conjured a vision of deaconesses as a mighty evangelistic force and expressed the hope that one day a legion of five hundred "will bring more souls to Christ and add more members to our Church in this city of New York in one year than all the Churches in the city to-day have added during the past ten years."[28]

Thoburn also addressed the deaconess movement in another book, *The Church of Pentecost*, published in 1901. He proposed that deaconesses, because of the contribution they could make to evangelism, should be sanctioned to preach. He appealed to the phrase, "forms of Christian labor," cited in the denomination's official description of deaconess work, and reasoned that these words could apply to preaching. For biblical validation, he turned to the story of Pentecost[29] and pointed out the inextricable link between women, prophesy, and the Holy Spirit in this verse: "In the last days it will be, God declares, that I will pour out my Spirit upon all flesh, and your sons and your daughters shall prophesy." (Acts 2:17). He then extrapolated that the verbs, "prophecy" and "preach," were interchangeable. He corroborated this semantic move with an appeal to the Old Testament prophet, Joel, who foretold that women would prophecy (Joel 2:28–29; Acts 2:17–18),[30] to Philip's four daughters who prophesied (Acts 21:9),[31] and the apostle Paul's instructions that women should cover their head when they prophecy (1 Cor 11:5).[32] To conclude, he reasoned that if women have received a divine commission to prophecy (Acts

26. Wheeler, *Deaconesses Ancient and Modern*, 300.
27. Thoburn, *Deaconess and Her Vocation*, 5.
28. Thoburn, *Deaconess and Her Vocation*, 123.
29. Acts 2:1–21.
30. "Then afterwards I will pour out my spirit on all flesh; your sons and your daughters shall prophesy, your old men shall dream dreams, and your young men shall see visions. Even on the male and female slaves, in those days, I will pour out my spirit."
31. "He [Philip] had four unmarried daughters who had the gift of prophecy."
32. "[B]ut any woman who prays or prophesies with her head unveiled disgraces her head—it is one and the same thing as having her head shaved."

2:17–18),[33] and if prophecy is preaching, then "women are anointed for this kind of service," i.e., preaching.[34]

Christian Golder, who was General Superintendent of German Methodist deaconess work in the US and oversaw its emergence and growth, authored two books on deaconesses in successive years: *The Deaconess Motherhouse* (1907) and *The History of the Deaconess Movement in the Christian Church* (1908). His book on the history of the deaconess movement begins with an introduction to the male diaconate in Acts 6:3, when "seven men of good report, full of the Spirit and of wisdom" were appointed by the apostles to oversee the distribution of food to Gentile widows. Deacons were subsequently tasked with evangelism and serving the sick and the poor. Curiously, in the next sentence, he introduced the term *deaconess* for the first time, yet without any explanation or biblical reference. He then ended the paragraph with this statement about deaconesses: "It is not improbable that these female workers, or servants (deaconesses), devoted themselves especially to their own sex. That this was done exclusively, however, is nowhere proven."[35] Despite this comment, he still persevered in presenting deaconesses as only able to minister to women. As we will see momentarily, Golder restricted the sphere of work in which deaconesses should be allowed to operate. Over the remaining several hundred pages, he cataloged the emergence of the diaconate after the Reformation, particularly among the Moravians, and he produced an ecumenical survey of the current work of deaconesses in several denominations in Germany, Switzerland, Sweden, England, Scotland, and the US.

In their very different approaches, these three clergymen authors set the deaconess movement within the vast expanse of Christian history, beginning with the exegesis of biblical texts and ending with the situation for deaconesses in their day. Through these publications, they advocated for its legitimacy and acceptance.

Benefactors

Finances proved a perennial struggle for most deaconess institutions; they existed on a shoestring budget and depended for survival on donations of

---

33. See n30.
34. Thoburn, *Church of Pentecost*, 124.
35. Golder, *History of the Deaconess Movement*, 19.

food staples, bushels of apples, beddings, and spare coins, like those given to Lucy Rider Meyer's Nickel Fund, to keep a deaconess training school, home, or hospital afloat.[36] Still, there were a few exceptions to these small donations when wealthy benefactors invested in deaconess work in their city. In Toronto, the financier was H. A. Massey, a devout Methodist who grew the H. A. Massey Company, a producer of agricultural implements, into a lucrative, international business. The Massey family, with its power and pocketbooks, emboldened the Toronto Methodist Conference to establish a deaconess home, complete with a training program so that women could come to the city, stay in the home, and be trained as deaconesses. A provision in Massey's will left the interest earned annually from a $10,000 donation to continue his financial support of deaconess work.[37] The largest employer of Methodist deaconesses in Toronto was the Fred Victor Mission, established in 1894 in memory of Massey's youngest son, who died while he was a university student. At the mission, deaconesses held gospel meetings, ran social activities, set up lodging for the homeless, and staffed a medical dispensary.

James Gamble, head of the Procter & Gamble Company, initiated and funded deaconess work in Cincinnati, Ohio. In 1888, he offered Isabella Thoburn, who was working at CTS at the time, a ten-room house and $1,000 a year for five years if she would come to the Queen City; she agreed, moved to Cincinnati, and opened the Elizabeth Gamble Deaconess Home. The next year, Gamble provided Thoburn and the other deaconesses an eleven-room, three-story house; this residence became the first location of Christ Hospital.[38] Gamble's son and namesake continued his father's financial support. The Gambles, like the Massey family, set up "bequests and financial donations [that] covered the ongoing expenses, mortgages and budget deficits of the deaconess movement in general and the training school specifically."[39]

Scarritt Bible and Training School in Kansas City, Missouri, founded in 1890 to train women as nurses, teachers, missionaries, and later as deaconesses, was named after its benefactor, Rev. Dr. Nathan Scarritt. In 1889, Scarritt offered to the General Conference of the MECS a section

---

36. Meyer devised The Nickel Fund as a fundraising strategy to encourage women in particular to donate their spare change, even as little as a nickel, to support Methodist deaconess work.

37. Thomas, "Servants of the Church," 378.

38. Dougherty, *My Calling to Fulfill*, 107.

39. McConnell, "Canadian Deaconess and Missionary Education," 33.

of his land, valued at $15,000, at the northeast corner of Askew Avenue and Harris Avenue (now known as Norledge Place), along with a cash gift of $25,000 "for the purpose of establishing a missionary training school under direction of the woman's board of missions on condition that an additional $25,000 be raised. This offer was formally accepted a few hours before his death on May 22, 1890."[40] Scarritt believed his gift to be divinely inspired. "While alone walking about his estate, a voice seemed to speak to his soul and say, 'Why don't you give this land to the Woman's Society for the training school.' He said that the thought had never before occurred to him, but the more he thought of it the more interested he became in it." He concluded his remarks with words from the well-known missionary, William Carey, which became the school's motto: "Attempt great things for God, Expect great things from God."[41] Scarritt became the MECS deaconess training school once the denomination established the Office of Deaconess in 1902.

Norman Waite Harris, a philanthropist banker in Chicago, gifted CTS in 1895 with a $20,000 parcel of land, which was "beautifully situated within five minutes' walk of Washington Park, and afforded ample space for the erection of three buildings, each larger than the one then occupied by the school."[42] During a dinner given in honor of WDO founder Thomas Bowman Stephenson, who was in Chicago while touring the US, Harris challenged attendees to donate to a new building by constructing an interesting mathematical equation.

> I am not very good at talking sentiment, but I am said to know something about figures, and I have just been figuring on this Training School. We are asked to put $35,000 into this new building. The interest on this at five per cent would be $1,750 a year. Now what do we get back for this? I see by the card in my hand that the students of the Training School gave last year 5,108 days to missionary work. The new building would accommodate three times as many students, and we could reasonably expect three times as much work. . . . putting it in round numbers, we would get at least 12,5000 days or over forty-one years service of a single person from these students each year, for our

---

40. Scarritt College Folder 1880–1892, 18.

41. Scarritt College Folder 1880–1892, 19. William Carey (1761–1834) was a British missionary to India. His influential book, *An Enquiry into the Obligations of Christians to Use Means for the Conversion of the Heathens*, helped to spur on the Protestant missionary movement in the early nineteenth century.

42. Horton, *Builders*, 135.

outlay of $1,750–an average of less than forth-three dollars a year. Can you get work done any more cheaply than that? I'm an American; I'm a Chicagoan; I'm a Methodist. . . . when we can get forty-one years of work done in the interests of our own church here in the slums of our own city for $1,750 I think it good business policy to improve the opportunity.

Evidently, his speech made an impact because subscriptions totaling $12,000 came in that evening to support the new building project at CTS.[43]

Harris's generosity to the international Methodist deaconess movement crossed continents to the Philippines when the Woman's Foreign Missionary Society of the MEC approached him for help to set up a deaconess training school in Manila. He "promised a donation of $5,000 with a condition that the Society would furnish the remaining $10,000 of the anticipated building cost of $15,000."[44] The school, which opened in its new location in October 1906, was named Harris Memorial Training School to honor his bequest. Within 25 years, Harris Memorial Training School had graduated 210 students.[45]

Husbands

Two deaconess leaders, Lucy Rider Meyer and Iva Durham Vennard, married men who would each relinquish their careers to work in the institutions founded and led by their wives.[46] Lucy Rider married Josiah Shelley Meyer, a secretary for the Chicago chapter of the Young Men's Christian Association (YMCA) on May 21, 1885. Within the month, the newlyweds were fully immersed in Lucy's vision for a women's Bible and training school that would become CTS. His salary supported the couple, her mother, and younger brother, as well as the school's start-up costs. In addition to his full-time job, he worked a double shift as the school's business agent. Eventually, he quit his YMCA job to devote his full energies and business savvy to CTS. "While Mrs. Meyer breathed

---

43. Horton, *Builders*, 136.

44. *Philippine Christian Advocate* (July 1905) 6; quoted in Robledo, "Gender, Religion and Social Change," 81.

45. Robledo, "Gender, Religion and Social Change," 95.

46. For more on Meyer's and Vennard's advocacy for the deaconess movement, see chapter 2.

her spirit into the Chicago Training School and made it a living organism, Mr. Meyer gave it its body."[47]

For many years, the couple worked amicably side by side, devoting their respective yet different talents to CTS, until enrollment began to decline after 1910. The increasingly difficult circumstances prompted inherent differences between them to escalate. According to her biographer, they had very different personalities. "Mr. Meyer, of sturdy Pennsylvania stock, was by nature conservative. He walked in the old ways and loved the old truths, and felt that they were being discredited by modern investigations and research." In contrast, she was "adventurous by nature" and greeted with alacrity "every new discovery in science, every new theory in metaphysics, every new experiment in social science.... 'More room! More light! Onward!' seemed always to be the cry of her soul."[48] Despite these obstacles, however, they remained steadfast in their support for CTS and the Methodist deaconess movement. A friend of the couple described their partnership in these words: "Seldom have husband and wife so intimately and successfully labored together in a common cause, as did these two people."[49]

The same was true for Iva May Durham and Thomas Vennard. Throughout their long courtship, she made it inextricably clear that she felt called to found Epworth Evangelistic Institute (EEI) and devote herself full-time to its success. She even postponed his marriage proposal for many years while she considered whether the demands of such an institutional endeavor would prevent her from getting married and having a family. Thomas's response at the time—and one that never wavered throughout their twenty-five years of marriage—was simply, "I am willing to be your background of support."[50] He was a successful architect who was highly sought after as Superintendent for the construction of large public buildings, including the Seelbach Hotel in Louisville. Like Josiah Meyer with his business knowledge, Vennard devoted his architectural prowess to overseeing the renovation of the main building of Chicago Evangelistic Institute (CEI), the second training school Iva founded. This was a career-ending decision because he had to relinquish his position in an architectural firm in the Chicago loop to work full-time on CEI's remodel. He had already anticipated this professional sacrifice during

47. Diekmann, "Lucy Rider Meyer," 5; quoted in Dougherty, "Meyers," 49.
48. Horton, *High Adventure*, 313–14.
49. Diekmann, "Lucy Rider Meyer," 5; quoted in Dougherty, "Meyers," 48.
50. Bowie, *Alabaster and Spikenard*, 98.

their courtship and wrote it in a letter to Iva: "I may be the janitor of an institution of which you are principal founder and controlling head."[51] As was said about Josiah Shelley, a mutual friend likened Thomas Vennard's support to lending strength to "the hands of his wife in the educational program to which the Lord had called her."[52]

Conclusion

Male advocates of the deaconess movement lent their influence, pen, ecclesial power, finances, votes, and practical expertise to help it launch and flourish. These men believed that deaconesses held the key to Methodism's outreach to the poor, sick, orphans, homeless, addicted, immigrants, factory workers, rural folk, and urban migrants. Some, like Thomas Bowman Stephenson and James Thoburn, went further to posit deaconesses as much more than servants and helpers; they envisioned them as a mighty, unstoppable evangelistic force to be unleashed by the church on behalf of God's reign. To this end, they flung the doors wide open concerning the sphere of work that deaconesses could pursue.

For instance, despite Stephenson's near plagiarism of all things from Kaiserswerth, one significant divergence is noteworthy. Fliedner the founder of Kaiserswerth, enumerated that deaconesses were to be servants in three arenas: 1. Of the Lord Jesus Christ; 2. Of the poor, the sick, and the young; and 3. Of her sister deaconesses. Stephenson introduced a significant modification to the second clause when he added a phrase that nodded to deaconesses in evangelism and preaching: Deaconesses "will be servants of His little ones, the sick He came to heal, and *the sinners He calls to repentance*."[53] This adaptation points to a wider (than Fliedner's) scope of work for the Wesley Deaconess Order (WDO) as "a 'soul-converting' agency. It must employ to the full all social influences and expedients, but in all, its object must be 'soul-winning.'"[54] Evangelism was one of "three great fields of usefulness" that Stephenson integrated into the WDO: "Evangelistic visitation, in connexion with circuits, with congregations, perhaps with groups of village congregations, and certainly in connexion

---

51. Bowie, *Alabaster and Spikenard*, 112.
52. Bowie, *Alabaster and Spikenard*, 109.
53. Bradfield, *Life of the Reverend Thomas Bowman Stephenson*, 424. Italics added.
54. Bradfield, *Life of the Reverend Thomas Bowman Stephenson*, 424.

with mission centres."⁵⁵ A WDO history recounts that "from the first they [deaconesses] were entrusted with evangelistic, pastoral and teaching work and that soon became their chief mission."⁵⁶

This wider sphere from Kaiserswerth also showed up in the WDO consecration service, which included a list of the kinds of work that deaconesses might be called to undertake. The list enumerated customary deaconess tasks, like teaching, feeding, nursing, and visiting. One more task on the list, not a common one for deaconesses, was preaching. For Stephenson, as with Thoburn, the rationale for deaconesses in preaching was grounded in evangelism. During the consecration service, the President of the Conference declared to the deaconesses gathered that "in all this you must be true evangelists of our Lord Jesus Christ translating your Gospel into the language of personal service, that it may be the better understood, not reckoning your ministry complete till those who you serve can say, Now we believe."⁵⁷ The leading example of a WDO deaconess evangelist was Sister Jeannie Banks, who held evangelistic meetings throughout the UK, including the Scottish Isles, from 1896 until she died in 1932.⁵⁸

Thoburn, like Stephenson, endorsed a wider scope of deaconess work, as is evident in the first source document in this chapter. To summarize here, Thoburn insisted that "the deaconess is not set apart for any one special form of work, but rather for any work which the Church can find for her." He continued, "I notice a persistent inclination on the part of the public generally to regard the work of the deaconess as simply and solely the duty of visiting the poor and nursing the sick; *but this is limiting her sphere in the most arbitrary way.*"⁵⁹

Not all male advocates agreed. Some worked enthusiastically on behalf of deaconesses but strictly limited their work to traditionally female roles, ones identical to Fliedner's three-part delineation above. For instance, in Golder's history of the movement, he differentiated two types of ministry, one for clergy and one for deaconesses, that he believed existed in the early church and should remain in place as the standard: "the ministry of helpful service [deaconesses] in contradistinction

55. Bradfield, *Life of the Reverend Thomas Bowman Stephenson*, 294.

56. *Wesley Deaconess Order*, 3.

57. "Order of Service for the Ordination of Deaconesses," 12.

58. For more on Banks, see Warner, "Wesley Deaconess–Evangelists," 176–90 and Evans, "'Noblest Ideals of Service,'" 197–210.

59. Thoburn, *Deaconess and Her Vocation*, 22. Italics added.

from the ministry of the Word [clergy]."[60] His rationale was the created order for each sex as presented in the first creation story in Genesis: "Each one after its own kind" (Gen 1:24). In other words, women and men—in their very nature and essence—were permanently differentiated. In his comment on Gen 1:24, he explained that to honor her sex, her "own kind," a woman must remain womanly.[61] Henry Wheeler, in his deaconess book introduced earlier, concurred, stating that "woman's own nature, implanted by the Creator's own hand, has made her 'the best of nurses, the gentlest of alms-givers, the tenderest of educators for the young of both sexes, and the great trainer and moral reformer of her own.'"[62] In other words, the support for deaconesses from male advocates, like Golder and Wheeler, remained enthusiastic as long as women's "ministry of helpful service" prevailed.

Even more, Golder positioned the deaconess movement as the appropriate organization to counter the "devious paths of the Woman's Rights Movement," a movement that represented, in his opinion, a "serious social danger."[63] He extrapolated that if the "woman question ever finds an outlet in the deaconess movement, [then] it is possible that the female diaconate will contribute more to the solution of the woman question than any other factor."[64] With these gendered boundaries intact, Golder campaigned vigorously on behalf of the deaconess movement.

In conclusion, by setting Golder and Wheeler alongside Stephenson and Thoburn, this chapter demonstrates that male advocates of the deaconess movement were not identical. While all of the men mentioned in this chapter were indeed advocates and strong supporters of the movement's emergence and success, their parameters for the work of deaconesses remained widely divergent, even contradictory.

Reflection Questions

1. What were the main objections raised by male adversaries to the deaconess movement? How did male advocates counter these arguments?

60. Golder, *History of the Deaconess Movement*, 18.
61. Golder, *History of the Deaconess Movement*, 531.
62. Wheeler, *Deaconesses Ancient and Modern*, 307.
63. Golder, *History of the Deaconess Movement*, 526.
64. Golder, *History of the Deaconess Movement*, 484.

2. In what ways did Methodist bishops and clergy support the training and advancement of deaconesses? What impact do you think their support had on the acceptance of deaconesses in various Methodist denominations?

3. With this multifaceted and enthusiastic support from many male advocates, why do you think the deaconess movement declined so rapidly?

THE DEACONESS AND HER VOCATION[1]

James Mills Thoburn

SINCE THE DAY OF Pentecost[2] God has anointed Christian women to pray and prophesy. The word "prophesy" as used in the New Testament is not limited, as common usage limits it, to predicting future events, and, indeed, rarely should be interpreted in that sense. It means, to speak by the aid of the Spirit of God, and, especially, to bear testimony to Jesus Christ by the aid of that Spirit. "The testimony of Jesus is the spirit of prophecy." Women are anointed for this kind of service.... I am talking now about a kind of service which has been recognized in Methodism since the days of Susannah Wesley.[3] At times this gift has almost disappeared from our midst, and then again it has revived. I feel assured that one of the most important departments of deaconess work in this country will be found in the line of those persons who succeed to the calling of Philip's daughters.[4] ...

But the claim of the deaconess movement to a recognized place in the Church does not rest upon mere considerations of policy. She has a vocation—a distinct and unmistakable call from the Lord of the harvest.[5] We all believe in the call to what we conventionally denominate

---

1. This excerpt comes from Thoburn, *Deaconess and Her Vocation*, 112–17, 119–23.
2. Acts 2:1–21.
3. Susanna (also spelled Susannah) Wesley (1669–1742) was the mother of John and Charles Wesley.
4. Acts 21:9.
5. Matt 9:37–38.

the ministry—that is, we believe that God calls men to the distinct work of preaching the word and assuming pastoral oversight of Christian churches. We must not, however, fall into the mistake, which I fear is too common in all the evangelical churches, of assuming that this one call to the ministerial office exhausts the divine prerogative in that direction. If there is any one doctrine clearly taught in the New Testament it is that man must not limit God's prerogative to call whom and when and how he pleases. Men and women have duties imposed upon them in one age to which they are not called in another. We ought to take a broad view of the whole subject and teach all our people to be prepared to hear the Master's voice at any time or in any place, summoning them forth to new duties and new responsibilities....

Now, we have to deal with some very significant facts, open to the inspection of the whole world. In the first place, we have nearly four hundred Christian women in our Church who believe that God has led them, not only by his Spirit, but by providential indications which have been to them tokens of divine guidance as clear as a visible pillar of cloud or fire, directing them to devote themselves to work in the Church on the deaconess basis. The four hundred of to-day will be eight hundred in a few more years. The seal of God is upon these women and upon their work. Many of them are achieving marvels. As John Wesley's mother [Susanna Wesley] said to her somewhat impulsive son, when he was about to restrain a certain layman from preaching, "God has as certainly called that man to preach as he has you"; so we may well say to every one who questions the reality of a divine call to these Christian women that if they have not a conviction received directly from heaven their clerical critics may well pause and examine their own credentials. They have, in the first place, a conviction deeply rooted in their own minds and hearts that God has given them this vocation. They have the approval of the Church, as signified by her highest council and by the general and cordial support of the great mass of our people. They have distinct and in many cases marvelous tokens in the shape of aid rendered them in their difficult work, and in addition to all these considerations they have the constant blessing of God descending and abiding upon them in their labors in a manner which none but the blind can fail to perceive. God is with them, and God will fully vindicate their right to a recognized place in our Church....

If any Christian living, by virtue of special obligations, becomes peculiarly consecrated to God it is a deaconess in the modern Church. There is nothing about her consecration which is in the slightest degree perfunctory or merely formal. It is very real to her. Those who question her consecration talk lightly of something they utterly fail to comprehend. She translates into action words which are often upon all our lips, sometimes in the form of testimony, sometimes expressed in words of sacred song, but too often not fully pondered or even understood. She gives herself up to the service of Jesus Christ alone. She separates herself, not in word, but in very deed, to follow her Master, as holy women did when he walked among the villages of Galilee.[6] She ministers to him in any and every way which presents itself to her. We read of those who in the days of his early life ministered to him of their substance. It would surprise the whole Christian world if they knew to what extent many of the deaconesses—especially those in England and Germany—are literally doing the same.... The sacrifices which many of our deaconesses have made will not be fully known in this world: but if any one thinks lightly either of what they give up or of what they take up it is merely an evidence that he has no practical acquaintance with either the work or the workers. God knows of the consecration of each one, and knows the value of the precious gifts which these sisters lay at their Master's feet, and he will not forget them in the great day when all the values of this world shall be readjusted and every service receive a stamp which shall express its exact value....

Their calling forms a new feature in our Methodist system, and it is too soon to try to settle the question of their ultimate progress. For one, however, I cannot doubt that their work has a great future before it. I see before me a band of only fourteen disciples who bear the already honored name of deaconess. I do not know how long God will permit me to live in this world, but I have a feeling within me—a hope which at times seems to assume the form of an expectation—that I shall yet live to do battle for my Master for many years; and I venture to say here to-night that I hope yet to see five hundred deaconesses working bravely and successfully for their blessed Master in this city of New York. That may sound like sheer extravagance to some of you, but I only ask that you remember my words in the years to come; and when this hope shall be realized—when five hundred Methodist deaconesses shall be walking these New York streets and entering these New York homes, witnessing for Christ, and daily and hourly striving to lead sinners to him as their Saviour—they will accomplish wonders which we do not dream of in these days of discouragement

6. Luke 8:2–3.

and despondency. Our deaconess of the future will become a constantly witnessing messenger of Jesus Christ, representing him in every circle which she joins and in every home which she enters, and striving every day to bring wanderers to a knowledge of Him who saves the lost. These five hundred anointed sisters of the future, when once fairly at work, will bring more souls to Christ and add more members to our Church in this city of New York in one year than all the Churches in the city to-day have added during the past ten years.

Reflection Questions

1. Thoburn emphasizes the divine call and unique vocation of deaconesses. How might his argument in support of women's spiritual authority challenge traditional views on church leadership?

2. Thoburn envisions a significant role for deaconesses in evangelism and church growth. How can his ideas about this "anointed" service of deaconesses inform contemporary strategies for outreach and pastoral care?

THE HISTORY OF
THE DEACONESS MOVEMENT
IN THE CHRISTIAN CHURCH[1]

Christian Golder

The slogan "Equality of Sex," which the Woman's Rights champions[2] have adopted, is a contradiction in terms, since sex presupposes inequality and difference. He who would wipe out this God-made distinction, or abolish it, would make man a woman, and woman a man. Who attempts it fights against nature, and is totally ignorant of the particular life mission of both sexes. True, the late denomination, "the new woman,"[3] is entirely agreeable to this view of things; but "the new woman" is not the divinely-created "Biblical woman," to whom the Creator has assigned a vocation for which she is fitted. There is in the present Woman's Movement an element which might be properly designated "Andromania." Many women have lost the womanly ideal, and are endeavoring to be men. They regard as their greatest triumphs to acquire the same rights as men and to be allowed to do what formerly belonged to the province of man alone. This does not mean that woman is to be barred from the profession of law, medicine, or teaching because for centuries these were

---

1. This excerpt comes from Golder, *History of the Deaconess Movement*, 532–33, 545–46.

2. For more on this movement, see chapter 1.

3. The term, new woman, rose to prominence beginning in the 1890s to describe the new freedoms women could enjoy in education, recreation, professions, and in their own independence. The Gibson Girl came to epitomize the new woman. Library of Congress, "Gibson Girl's America."

practiced exclusively by men. But when it is assumed that every vocation in life is to be open to woman on the ground that in all things she has equal rights, an injustice is done her sex. This position is just as wrong as that ultra-conservative opinion which maintains that, because Hannah, the mother of Samuel,[4] had no access to a judicial position, or because Phoebe, the first deaconess,[5] was not allowed to cast her vote, these same conditions should prevail at the present day. In both cases the inference is wrong. We totally misapprehend the distinction of sex and the designs of God by asking: "If a man is entitled to this and that, why not the woman? If the son has chosen this vocation, why not the daughter? If the husbands go to war, why not the wives?" The Scriptures give to us an entirely different idea of the essence of woman, and show us how the Creator assigned to each sex a particular sphere of action. If we would hold more to the Word of God, the woman question would be less complicated and easier of solution. It appears to us that even to-day, after a lapse of six thousand years, man does not yet understand the essence of woman, and it would also seem that woman has not yet learned to know herself. The Bible tells us that all reforms must begin with the cradle, and that in the family must be sought the foundation of all temporal happiness and the support of all that is great and beautiful and noble on earth. The family is society, State, and the Church in embryo, and the spirit of the household, its happiness, the progress of the people, the hope of the future, and the prosperity of the Church, all depend upon the queen of the house—the mother. The mother, sitting at the cradle, makes history, and her hands rule the world. The emancipation of woman can, therefore, only lie in the direction that is pointed out by the Scriptures. The so-called "emancipated woman" forsakes the vocation given to her by the Creator, and thereby finally abandons herself to unbelief, as is abundantly proved by the example of Elizabeth Cady Stanton[6] and other leaders in the Woman's Movement, conspicuously the socialistic women of Europe....

Summing up the whole in a few theses, we have the following result:

1. Woman is on a plane of perfect equality with man in the religious domain; that is, both sexes were redeemed by Christ, and have,

---

4. 1 Sam 1–2.

5. Rom 16:1.

6. Elizabeth Cady Stanton (1815–1902) was the leading intellectual light of the first wave of feminism, beginning in the mid-1800s in the US, and a convenor of the first women's rights convention in the US, held in Seneca Falls in 1848. She spearheaded the publication of *The Woman's Bible*, published in two volumes in 1895 and 1898.

as children of God, the common duty to build up the kingdom as best they can. "There is neither male nor female: for ye are all one in Christ Jesus."[7]

2. Woman has the mission in the gospel to build up the kingdom according to her special gifts and faculties, particularly through the service of love. In this relation she is more like the Savior and accomplishes greater things than man. The Church, in the Deaconess Work, has given the female sex a wide field of fruitful usefulness, even within its inner portals.

3. The order of creation has placed upon woman, on account of her natural endowments, certain restrictions which can not be removed without injury to her highest interests. She should, therefore, not push herself forward and lord it over man. Neither in social nor commercial nor political relations can she usurp the lead without changing the nature of her being and forsaking her God-given vocation.

4. The calling best suited to womanly nature is that of wife and mother, and unto this the female sex ought to be specially educated, and man should have a conscientious care that their duties be not disregarded or depreciated.

5. Both the Scriptures and nature assign to woman the family circle as the principal sphere of her calling, and it is only from this standpoint that the woman question may be safely discussed. The Scriptural passage, "The husband is the head of the wife,"[8] speaks only of his authority in the family circle, and determines nothing for public life.

6. The precept of the apostle, imposing "silence" upon woman, was not at variance at that time with her highest interests, and while the necessity of her "silence" by the force of changed conditions has passed away, her highest interests may nevertheless be conserved. It is, however, certain that woman was debarred from ordination to the ministry, although the passages in question (1 Cor. xiv, 34,35)[9] say nothing of the boundaries within which woman is to move in public life.

7. Gal 3:28.
8. Eph 5:23.
9. "[W]omen should be silent in the churches. For they are not permitted to speak, but should be subordinate, as the law also says. If there is anything they desire to know, let them ask their husbands at home. For it is shameful for a woman to speak in church."

7. It is clear that, if the world is to be saved, woman must at the present day be drawn into a much more expanded and general circle of activity, and it devolves upon the Church in an entirely different manner than has happened for the past two thousand years to return to the principles of Holy Scripture and the Apostolical Institutions. The Deaconess Movement opens up for woman a blessed usefulness outside of the home, and this in the direction of practical charity and service to mankind. When it is considered that the women of paganism can only be reached by female missionaries, that in the home Churches two-thirds of the membership belong to the female sex, and, finally, that their social and ecclesiastical relations, as well as their intellectual and educational progress, are far ahead of the apostles' times, it must be acknowledged that the Church needs in a great measure the enlightenment of the Holy Spirit on the question of the proper position and sphere of a woman.

Reflection Questions

1. How does Golder's interpretation of gender roles challenge the Woman's Rights Movement? How does he propose the deaconess movement as the solution?

2. How do Golder's views oppose or support perspectives on gender that we encounter in our faith communities today?

Anna Hall, Deaconess, Methodist Episcopal Church

FIRST DEACONESSES OF METHODIST EPISCOPAL CHURCH, SOUTH, CONSECRATED AT ATLANTA, GA., 1903.

First Deaconesses of the Methodist Episcopal Church South

Chapter VII

NEGOTIATING "ANDROMANIA" AND OTHER DISPUTED BORDERS IN THE METHODIST DEACONESS MOVEMENT[1]

Overview

THIS CHAPTER STRIKES AT the heart of the thesis of *No Man's Land*, that deaconesses never found, in any country, in any Methodist church, a secure place where they were fully embraced and respected as church officers. As such, they occupied no man's land. The deaconess order, as presented in chapter 1, was contested from the start, and in some churches, only passed by a slim vote. Even then, critics were not silenced; they continued to search for inroads to curtail or shut down altogether any aspect that, in their opinion, crossed over the line into roles assigned to clergymen. The two source documents, taken from the *Deaconess Manual of the African Methodist Episcopal Church*, published in 1902, show both sides of this ongoing conflict. On the one hand, the "Ceremony of Consecration" makes clear that deaconesses were called by God and were "deemed worthy" by the pastor and Official Board. Then, they were publicly consecrated to their office by the laying on of a bishop's hands along with recitation of the Trinitarian invocation. On the other hand, the second

---

1. This material was first presented in my presidential lecture at the 2018 Wesleyan Theological Society meeting. The meeting's theme was "Borders: Bane or Blessing?" The lecture was published in the *Wesleyan Theological Journal* 54 (2019) 7–24. Changes to this version eliminated duplication with material included in earlier chapters.

document, "Special Instructions," lines out exactly what deaconesses were allowed to do—and not to do—in the sick room and at the bedside of the dying—lest she overstep the clergyman's authority.

The Rev. Dr. Charles Parkhurst, senior minister of Madison Square Presbyterian Church in New York City, coined the term *andromania* for a February 1895 full-page article in *The Ladies' Home Journal*. The article's one-word title was simply, "Andromaniacs." What is an andromaniac? A woman who suffered from andromania. What is andromania? "A passionate aping of everything that is masculine."[2] More than an affliction, Parkhurst diagnosed andromania as a disease with these symptoms:

> It is an attempt on the part of those affected with the *disease* to minimize distinctions by which manhood and womanhood are differentiated, whether as regards their culture, their interests or their activities. It is that animus which permits a woman to imagine that she has achieved a great triumph if she succeeds in doing something that only man has hitherto been accustomed to do, but that no woman has hitherto availed to do. It is that animus which excepts to having woman's public activities along any line distinguished by any designation of sex.[3]

By way of illustration, he cited an existing case of andromania exhibited by women in a nearby city, who objected to their organization's being labeled "The Women's Board of Aid" when the corresponding men's organization did not bear a label designating it as "The Men's Board of Aid."

Andromania as a term did not catch on in the English language, as predicted by an editor of the journal, *Medical Arena*, who wrote a favorable op-ed on "Dr. Parkhurst's New Word."[4] Nonetheless, andromania did make its way into the deaconess annals when Rev. Christian Golder referenced it in his history book on the movement.[5] As noted in the previous chapter, Golder championed the deaconess movement as the solution to the problematic Woman's Movement, a movement he denounced for exhibiting symptoms of andromania. He voiced concern lest the disease break out like an epidemic in the deaconess movement, and deaconesses afflicted with it would want to act like clergymen.

2. Parkhurst, "Andromaniacs," 15.
3. Parkhurst, "Andromaniacs," 15. Italics added.
4. "Dr. Parkhurst's New Word," 27.
5. Golder, *History of the Deaconess Movement*, 532.

This chapter focuses on the gender and church office borders that deaconesses had to negotiate. Despite the time and energy on these negotiations, as we have seen in previous chapters, deaconesses came away from them with no precise sphere of work, no precise status in ministry, no precise financial underpinning, and no precise ecclesial position. Given the multiple, constantly shifting borders that intersected their daily lives and ministries, it is no surprise that the deaconess movement succumbed to a steep decline within a generation of its beginning.

The negotiation of these borders by deaconesses overlapped with titanic changes for women in many countries, as presented in chapter 1. In the US, for example, these decades pulsed with the beat of sweeping social change, bold legislation, and audacious innovation, from settlement houses and neighborhood playgrounds to the nineteenth amendment for women's suffrage, from the income tax to the Social Gospel, from the assembly line to the movie theatre. No segment of American life, no crevice of American culture, no stratum of American society stalled this explosion of innovation. During these decades, as documented in chapter 3, the number of women in educational institutions positively boomed. Women's colleges and coeducational land grant institutions experienced a large influx of women students.[6] Simultaneous with advances in education came an increase in women entering the workforce, a decrease in women's fertility, and an increased agitation over "the woman question."[7] This collocation of women's realities pressured Protestant denominations to create a space, an outlet, for women—especially unmarried women—to serve the church more programmatically. Creating the Office of Deaconess appeared as the solution to what Golder and Parkhurst perceived as the "problem" of the woman question and the cure to andromania.[8] Did it work? Let's take a look.

6. Rury, *Education and Women's Work*, 4, 19. The founding of a handful of Eastern women's colleges, including Vassar (1865), Smith and Wellesley (1875), Radcliffe (1879), and Bryn Mawr (1885), bolstered women's access to education. In Midwestern states like Wisconsin, Iowa, and Michigan, women enrolled at coeducational land grant colleges, built on public lands established through the Morrill Act of 1862. Colleges also opened for Black women, like Bennett College (1873), originally founded as a coeducational institution, and Spelman College (1881). For Roman Catholic women, the College of Notre Dame in Maryland opened in 1899; fifteen years later, the number of Catholic women's colleges had jumped to nineteen.

7. For example, see Golder's agitation over "the woman question" that he returned to multiple times. Golder, *History of the Deaconess Movement*, 526-46.

8. The word *problem* appeared frequently in discussions about women's work in the church. For instance, the German Wesleyan Methodist church "felt the need of

Gender Border

Gender is a "powerful means of orienting world and self"; it is inextricably tied up with the social construction of what it means to be male and female.[9] One learns about gender roles through instruction and observation of family, society, church, school, and other such institutions.[10] For Parkhurst, gender was fixed from the moment of creation, therefore, it remained immovable. God set it up in the way God intended it to be, and only those who suffer from the disease of andromania would question its eternal veracity. "It is well enough for her [woman] to say that she wishes she were a man; but she is not," declared Parkhurst, "and till she is, she might as well succumb to the fact that God and Nature had very different intentions for her from what He had for her brothers, and that He recorded His intentions in a way that He has taken some pains to prevent her being able to forget."[11] No doubt his mention of "pains" references childbirth because women's role, according to Parkhurst, orbited around birthing and training children; that's what "she was specifically endowed and ordained to do."[12] Nonetheless, not all could be left up to the natural order of creation; he recognized the impact of nurture and discipline on gender roles. So, he instructed readers to use their influence in such a way as to make "the differences between manhood and womanhood greater, not less."[13] To this end, he deemed that education must be gender-specific to separate clearly and cleanly womanhood from manhood. He considered such an education to be essential because "the female student is quite a distinct species of intellectual creature from its male counterpart."[14] If this did not succeed, if andromania spread and women became more like men, the outcome portended such horror for Parkhurst that he asserted without equivocation, "Any civilization that transforms or tends to transform a woman into the female duplicate of a man is a false civilization."[15]

---

providing a career for women in the church. A committee was appointed in 1887 to study the *problem*." The remaining paragraph discusses deaconess work as a means to solve the problem. Douglass, *Story of German Methodism*, 197. Italics added.

9. Bendroth, *Fundamentalism and Gender*, 6.
10. Sapiro, *Women in American Society*, 68.
11. Parkhurst, "True Mission of Woman," 15.
12. Parkhurst, "True Mission of Woman," 15.
13. Parkhurst, "Andromaniacs," 15.
14. Parkhurst, "College Training for Women," 15.
15. Ironically, he argued that in a true civilization, women were the superior sex,

I presented in detail Parkhurst's stringent beliefs about the gender border because some male advocates of the deaconess movement, like Golder, perpetuated them. It was Golder's use of the word *andromania* in his deaconess history that first alerted me to its existence. Still, for five hundred pages before the Appendix, where he zeroed in on the woman question in light of the New Testament, Golder campaigned vigorously on behalf of the deaconess movement. Why? Because he extrapolated that *if* the woman question "finds an outlet in the deaconess movement, [then] it is possible," he continued, "that the female diaconate will contribute more to the solution of the woman question more than any other factor."[16] Deaconesses, he assumed, would naturally obey the gender border and automatically restrict their work within its confines.

If you are wondering why the focus thus far is on male church leaders, it is important to remember that this is necessary precisely because men set up the parameters of the deaconess movement, they comprised the church legislative bodies, and they were the ones to vote on its approval. Therefore, deaconesses had to negotiate the gender border that men constructed for the movement.

The impact of the gender border showed up in the division of labor between the clergy (men) who "pursued the ministry of the Word in preaching and Bible teaching," and the deaconess (women) who engaged in the "removal or mitigation of sorrow, poverty, and pain."[17] Or, as Golder phrased it, deaconess labors were delineated along the lines of what is "especially adapted to the nature and capacity of woman."[18] Golder went on to claim that the man at the heart of the Protestant diaconate revival, Kaiseserwerth's Theodore Fliedner, "understood woman better than she understood herself." Fliedner, explained Golder, capitalized on his "marvelous" understanding of "the female character" to develop deaconess work along the lines appropriate for women.[19] Most deaconesses negotiated this border successfully by remaining on their side—the woman's side—of the gender border. Even a more progressive thinker, like Lucy Rider Meyer, as noted in chapter 4, promoted maternalism as the pivotal strategy for the movement.

---

but they retained their hold on superiority only if they "cherish their femininity with some considerable measure of caution." Parkhurst, "Andromaniacs," 15.

16. Golder, *History of the Deaconess Movement*, 484.
17. Ames, "Lucy Webb Hayes National Training-School," 137.
18. Golder, *History of the Deaconess Movement*, 334.
19. Golder, *History of the Deaconess Movement*, 54.

Still, it remained for individual deaconesses to negotiate the gender border, and some got caught in its web. Take Iva Durham Vennard who, as set out in chapter 2, challenged the gender border and angered male opponents because of her relentless commitment to evangelism. At her deaconess training school, Epworth Evangelistic Institute, she emboldened students to preach and be engaged in public evangelism, and her daring—andromania, really—roused prominent Methodist clergymen and laymen in St. Louis to label her a dangerous and powerful woman. Then, while she was on maternity leave attending to motherhood in earnest, these men led a coup to oust her as principal. Their paramount complaint? That Vennard and her faculty, staff, and students had succumbed to the disease of andromania.

Church Office Border

In 1888, the Methodist Episcopal Church (MEC) became "the first branch of the Church of Christ in modern times that . . . made the deaconess an officer of the Church by its organic law."[20] What in reality, though, did this phrase, an officer of the church, mean for the status of deaconesses in the church? The pivotal question to be considered is, Were they clergy or lay? The short answer: Neither. Despite having a designated church office, they remained encased in a nebulous border region—a no man's land—that required continual negotiation and diplomacy.

Deaconesses Were Not Clergy

Methodist deaconesses were consecrated in an official, public worship service that closely resembled the ordination service for clergymen. Both services took place in the church, and both services included prayers and hymns, questions to the candidates, and the charge to be faithful to their respective callings. Both services also involved clergy—and often a bishop—laying hands on each candidate along with pronouncement of the Trinitarian invocation. In the first source document in this chapter from the African Methodist Episcopal Church (AME), deaconesses were to respond affirmatively to three questions, then they knelt before the bishop, who in turn, took each candidate by the hand and pronounced these words over her: "Be thou consecrated to the office and work of a

---

20. Wheeler, *Deaconesses Ancient and Modern*, 293.

Deaconess in the African Methodist Episcopal Church, in the name of the Father, and of the Son, and of the Holy Ghost. Amen."[21] This ecclesial gesture and wording consecrated deaconesses, whereas the same gesture and nearly the same wording ordained clergy. The difference between consecration and ordination, however, was more than semantic. Clergy were ordained into a clearly designated space of church authority; deaconesses were consecrated into a nebulous space, literally a no man's land, with male opponents holding on tightly to their side of the gender border. That there existed no intention to ordain deaconesses became clear at the same MEC General Conference where the Office of Deaconess was approved, because the same voting body declined the ordination of deaconesses in India, despite the strong support of Bishop Thoburn. The juxtaposition in this same General Conference of a yes to their consecration but a no to their ordination, even in far-off India, reinforced the church office border between deaconesses and clergymen.

The difference between deaconesses and clergymen is also evident in the second source document in this chapter, where it is stipulated that a deaconess "shall be subject to the general direction of the pastor." Then, as we saw in chapter 1, deaconesses working in the Sick Room were to follow specific instructions that boiled down to this admonition: "Be quiet and let him [the pastor] have 'the right of way.'" What then could the deaconess do when tending the sick? She was to clean up the room and change the bedding.[22] These instructions were preceded by an overarching statement in the manual affirming the submission of deaconesses to clergy: "Woman is pre-eminently the helper of man—his second self."[23] To ground this sentiment biblically, the manual included brief descriptions of female biblical figures, and each description pointed to woman's role as man's helper. The Shunammite princess in 2 Kgs 4:8, for instance, received praise because she "reverenced holy men and believed it her duty to support them."[24]

Vennard railed against clergy who consigned deaconesses to trifling administrative tasks instead of taking advantage of their prowess for and training in evangelism. She vented this opinion in an editorial in the *Deaconess Advocate*. "If the pastor needs a stenographer let him hire one. If the church needs some one to collect funds for the preacher's salary or

21. Grant, *Deaconess Manual*, 30.
22. Grant, *Deaconess Manual*, 29.
23. Grant, *Deaconess Manual*, 11.
24. Grant, *Deaconess Manual*, 14.

other expenses let stewards be appointed. A deaconess trained in soul-winning is too valuable to be used in such routine."[25] We have already seen, though, what happened to Vennard with the male takeover of her school because of her border-crossing opinions.

Deaconesses Were Not Laity

Deaconesses were not clergy, but they were not laity either in the sense that they were consecrated, set apart from other laity, as church officers. The process of consecration began when they received a call from God to become a deaconess. These calls were transformative, often with a complete change of direction. For instance, due to the divine call she received, Louise Semple altered her plan from pursuing her artistic talent to becoming a deaconess. She recalled, "When I became convinced that the call was from the Lord, I could only say, 'Here am I, send me'[26] and I never for a moment regretted the decision."[27] Similarly, Louise Golder, who joined her brother, Christian, to promote deaconess work among German Methodists in Cincinnati, described her call in these words: "The more I prayed about it, the more my inner joy and impulse grew and was so strong that I felt, if I didn't obey the voice, I would be going against God's will."[28] To respond to the call, the would-be deaconess enrolled in the required course of study. As set out in chapter 3, the course of study curriculum combined theological education with practical work experience. These aspects in aggregate—the divine call, the advanced education, and the consecration service—set the deaconess apart from the laity and more closely resembled the process of becoming a clergyman.

Thoburn wrestled with this question as well—were deaconesses clergy or laity? His response was to suggest that deaconesses and clergy be treated similarly. In response to a question he must have heard often—"What is the use of all this? If a woman wants to work there is nothing to hinder her"—he answered, "It is a very easy thing to say that if a woman wants to work she can easily find a place, but do you deal that way with ministers? If a man wants to work for God the church takes him and trains him and tries him and sets her seal upon him, and finds him work and

---

25. Vennard, "Editorial," 6.
26. Isa 6:8.
27. Dougherty, *My Calling to Fulfill*, 2.
28. Dougherty, *My Calling To Fulfill*, 2.

sets him at it."²⁹ His unspoken yet obvious inference was that deaconesses should be respected and valued much more than they have been by the church, certainly as if they were clergy. Instead, what he often witnessed was deaconesses being treated with no respect, as retainers to be used or disposed of at will. Thoburn believed the opposite was true.

However, his opinion did not prevail. Deaconesses remained in no man's land, neither clergy nor laity, and their occupation of this nebulous border region resulted in long-lasting, negative consequences. In her dissertation on Methodist deaconesses in the Philippines, Liwliwa T. Robledo explains the struggle over the classification into the late twentieth century: Were deaconesses clergy? Laity? Or neither? The issue at stake revolved around membership in the annual conference, which only allowed for two categories: clergy and lay. According to Robledo, "Bishop Emerito P. Nacpil said that deaconesses do not want to come in as ministers, they do not want to come in as lay, they want to come in as deaconesses. This, he asserted, was an entirely new thing. 'And I don't see that there is a third category for membership in the Annual Conference. The whole thing is very structural.'"³⁰ The bishop's words underscore the church office border that deaconesses had to negotiate. They were neither clergy nor laity; rather, they were an "entirely new thing" that even after more than a century remained unresolved.

Conclusion

In 1970, the United Methodist Church convened a study project on "Attitudes of the United Methodist Deaconess" to ascertain from deaconesses how they viewed their role. I read through the study with a particular eye to border issues, and I found to my chagrin that they were still present for these deaconesses to negotiate. Consider, for instance, this comment by an anonymous deaconess: "As a deaconess, a woman is no longer a full human being." The gender border is there in her words that she is not a woman; she is not even fully human. She goes on to say, "She [a deaconess] is accepted as a kind of maiden aunt, to be pitied, or step-daughter, to be looked after—but from her the church expects little."³¹ Here, again, is

---

29. Thoburn, *Deaconess and Her Vocation*, 73.
30. Robledo, "Gender, Religion, and Social Change," 254.
31. Wilson, *Attitudes of the United Methodist Deaconess*, 13.

a woman, a deaconess, who feels like others treat her as a dependent, as if she were not a fully formed adult with her own agency.

This same deaconess then pivoted to comment on the church office border, "She has already been eliminated in regard to her own Annual Conference. . . . there is now no structure for her. She has to struggle, and make a point of it, even to be recognized." The deaconess, who is neither clergy nor lay, remains in limbo, in no man's land with no place structurally to belong. Not surprisingly, with great pessimism, she concluded, "In this context, I see little future."[32]

Borders required constant negotiation by deaconesses. The gender border meant that when a deaconess, like Vennard, stepped across the border to preach, or even more unthinkable, to train other women to do the same, she received the whip of male disapproval and fell captive to their coup. The church office border remained a fickle one. The result: deaconesses labored tirelessly to visit the poor, to care for the orphan, to preach the gospel, and all of this in-between borders, in an isolated, still contested no man's land, without a safe sanctuary to call their own.

Reflection Questions

1. How did andromania influence the perceptions and limitations placed on deaconesses? Where do you see andromania still operative today in the church? In society?
2. In what ways do you think that the conflicting borders of gender and church office contributed to the eventual decline of the deaconess movement? Do you see remnants of these borders for women in church leadership today?

---

32. Wilson, *Attitudes of the United Methodist Deaconess*, 13.

"CEREMONY OF CONSECRATION"[1]

THE DEACONESSES.

(This office was created by the General Conference in 1900.)

QUALIFICATIONS: A woman, to be admitted to the office of Deaconess, should not be younger than eighteen years nor older than thirty-five, unmarried, or, a widow, possessed of good reputation, good English education, a full membership of at least two years in the A. M. E. Church, and general adaptation for the work.

HOW CONSTITUTED.

A woman feeling herself called to the office of Deaconess may state the same to her pastor. If the pastor regards her as a suitable person for Deaconess, he shall present her name to the Official Board. If the Official Board regard her as worthy, it shall elect her Deaconess and select a committee of three Stewardesses[2] to arrange for her consecration. On a day appointed by the Bishop, for consecration of Deaconesses, all persons to be consecrated shall appear in full Deaconess garb. The Bishop, or some person appointed by him, shall deliver an address or sermon, setting forth the importance, responsibilities and duties of the Deaconess.

The committee of Stewardesses shall conduct the candidates to the pastor, who shall present them to the Bishop.

---

1. This excerpt comes from Grant, *Deaconess Manual of the African Methodist Episcopal Church*, 23–25.

2. AME stewardesses prepare the sanctuary, particularly the altar, for worship services. During the consecration service, they bring deaconess candidates to the pastor.

CEREMONY.

Pastor: "Reverend Father in God, I present these holy women to be consecrated Deaconesses."

The Bishop: "Take heed that these women whom you present be proper persons to perform the work of a Deaconess, and that they be of sober mind, modest in all their ways and possessed of large charity."

Pastor: "They have been examined and are believed to be well qualified to enter upon the sacred duties of Deaconess."

The Bishop: "It becometh the Deaconess that she shall be pious, chaste, temperate in all things, modest, humble, industrious and devout, as she is to serve the Church of God to His praise and glory. Throughout the history of the Church God has been pleased to call and qualify certain women for the gentler and holy service of ministering to the Church and the ministry. Such women were Deborah,[3] Mary the holy mother,[4] Eunice,[5] Lois,[6] Priscilla,[7] Lyddia[8] [sic] and Phoebe.[9] And in the latter days He has been pleased to own and bless the labors of Sister Sarah Gorham and many others.[10] May the Lord bless and acknowledge these persons according as He has blessed the ministrations of all holy women. May they withdraw themselves from all worldly cares and vocations and give themselves up entirely to ministrations to the Church and to suffering humanity."[11]

Then shall the Bishop inquire of the candidates as follows:

3. A prophet, poet, and judge in Israel. See Judges 4–5.

4. The mother of Jesus Christ. See Luke 1–2.

5. The mother of Timothy, a disciple of the apostle Paul. See Acts 16:1 and 2 Tim 1:5.

6. The grandmother of Timothy. See 2 Tim 1:5.

7. A coworker of Paul's along with her husband, Aquila. See Acts 18, Rom 16:3–4, 1 Cor 16:19, 2 Tim 4:19.

8. A seller of purple cloth who set up a Christian church in her home. See Acts 16.

9. A deacon (also translated as deaconess or servant) in the early church. See Rom 16:1–2.

10. Sarah Gorham (1832–1894) was the first single AME woman to be sent as a missionary to a foreign field. In 1888, at the age of 56, she traveled to an AME mission station in Magbele, Sierra Leone. She established there the Sarah Gorham Mission School, which offered religious and industrial training to Temne women and girls. She died in 1894 after a bout with malaria.

11. For more on this collect today, see the introduction.

"Have you duly considered the sacredness, the ex-actions and responsibilities of this office which you have come to enter?"

Answer: "I have considered them all."

Bishop: "Are you determined to observe all the rules for a Deaconess, give yourself up to such life and duties as these rules require, and keep yourself unspotted from the world, all its vanities and frivolities?"

Answer: "I am so determined."

Bishop: "Will you be governed by the discipline of the A. M. E. Church and subject to the direction given in the discharge of the duties of your office?"

Answer: "I will be so governed."

Then shall the persons to be consecrated kneel. The Bishop, taking each candidate by the hand, shall say to her:

Bishop: "Be thou consecrated to the office and work of a Deaconess in the African Methodist Episcopal Church, in the name of the Father, and of the Son, and of the Holy Ghost. Amen."

Reflection Questions

1. How does this consecration service for AME deaconesses reflect the gendered expectations and roles which they had to negotiate?
2. What does the inclusion in the service of biblical women's names, such as Deborah, Priscilla, and Phoebe, suggest about AME male church leaders' view of deaconesses? Do these biblical women confirm their view of women's roles or complicate it? What about the inclusion of Sarah Gorham's name?

"SPECIAL INSTRUCTIONS"[1]

1. THE SICK ROOM. You are expected to visit the sick, those who are distressed and often crazed with pains, aches, and delirious with hot, scorching fevers. They may often appear cross and peevish; often in discouragement and despair; in their desperate struggles with disease and losing hope, may look with disfavor upon your ministration as a worker of the Church. You are expected to fortify and harden yourself against rebuke and peevishness; put your feelings aside and assume a cheerful manner and voice; mournful looks and tones are not good antidotes of sicknesses. Do not be too inquisitive and volunteer superfluous advice in recommending various drugs, roots, herbs and patent medicines. Be gentle in touch and step; avoid loud talking and needless standing over the sick, or, moving about. Use tact in presenting the claims of the Bible; remember that God speaks to men in "a still, small voice";[2] too much talk may nauseate and cause the patient to wish you gone. Do not go to gather up "dying testimony," but be more concerned to get living testimony; oftentimes, through effect of strong medicines and fever, the sick may give utterance to peculiar and irreligious words and expressions, to which you are to pay no heed. Protect the sufferer as much as possible, in both mind and body. The undertaker will bring a coffin when the time comes, so let your mission be to bring good tidings. Acquaint your pastor of all cases needing his attention. He can do his work much better than you. And do not argue about religion with the pastor as to what you do, or, do not believe in the sick room; be quiet and let him have the "right of way." Arrange

---

1. This excerpt comes from Grant, *Deaconess Manual of the African Methodist Episcopal Church*, 28–32.

2. 1 Kgs 19:12.

the disordered room and the bedclothes; if the bedding require it, try and effect a change. Let pity prompt every service of yours.

2. THE BED-CHAMBER OF THE DYING. You are to stand by the bedside where a soul is loosing its moorings to its fallen tabernacle, and breaking every human tie, and fast losing consciousness of its surroundings. The spot is sacred and the occasion one of the deepest solemnity and gravity. Why ply the departing soul with numerous and useless questions, when, perhaps, it may be communing with its Maker or gathering strength for the outward sweep into the Eternal Beyond? Stand near, in attentive silence, and wait to hear the call, the expressed want, the muttered prayer and join it; give it time; do not get excited; be the example of dignity and Christian faith for the agonized husband, father, wife, mother, brother or sister, whose heart, in its sorrow, seems ready to burst in agonized grief; try and calm that storm and encourage the wounded heart. When death has come do what you can in preparing the body at once for its burial. Avoid the superstition of covering up the pictures and looking-glasses with cloths. Close the eyes and tie a cloth about the face to close the mouth. In regard to funeral arrangements, consult with the family about seeing the pastor, so as to avoid coming into conflict with any previous appointment he may have made, thus causing embarrassment.

3. THE UNFORTUNATE. Men and women are losing their property by fire and water and wind; their money by speculation and otherwise; their pride suffers; they are sensitive and downhearted. Some are crippled in limb, blind, deaf, dumb, simple and idiotic, deformed, and they are often mocked and made sport of. Only by kindness and loving words can they be reached and brought within the house of God. Or, they may be found isolated in lonely places; these are indeed the ones of "the highways and hedges"[3] that the Christian worker is to find, in the lanes and alleys; they are ekeing [sic] out of sad existence, feeling keenly the humiliation of the world. Will you not be a friend to them? This is the class the Master largely sought out—the "weary and heavy laden."[4]

Over yonder, in an almost desolate place, is the "poor-house," and within its cheerless confines are those who once were light, happy and gay, but they are now "upon the cold charity of the world." They need your visitation and godly communion. In the hospitals, lying upon their

3. Luke 14:23.
4. Matt 11:28.

cots suffering, are many who have neither "kith nor kin" to visit them; some will never again walk forth in life. The voice of God calls and says, "Comfort ye my people; comfort ye my people!"[5] The wounded Samaritan is there,[6] the prodigal son[7] and many wandering daughters, who would be happy if they knew of Christ. Why not take a companion in there and speak of Jesus and offer a short prayer. The jails and prisons await your coming. These are among the unfortunate; they see no star of hope, but you can point them to "The Bright and Morning Star."[8] You can carry little tracts[9] and Scripture truths. Some you may get pardoned, and thus save a valuable life by a judicious intercession. Go to those who hear naught but the iron bolts moving, and rattling of prison chains, with armed and stern guards about them, while in their narrow cells. They need you.

4. THE HUNGRY AND NAKED. This class you must, in the main, look up. Some are too old to work and are left to starve in desolate places; others, on account of sickness, are unable to work; others, again, in the big cities, are out of work and money; they cannot get any food for themselves and little ones; they should be reported to the Church or any other institution which should feed the hungry poor.

Then there are the little half-clothed and shoeless children who never see inside of a church or Sunday school, who could be clothed by garments made by you; clothes and cast-off shoes could be solicited and given them. Such attention would win many. We must learn to minister to bodies in order to reach souls. Fine churches, organs, choirs, eloquence and such like are good when men are fed and clothed, but these are forgotten when they are hungry and naked, with suffering children around their knees crying for bread.

5. HOMELESS PERSONS. This refers principally to females, who are stranded in the city; who are without work, and often in despair go to the bad; little boys and girls deserted by faithless parents or guardians, and often still in the hands of careless parents and guardians. Homes should be sought and places of work. If we have a Deaconess Home, work in sewing

5. Isa 40:1.
6. Luke 10:25–37.
7. Luke 15:11–32.
8. Rev 22:16.
9. A brief written summary of the Christian gospel handed out for evangelistic purposes.

and such like could be given them until a place could be found. Many such females can be met at the depots from off the trains and at steamboat landings. Without money, they know not where to go. The saloons and other places have their doors standing invitingly open, while the church is closed. We must set before this class "an open door."

6. FALLEN WOMEN.[10] They are human. Many of them have said to themselves, "No one cares for my soul," and so they plunge deeper into disgrace; others there are who long to get away from their awful and horrid surroundings, but have no one to encourage them to make an effort. They cannot be reached at the "end of a long pole"; personal contact is the essential. Let the Deaconesses go in company to these homes of sin,[11] in the name of the Lord, and go as a sister. Talk to them and urge them to begin life over again. Do not stop because fruits are not immediate. Sometimes they may be found upon the streets, wandering about. They have hearts that can be touched, "chords that will vibrate once more."[12] Why should we not speak to the woman that is "a harlot?" Are we purer than the Master? There is no class of individuals who are regarded with more contempt and shunned. Should they wish to do so, society would willingly excuse a neglect of visiting this class of people by pious women; but duty calls to go to them and carry a message of peace and pardon.

Reflection Questions

1. How did the special instructions for deaconesses in the sickroom and with the dying reflect broader societal expectations of women's roles in caregiving during the early twentieth century?
2. In what ways did the duties outlined for deaconesses in caring for the unfortunate and fallen women demonstrate the church's approach to social outreach and moral reform in their day? Are these same duties appropriate today for the church to pursue?

---

10. Prostitutes and unwed mothers.
11. A brothel.
12. This phrase comes from Fanny Crosby's hymn, "Rescue the Perishing."

Sister Elise Searle, Deaconess, Wesley Deaconess Order

Sister Olive Jeffrey in foreground, Methodist Church of New Zealand

EPILOGUE

A Deaconess Blueprint for the Revival of Methodism Worldwide[1]

THIS EPILOGUE STARTS WITH my breaking a cardinal rule for historians as cited by our colleague, Martin Wellings, in his article for a book that ruminates on the future of the British Methodist church: "Historians tend not to be builders of grand systems and purveyors of sweeping generalizations, much less predictors of the future in the light of the past."[2] Martin then proceeds to break this cardinal rule himself, so I am joining good company! While I am not going to attempt a future prediction, I will *map a way forward* for Methodism in light of a movement from the past with remarkable promise and fortitude, which, tragically, was never realized. I am speaking of the international Methodist deaconess movement. So, in this epilogue, I will push the "so what" question of the historical narrative to provide what I believe can be the "grand system"—the blueprint—with five core elements for the revival of Methodism worldwide.[3]

A Snapshot of the Methodist Deaconess Movement

A journalist in 1898 provided this synopsis of a deaconess's average day:

---

1. This epilogue was first presented in a plenary lecture at the 14th Oxford Institute of Methodist Theological Studies. It was then published in *Thy Grace Restore* with other conference plenaries. Changes in this version eliminate duplication with previous chapters.

2. Wellings, "'Time to Be Born and a Time to Die'?" 149.

3. I am using the word, revival, as defined in the online Oxford Dictionary: "an improvement in the condition or strength of something."

> In the morning she will, perchance, visit a sick man, grumpy and ungrateful, recovering, it may be, from the results of a debauch. It is hers to speak comfortable words to him, to dress his wounds if he have any, and to pave the way for a reconciliation with his wife. . . . Perchance it is a widow she visits in the afternoon, accustomed to earn her scanty crusts as charwoman. Then it is as often as not a case of going down on her knees—not to pray, at least not just now, but to scrub the room out. Or, it may be, a weak mother needs fresh air. Then our Deaconess becomes nursemaid to the infant, and the ailing mother has a day in the country or a ride on a farm. To paper a room, nurse a fever case, make it up between lovers, conduct a service, fire a prayer-meeting, expound the Scriptures, advise in family crises—these are the items that make up a Deaconess' work. A bit of a judge, a bit of a lawyer, a skilled nurse, a preacher, and above all a lover of her kind—all this must a Deaconess be; and it is not easy to find such a combination.[4]

Adapting to these wide-ranging needs became second nature to deaconesses who lived among those to whom they ministered. "We are in the heart of our work," wrote a deaconess in Salford, England. "The people we want to help live all around us. They pass our doors in their clattering 'wooden shoon,' at a quarter to six every morning; we hear their loud laughter, and alas! sometimes their drunken cries late at night."[5] The daily work of deaconesses in their neighborhood was grueling and often heartbreaking. Scenarios of human misery, for example, fill the pages of Elizabeth Ann Pitts's 1900 diary (see Appendix A) during her daily visitation rounds in London when she was a student at Mewburn House, the first training school for the Wesley Deaconess Order (WDO). Here is a snippet from one day's visitation:

> The next was Mrs. Cooper, she seemed to be worn down with work, having 9 children the baby only 7 weeks old, so I did not think it wise to hinder her from thronging duties, so after expressing my sympathy offered a few words in prayer, she appeared very thankful. . . . The next place was Mrs. Arrowsmith No 69, it is a sad poverty stricken home, her husband gets work now & then at the docks, the eldest child was kept in because she had not any boots to wear, the second child is suffering from

---

4. "Much the Same in America," 164.
5. "Deaconess Work in Salford," 38.

ulcerated bowels, also Whooping Cough; the Mother with infant in arms looked weighed down with care.[6]

The strain on deaconesses of these daily encounters showed up physically in illness or exhaustion so much so that Thomas Bowman Stephenson, WDO founder, was often asked, "'Why do so many of your Deaconesses break down in health?'" He responded that such a question "reveals at once the fact that the querist is ignorant of the strain under which the worker, at any rate among the slum population, often lives."[7] This daily trauma took its toll on Sister Thirza Masters, and after more than a decade of visiting the destitute and the hopeless, she had a complete breakdown. In her diary (see Appendix B), she details her total despair while undergoing in the hospital—what she calls "her prison"—the infamous "rest cure," often prescribed in the early twentieth century for women in her condition.[8]

It is difficult from our vantage point to imagine what Masters, Pitts, Isabel Sinclair, and other Methodist deaconesses encountered day after day on their visitation rounds. "There was little or no national medical service, no maternity service, no pre-natal or child welfare clinics or district nurses. There was no financial aid from the State during sickness, unemployment or old age. The Sisters met a level of destitution which we do not know to-day."[9] To compound the strain of encountering the depths of human suffering and their frequent ill-health, they worked within an indifferent, even hostile church that, as evident in chapter 7, treated them like a third species, neither clergy nor laity.

Why, then, should we look to the deaconess movement, whose heyday occurred more than a century ago, for a revival blueprint today? This is a valid question, and one I asked myself countless times after committing to this topic in an unguarded moment of optimism. I wanted to change it, but to be honest, I am glad I kept with it, because from the margins, the misunderstood, the alienated—rather than those in the center of power—often come the idea, the blueprint that shows us the way forward. Such was the status of the international Methodist deaconess movement. It occupied, for a time, a counter-cultural outpost on the margins that was increasingly less attended to by the institutional church as it became more

---

6. Pitts Diary, unpaginated. For more from the diary, see Appendix A.
7. "In Perils Oft," 201.
8. See Appendix B, n22.
9. Wesley Deaconess Order pamphlet, 6.

bourgeois and respectable. This is not to say that the deaconess movement was without its flaws and shortcomings. Not at all. Deaconesses could be condescending to the poor, expecting them to pull themselves up by their bootstraps if they only applied themselves and worked harder. And deaconesses were stuck in nineteenth-century revivalism as if that approach was the only one to follow for evangelism and outreach. There is more to be said on these topics; however, here, at the close of this book, we will consider five core elements of the deaconess movement that—when put into practice—will spark revival in our time.

Unite Knowledge and Vital Piety[10]

WDO Deaconess, Sister Thirza Masters, wrote the following about the Christian conversion she experienced:

> A great longing possessed me to know Christ as a living, bright reality.... Early and late I sought for this happy experience, wrestling and praying for hours.... There followed soul struggles, and it seemed that God had hidden His Face from me. For 18 months I scarcely smiled. [Then after reading Hannah Whitall Smith's bestselling book, *The Christian's Secret to a Happy Life*][11] ... the mists cleared and the scales fell from my eyes. I saw that my efforts and soul chastening had been in vain, and that I had simply to surrender myself and my doubts to Christ.[12]

Deaconesses, like Masters, testified to an experience of a definite conversion. Most were raised in religious homes and the Methodist church, thus they were surrounded from birth by a Christian environment. Masters, for example, was raised along with thirteen siblings in the Wesleyan Methodist Church in the UK. Still, a moment happened when God became real in a new, intimately personal way, as Masters's account demonstrates. Deaconesses also experienced a definite call to

---

10. This phrase is my adaptation of a line in Charles Wesley's hymn, "Come Father, Son and Holy Ghost." The line reads: "Unite the pair so long disjoined, Knowledge and vital piety."

11. Hannah Whitall Smith (1832–1911) was one of the most prominent public women in the late nineteenth and early twentieth centuries. A Philadelphia Quaker, she was a founding member of the Women's Christian Temperance Union, a leading supporter of women's suffrage, an evangelist, and a bestselling author. Her book, *The Christian's Secret to a Happy Life*, sold over two million copies in its first printing in 1875. It continues to be reprinted and widely read today.

12. Masters, "Lives of Wesley Deaconesses," 168. See also her diary in Appendix B.

serve God in full-time religious work. WDO deaconess Dora Stephenson explained that the divine call for a deaconess acts as a "definite and prayerful covenant with God to do the work to which she believes He has called her."[13] Masters's call to deaconess work began when her "sympathies were stirred and I longed to devote my life to the easing of others' burdens." She followed up this stirring by considering the available options, including the Salvation Army, for women in full-time religious work. Then came the serendipitous timing of the Methodist deaconess launch: "It was about that time that Dr. Stephenson was divinely led to open the way more widely for Women's Work in the Methodist Church. And, seeing his request for Christian women to offer for Training for Deaconess Work, I responded. Instantly I saw that God did want me, and that He was opening the way for me."[14]

What these deaconesses exemplified in their conversion and call is *vital piety*. Is this word still meaningful today? This question is an appropriate one because in the same lands where the deaconess movement once flourished, vital piety—as in conversion and consecration of one's life—is rarely mentioned in Methodist churches today. *If* such talk ever happens, it feels embarrassing, and there is often a pregnant silence when we look down at our feet and hope for someone else to say something in response. Today, we seem to operate from a Bushnellian point of view on vital piety. Horace Bushnell, a Congregational pastor and theologian in the US, exercised a significant influence in tamping down vital piety talk during the mid-nineteenth century. He criticized "emotional revivalists" for their insistence on the "radical breach-making character" of conversion and advocated instead for an imperceptible growth into the Christian life, where "the child is to grow up a Christian, and never know himself as being otherwise."[15] Bushnell's perspective on conversion, recently described as "organic," relied on a steady, long-haul Christian influence at home and church rather than a speedy, spectacular one.[16] Mainline Protestant seminaries jumped on Bushnell's ideas and advanced a curriculum with religious education replacing evangelism as "the new paradigm for ministry" for an educated clergy.[17] And now, even religious education in

13. Stephenson, "What Is a Deaconess?" 219.

14. Masters, "Lives of Wesley Deaconesses," 168.

15. Marty, *Protestantism in the United States*, 192. See Bushnell, *Discourses on Christian Nurture* and Macleod, *Building Character in the American Boy*, 23.

16. Albanese, "Horace Bushnell," 616.

17. Taves, *Fits, Trances, and Visions*, 343.

the church is often marginalized. So, the question for us to consider is, Where and when does talk about vital piety happen? Even initiating these kinds of conversations, which were commonplace among deaconesses more than a century ago, could provide a spark toward revival.

The other word, knowledge, was also a serious commitment for deaconesses. In the training school or deaconess home, their vital piety was balanced with knowledge and training for the work. Here, for example, is the curriculum for the course of study offered at Harris Memorial Training School in Manila.

> **First Year:** Old Testament-History; New Testament—Gospels; Catechism; Methodist Discipline; English—Reading; Writing; Arithmetic; Weekly Sunday School lesson; Music—Vocal.
>
> **Second Year:** Old Testament—History; New Testament—Book of Acts; Catechism; Methodist Discipline; English—Grammar; Geography; Arithmetic; Physiology and Hygiene; Weekly Sunday School lesson; Music—Vocal.
>
> **Third Year:** Old Testament-History and Prophesy; New Testament—Epistles; Bible Study by Topics; Church History; English—Composition; Physiology and Hygiene; Weekly Sunday School lesson; Music—Vocal and Instrumental [18]

Along with these courses, the curriculum integrated practical work as the other major component of deaconess training. Training schools, as noted previously, were set up in cities, like Sydney, London, Frankfurt am Main, Toronto, Chicago, Boston, and New York City, where students worked in city missions, jails, courts, hospitals, workhouses, Travelers' Aid ministries, and settlement houses. However, even in the rural setting of the WDO training school in Ilkley, West Yorkshire, students still visited in the community one afternoon a week on Wednesdays. "Shortly before one o-clock every Wednesday," wrote a student, "we wend our way, a blue-cloaked band, to the station. The afternoon is spent in Bradford, and the surrounding villages. Meetings are conducted, and sick people visited, thus affording a foretaste of the work awaiting us in the future."[19] Today, a foretaste of the work awaits us as well, and our commitment to unite

---

18. *Third Annual Session of the Woman's Conference of the Philippine Islands*, 32; quoted in Robledo, "Gender, Religion and Change," 97–98. See also chapter 3 which explores the deaconess training school in greater depth.

19. "Student's View of College Life," 73. See the source document in ch 3.

knowledge and vital piety in word and deed, like the deaconesses, would be a pivotal step forward for the revival of Methodism worldwide.

Live Simply, Even Communally

> Deaconess work and the mode in which Deaconesses live is a protest against the utilitarian standard which pervades all our civilization. The poor appreciate it. It is a revelation to them that here are women who are working for the love of Christ, and who know something of the limitations of poverty as well as the people among whom they labor. 'He became poor for our sakes.'[20] It is a voice in this modern age, saying to the multitude, there is something more precious than dollars and cents. There is a wealth of life more to be desired than silver and gold.[21]

Methodism in the late nineteenth century became increasingly middle-class in outlook, architecture, and worship style. In 1877, an MEC minister in Chicago described its bourgeois ascent: "Methodism is in transition; moving up out of poverty into wealth; out of obscurity into notoriety; out of her plain garb into the latest fashions; out of the log-cabin into the white house; out of the old camp-grounds into the 'Ocean Groves' and the 'Lake Bluffs;' out of the plain old meeting house into the grand new church with organ and quartet-choir, and all with the ornamentation of a heavy mortgage."[22]

Deaconesses embodied—literally!—the opposite. They stood against materialism by doing without. They did without a salary; they only received pocket money, as enumerated in the source document from the Martha-Maria deaconess organization in chapter 4. Living without an income silenced accusations that they worked for pay or that deaconesses cost the church money that was better spent elsewhere. "Money is . . . crystallized power," wrote Meyer, "and God's children should hold it sacred for God's work, using only so much of it for their own comfort and adornment as will make them better workers for God."[23]

---

20. 2 Cor 8:9.

21. Wardle, *Report on Deaconess Work*, 11. Ps 19:9–10.

22. Burns, *Northwestern Christian Advocate*, 6. For a similar story in the UK, see Armstrong, *Church of England, Methodists and Society*, 207; Field, "Social Structure of English Methodism," 199; and Rack, "Wesleyan Methodism 1849–1902," 3:127.

23. Meyer, *Deaconesses*, 236.

In addition, deaconesses also did without a closetful, even a drawerful, of clothing. Look again at the minimal amount of clothing provided to Martha-Maria deaconesses, as listed in the same source document. They only received a new grey dress every two to three years; the cheaper, calico dresses were provided as needed. In total, though, there would be no more than five dresses hanging in the closet. Further, their uniform—the distinctive deaconess dress—signified to the church and society their complete commitment and the foregoing of luxuries or anything in excess.

Deaconesses also did without a home and family of their own. Instead, they lived among a sisterhood, a company of like-minded women. The deaconess home provided a sacred place set apart from the world to which they returned after a long day of visiting in overcrowded tenements or nursing the infirmed. As a community, they gathered to eat, discuss the day's events, share each other's burdens, worship together, and pray over the difficult situations they tended to throughout the day. In this home, deaconesses lived communally as a family. For WDO deaconesses who lived more on their own, the annual, week-long convocation became the high point of the year when they met with those who understood their work as no one else did. They spoke in longing terms of the convocation as breathing new life into their work and giving them strength to return and resume the work.[24]

The *esprit de corps* among deaconesses, whether in daily communal living or the annual convocation, enabled these women who had relinquished home and family, fashionable clothes, and modern conveniences, to persevere in simplicity and shared purpose. They did not view themselves as separate individuals but as a sisterhood, even across national boundaries and different denominational communities. One illustration in particular encapsulates this international connection. Mina Fliedner, who carried on her father's work at the Kaiserswerth Motherhouse, was asked if she had a message of greeting for the WDO's Annual Convocation of 1904. She replied, "'No, I think I can send them no message, as I do not know them well enough, but you may tell them that I love them all in the Lord Jesus, and that while their Convocation is meeting, I shall be praying for them night and day.' . . . Two days afterwards, Sister Mina was found in her room, dead, on her knees. She

---

24. David Clark lifts up similar themes, including the importance of the annual Convocation, for the men and women in the Methodist Diaconal Order in British Methodism today. Clark, "Hallmark of the Methodist Diaconal Order," 6.5–6.6.

had passed away in the very act of prayer."[25] This portrait of a deaconess in Germany on her knees in prayer for deaconesses in the UK, women she did not know and would never meet, underscores powerfully for us today the potential strength of our international connection. Let's build on it—at the very least—by praying for each other across international borders for the revival of Methodism worldwide.

The deaconesses also set us an example of doing without for Jesus's sake so that more resources can be shared for God's work throughout Methodism. Lucy Rider Meyer took this admonition to heart and set up an organization called the "Do Without Band." It had a twofold purpose: to encourage self-denial for Jesus's sake and to raise funds for deaconess work. She explained the genesis of the organization in these words: "The Band, it was decided, should have no membership fee; and any one, informally taking the simple pledge: 'I will look about for opportunities to do without for Jesus sake,' should be a member. . . . The Motto chosen was that which has since been adopted as the general motto of the Deaconesses themselves: '*For Jesus' Sake.*'" A badge with the initials, FJS, on it was designed for members to wear, and issues of the newsletter included an envelope in which all "Do Without Money" was to be deposited for safe-keeping until it was sent to the Office at 114 Dearborn Avenue, Chicago."[26] Consider for a moment what a Methodist "Do Without Band" might accomplish today for Jesus's sake!

Unify Evangelism and Humanitarianism

Sister Elise Searle, a WDO deaconess elected by popular vote to the Board of Guardians in Norwich, engaged in political lobbying to make substantive changes to improve the food served to residents at the workhouse and to increase the supply of towels at the local hospital. "These details may seem very trivial to an outsider," Searle stated, "but they mean a great deal to the respectable poor, many of whom, through sickness and adversity, are forced to shelter their declining days in our workhouses."[27] But that is not all she did. She engaged in evangelism with the people applying to the Board of Guardians for welfare aid. As recipients waited in line to submit their aid applications, Searle would

25. "Pathetic Incident," 85.
26. Meyer, *Deaconesses*, 140–42.
27. Searle, "Notes from Norwich," 119.

slip out of the board meeting and lead them in hymns, like "Jesu, lover of my soul," or "Safe in the arms of Jesus." She explained, "Between the hymns I have a little homely talk with them, about the Jesus to whom we have been singing, and it is delightful to see some of the sin-hardened faces relax, and a new light dawn in the dim eyes, as we speak and sing of the love of our Savior."[28] In other words, she united evangelism and humanitarianism to reach people physically and spiritually.

The integration of evangelism and humanitarianism showed up in the WDO consecration service. A short statement read by the President of the Conference listed various kinds of humanitarian work that deaconesses might be called to undertake, including preaching, teaching, feeding, nursing, visiting, and rescuing. Then, the President declared that "in all this you must be true evangelists of our Lord Jesus Christ translating your Gospel into the language of personal service, that it may be the better understood, not reckoning your ministry complete till those who you serve can say, Now we believe."[29] In other words, humanitarianism and evangelism—together—helped people see the gospel at work and to believe it.

The unity of evangelism and humanitarianism might seem antiquated today. Particularly the word *evangelism* the "e" word, raises hackles or at least discomfort in many churches. In the words of a local church evangelism committee member, "The word *evangelism* kind of unnerves me and I think it unnerves a lot of people. . . . When you say 'evangelism,' people think Holy Roller."[30] Instead, many church members want to focus on humanitarianism to the neglect of evangelism. This preference comes up every time I teach an evangelism class to seminary students. Not too long ago, a well-meaning, earnest student asked this series of questions: "If the T-shirt I wore when I helped with the clean-up after the hurricane had my church's logo on it, then did I evangelize? Did I have to say anything about Jesus or the gospel? Doesn't the church's name speak for itself and identify me as a Christian engaged in hurricane relief work?" Inevitably then, someone quotes St. Francis's famous quip (which many scholars do not think he ever said): "preach the gospel and when necessary use words." As Jonathan Merritt explains to those quick to invoke the saint to confirm their bias against evangelism, "Words are far more necessary than this

---

28. Searle, "A Unique Congregation," 136.
29. "Order of Service for the Ordination of Deaconesses," 12.
30. Sider et al., *Churches That Make a Difference*, 64.

quote leads us to believe. The Christian faith would not exist—it cannot exist—without words."[31]

Still, what my student expressed in her question is confirmed by Robert Wuthnow, who conducted a comprehensive study of churches in the US and found powerful "social pressures to emphasize service rather than evangelism."[32] Nevertheless, as a church leader in Wuthnow's study commented, "Evangelism is part of the Christian faith. It might be intrusive and it might step on the toes of some folks who don't think it's right, but it's there and we have to recognize that it's there."[33] Certainly, the deaconesses did, and for them, attending to evangelism and humanitarianism was a seamless venture.

Move Out Beyond the Church Walls

> There are important classes of the community, which, by the hard demands of modern society, are practically excluded from anything like regular attendance at the House of God. Such are the police, the railway men, and the firemen. If the demands of the modern social system are to be met, such men must surrender much of the happy freedom of the Sabbath holiday. In such circumstances, how is their religious life and sympathy to be maintained?[34]

How indeed was their religious life to be maintained when a worker's livelihood required them to work on the Sabbath? Enter the deaconess who recognized the conundrum and brought the religious gathering to them, often in their place of work. One WDO deaconess described her resolve in these marching orders, we "shall go to them, not wait for them to come; it shall suit the convenience of *their* work; not demand that it shall bend to ours; it shall provide for them religious services and influences which shall fit into the corners and crannies of *their* lives."[35] So, for the firefighters who had to stay at the station on the Sabbath to be ready in case of a fire, deaconesses came to the station and held services there.

Listed below are seven more examples of religious gatherings, initiated and staffed by WDO deaconesses, that convened outside the

---

31. Merritt, *Learning to Speak God from Scratch*, 49.
32. Wuthnow, *Boundless Faith*, 242.
33. Wuthnow, *Boundless Faith*, 241–42.
34. *Highways and Hedges*, 212.
35. *Highways and Hedges*, 212.

brick-and-mortar church and were held at convenient times for each audience:

For female factory workers in Liverpool, a deaconess opened a dining room in the basement of the Liverpool Mission Hall, where on their lunch break they could eat and rest inside rather than out in the elements and make tea with the hot water provided. The deaconess joined them to sing with them and talk about Jesus.[36]

For ballerinas performing at the local theater, a deaconess arranged permission to meet them in their dressing area, where she hosted a nice tea. After tea, she led them in singing hymns followed by a short talk. Being "behind the scenes" where the ballerinas spent so much of their time gave the deaconess a better understanding of their daily lives.[37]

For children in Rotherhithe, an impoverished area in London, a deaconess planned "activities, including 'play' hours and guilds for both boys and girls where they could use books and games and see lantern shows."[38] She also served more than 2500 breakfasts to school-aged children who would otherwise go without breakfast to school.[39]

For young women—fifteen years of age and older—who labored in Nottingham warehouses and factories, a deaconess organized a weekly evening gathering intended simply to bring joy and light into lives filled during the workday with "long, grey, monotonous drudgery." She cleared the schoolroom of desks and chairs and filled it with lights, table games, music, singing, and sewing. She noticed that some of the girls looked pale from their factory work, so she started a Rambling Club and took them on countryside hikes every other week. "One gets to know and understand them better, for it gives the opportunity of a chat about their homes and factory life. . . . we are hoping this year to take a few excursions by train, and even hope for a glimpse of the sea, many of them not having yet seen it."[40]

For construction workers far from home while building a London hospital, a deaconess held a dinner-hour service. "For nearly two years, they have held a simple meeting—talking to the men, singing to them, praying with them."[41]

36. "Some Wesley Deaconesses and Their Work," 77.
37. "Letter from Leeds," 154.
38. For more on lantern shows, see 155n8.
39. Graham, *Saved to Serve*, 37.
40. Harbord, "Girls' Clubs," 19–20.
41. "Dinner-Hour Service," 260.

For young women working in a large woolen mill in Bradford, a deaconess came at dinner time with hymn sheets to hold a brief service. Some 60–70 girls sat on improvised seats to sing, hear a short talk, and pray until the bell rang. Then, "the machinery starts; the girls take their places at the looms, and all is clatter and noise."[42]

For travelers in a busy railway station, "from seven each morning till late in the evening, she [a deaconess] is here to lead the blind, to help the lame, to advise the wandering, to comfort the sick, to protect girls and women, and to speak, as opportunity offers, a word for Jesus."[43]

Today these outside-the-church-wall gatherings might be labeled "Fresh Expressions." Ever since the 2004 Mission Shaped Church report from a working group of the Church of England's Mission and Public Affairs Council introduced the term, a growing movement of practitioners and pioneers have formed Fresh Expressions of Church in many countries. These ministries revolve around the foundational belief in God's prevenient grace, as Wesleyans understand it, that God is already at work in the world in advance of our efforts. Michael Adam Beck and Jorge Acevedo tease out the connection between the early Methodist movement and Fresh Expressions. Like the Methodist pioneers, "Fresh Expressions is a form of disruptive innovation. It puts us directly in the living rooms, running groups, restaurants, fitness clubs, tattoo parlors, and social spheres where people are doing life together, connected by flows. Jesus loves the people of those communities, and he created the church as an instrument to reach them."[44]

Moving out beyond the church walls circumscribed everything about the deaconess movement from the outset. Long before the Fresh Expressions movement, deaconesses set up sacred spaces in courthouse waiting rooms, fire stations, factory floors, and railway stations. At the same time, however, not so fresh were the services put on by them because they repeated nineteenth-century revivalism *ad nauseum*, relying on the standard gospel hymns followed by an evangelistic talk. Nonetheless, deaconesses showed up among the poor, with factory workers, and alongside children in poverty, thus making church visible beyond the walls.

---

42. "White-Striped Veil," 71.
43. "Mission Field at Home & Abroad," 232.
44. Beck and Acevedo, *Field Guide to Methodist Fresh Expressions*, 72.

Share Knowledge and Experience Across a Worldwide Network

The Wesley Deaconess Order (WDO) badge, even in its petite size, captured this fifth and final element, which is the generous and free sharing of knowledge and experience, what we now call intellectual property. On the reverse side of the badge, three words were inscribed: For Jesus' Sake. These words were the motto of the Chicago Training School (CTS), and as such, they represented the US deaconess movement on the WDO badge. On the front of the badge was a dove, representing the deaconess work at Kaiswerswerth in Germany.[45] Added together, on this one small badge, three deaconess communities, three nations, two languages, and two ecclesial traditions (Methodist and Lutheran) were symbolized. Truly, this one small token from the WDO quintessentially encapsulated the sharing of knowledge and experience across the international network of the Methodist—and ecumenical—deaconess movement.

Further, this international exchange occurred without any concern about plagiarism or the need for extended footnotes to cite the source. Any idea or document produced in one place was freely exchanged, as is evident in the following examples:

- The WDO consecration service was copied, with some modifications, from the Kaiswerswerth service.[46]
- *Flying Leaves*, the title of the WDO monthly newsletter, was the English translation of Kaiserswerth's journal, *Fliegende Blätter*.[47]
- Deaconesses in the US and the UK followed the daily Bible reading plan set up by deaconesses at Kaiserswerth. An aggregate in 1906 of deaconesses in these three countries added up to "twelve hundred Deaconesses at Kaiserswerth, the Methodist Episcopal Deaconesses of America, and the Wesley Deaconess Order, with many Associates and friends, are all united in such a spirit of faith and prayer and meditation as will be produced when we daily tread together the same sacred path of Bible Reading."[48]

---

45. "True," 102.
46. "Recognition Service," 178.
47. Bradfield, *Life of the Reverend Thomas Bowman Stephenson*, 407.
48. "Our Bible Reading Table for 1906," 14.

- Editors of deaconess newsletters freely published articles from other newsletters without concern for copyright or plagiarism. Stephenson issued this statement in acknowledgment of this free exchange: "We are glad that Mrs. Meyer feels free to reproduce in its pages, occasional paragraphs from *Highways and Hedges*; and we are still more glad to know that we are welcome to use anything from *The Message* which may be useful and opportune for our purpose."[49]

Deaconesses not only believed but also put into practice the sentiment that we are all part of one movement, so let us do all we can to make each other better. Feel free to use our consecration service and adapt it for your context. Feel free to use any articles published in our newsletter that will help secure support and enthusiasm in your context for deaconess work. Feel free to come stay in our deaconess home when you are in town, and so on. Even more amazing to consider is that this international sharing of resources occurred before email, internet, cell phone, and social media. Deaconesses regularly and freely communicated with each other nationally and internationally so that the work of God everywhere would be strengthened and invigorated. Imagine for a moment the impact of such an open-access approach to sharing knowledge and experience around the international network of Methodism today.

In closing, I contend that this courageous, always contested, nearly forgotten international women's movement holds the key, if followed assiduously, to the reawakening, reimagining, and revival of Methodism worldwide as a vital force in our time. So, let us follow their lead and practice these five steps:

> Unite knowledge and vital piety
>
> Live simply, even communally
>
> Unify evangelism and humanitarianism
>
> Move out beyond the church walls
>
> Share knowledge and experience across a worldwide network

---

49. "Our American Sisters," 234.

Appendix A

DIARY EXTRACTS— ELIZABETH ANN PITTS

Overview

THE EXTRACTS FROM ANNIE [Elizabeth Anne] Pitts's diary narrate her experiences beginning in 1900 when she is a student at Mewburn House, the Wesleyan Deaconess Order (WDO) training school in London. Her mornings begin with chores—what she labels as Time Table—then she lists reading assignments and lecture topics. Lecture topics range widely; on one day, she practices bandaging and studies for a theology class, then she writes down "prophecies from the Old Testament, relating to the birth, sufferings, and death of our Lord." Entries from the afternoons describe in detail her practical work experiences as she visits the poor and the sick in the neighborhood near the training school. Many evenings, she helps with religious services in Gordon Hall Mission.

At several points in the diary, there are marginalia written in a different handwriting from hers. The following comment gives the impression that keeping a diary is a requirement for Mewburn House students: "An excellent Diary, well written in every way. I am much pleased by the way in which you record your visits. A.E.G."[1] After she completes the training at Mewburn House, she receives an assignment to work in the Methodist circuit at Denaby, in south Yorkshire. This is the shortest portion of the diary. The last entry in October 1903 is brief yet poignant; it depicts in

---

1. These initials belong to Rev. A. E. Gregory, who gave lectures on the Bible to Mewburn House students. Graham, *Saved to Serve*, 305.

seven words the devastating impact of the Denaby Colliery strike on the community: "Strike–scattered the people/Poverty–still suffering."

Included with the diary is a letter from her daughter regarding the donation of her mother's diary. The letter, dated September 18, 1975, confirms that her mother left the WDO before completing her probation to get married.

> I am so glad you would like the diary. Please do not send the postage as it gives me such pleasure to do this and feel that the diary is of some use.... Of course when she married she had to leave the Order, but they could not get another Deaconess. The [Denaby] Circuit invited mother to go on with her work and the Circuit would pay her. I think she said the wage then for a Deaconess was £1 per week. Mother continued in this work for 18 months after her marriage.
>
> Yours sincerely,
> Edith Goman (Miss)

1900 Friday Jan. 5th

I arrived at Mewburn House[2] about 3.30 p.m. and was received very kindly by all, it cheered me greatly to meet one familiar face amongst the number; (Sister Rose) notwithstanding the natural depression of leaving lov'd ones ill at home; yet I realized I was in the atmosphere of love and true sympathy. About 8 o/c Sister Elizabeth,[3] with Sister Elsa kindly accompanied me to a prayer meeting at Gordon Hall;[4] Miss Ayles[5] led the meeting; God's presence was very real, and with playing the Harmonium,[6] and engaging in prayer I felt thoroughly at home in the midst of strangers....

2. Mewburn House, opened in 1890, was the first WDO Deaconess House. When Pitts arrived in 1900, it was located at 84 Bonner Road in London.

3. Sister Elizabeth Barraclough was the Sister-in-Charge of Mewburn House in 1900.

4. Gordon Hall was a Wesleyan mission room on Globe Road, Mile End (in the East End of London). It was formerly a Methodist church known as Globe Road Chapel. "Acknowledgments and Appeals," *The Methodist Times* (June 5, 1890) 570. I am grateful to Martin Wellings for this reference.

5. Sister Ayles, a WDO deaconess who died in 1946, bequeathed a row of houses to be left for the financial benefit of older, retired deaconesses. Graham, *Saved to Serve*, 323.

6. Also called a reed or pump organ, it is a keyboard instrument that can be foot or hand-pumped.

Sunday 7th

Time table.[7] Attended service at Victoria Park Church[8] in the morning, and Covenant Service[9] in the afternoon. About 6.15 p.m. I went to the Cripple Church played the instrument, and gave an address from St. John's Gospel 11.9.[10] The children paid great attention, one sang a solo, "The Beautiful River,"[11] it was a touching sight, to see one so frail in body, using the small talent given her, by singing the praises of God. I never remember looking upon such a number of sad, and deformed little ones before, the sight moved my whole being in love and compassion for the welfare of their precious souls.

Monday 8th

Time Table until 10 o/c. About 3 p.m. Miss Ayles and I went to Gordon Hall, to cut up and prepare for the Mother's Tea Meeting; on our way there we called to see Mrs. Allen. She was greatly disappointed at not being able to go to the Tea; her husband was just recovering from Bronchitis, therefore she was obliged to finish peeling a sack of onions, to raise sufficient money to pay the rent; that same evening; on making enquiries I found she was paid 1/8 per sack (1 cnt]) 2d carriage to the factory, leaving 1/6 nett profit, which would take 3 days in spare time.

At 6 o/c the Mothers arrived in large numbers (about 100.) and thoroughly enjoyed the provisions prepared for them, after giving thanks they all sang very heartily "What a Friend We Have in Jesus," then Sister Dora Stephenson[12] kindly entertained them, with the help of a few children from the "Home;"[13] one recitation in particular (given by a little boy) highly amused the Mothers, I forget the title but it finished by asking God to come and finish the baby, as it had not any teeth. About 7.45 we handed oranges round to all in the room; then I was obliged to leave,

---

7. Time Table refers to the daily chores assigned to the students.

8. This church is located just south of Victoria Park in London's East End.

9. John Wesley introduced in 1755 the annual covenant renewal service to be used on or near January 1 in Methodist societies.

10. 'Jesus answered, "Are there not twelve hours of daylight? Those who walk during the day do not stumble, because they see the light of this world."'

11. The hymn, "Shall We Gather By the River," was composed by Robert Lowry (1826–1899).

12. Dora Stephenson was the daughter of the Wesley Deaconess Order (WDO) founder, Thomas Bowman Stephenson, and the first consecrated WDO deaconess.

13. The Children's Home was founded by Thomas Bowman Stephenson in 1869.

having to lead the Womens Bible Class, there was a nice little instrument in the room, which put more life into our singing, we took the subject of Prayer, and had a very blessed time.

Tuesday 9th

Time table until 10 o/c, then we met in the study for reading (alternately aloud) "Praying and Working,"[14] we spent a most pleasant as well as profitable time together. 2.30. Miss Ayles and I commenced visiting, we first called at Mrs. Pope's Queens Buildings found her suffering from dropsy,[15] her son had been out of work 10 weeks, the younger one for a few weeks, and most of her husbands small earnings were spent in drink, on asking if he could not be persuaded to sign the pledge, she replied that he has done so many times, and wept like a child, then the craving for it would gain the mastery, she cried bitterly while telling us she was brought up by good parents; and to look upon her little ones, and think they would soon be left to the mercies of a drunken Father, was more than she could bear, after speaking to her of Christ as her Saviour and Friend, Miss Ayles offered prayer; I was glad to find her sons were total abstainers.[16] . . .

Thursday 11th

From 10 a.m. to 11.30 we read from the "Pilgrims Progress,"[17] each of us taking up the different characters, which made it most interesting, and more easy to understand. . . . [Visited] Mrs. Growhurst No. 4 Harrold St., she seemed very cast-down, her sons had been out of work for some time: like a Mother she did all in her power to help them, so arranged with a hospital to scrub the floors so many days a week, instead of it really being a help, she has been obliged to spend most of it for doctoring; her strength gave way under the extra pressure; I read a few verses and prayed with her, she said she was glad to have someone to tell her trouble, and hoped to see me again very shortly.

---

14. Stevenson, *Praying and Working*, includes two chapters on Kaiserswerth.

15. An older word for edema, a condition in which excess fluid collects in bodily tissues.

16. In the margin in pencil is written the following: "This is too detailed. Leave out unimportant things to make room for what is of value."

17. John Bunyan's *The Pilgrim's Progress*, published in 1678, is an allegory about Christian, the main character, who journeys from this world (the City of Destruction) to heaven (the Celestial City).

No. 8 in the same St. was also on my list by mistake, but the woman asked if I would be kind enough to go in, as her niece was very ill, after offering a short prayer, and reading a few verses at once, so as not to weary her, to my joy I found she was trusting in Jesus, she buried her Mother the week previous; her little girl was in the Childrens Hospital, some time back she lost a child by death, & a little delicate infant – 14 months was by her side in bed, her Aunt said her life has been one of continual trouble, but they were thankful to say her husband was a steady man although his wages were small. The last I visited was Mrs. Maynard 25 Ash St., had a good time there also. . . .

Tuesday 23rd

Time table until 9.30, when Sister Elizabeth gave a most helpful "Bible Lesson" from first epistle general of John; I was greatly bless'd while studying what "Manner of Love."[18] 2.30. Sister Rose and I visited the "Infirmary." I was struck with the size and cleanliness of the place going in, but coming out the marked difference of expression on the face of those that were Christians and those that were not, impressed me greatly. A young married man was suffering from "Consumption of the bowels,"[19] it was sad to see him looking so ill and ghastly, but he was peacefully trusting in Christ as his Saviour which was expressed in his countenance. A dear aged Christian was ill in bed, had buried her husband 4 days previous, but knowing he was safely landed in the "Home" above she promised not to dwell upon her loss and loneliness, but to think of Heaven and the time when they would reunite.

Another woman had been burned by a lamp, one eye was burnt out, ear off, and face altogether in a dreadful cond[ition.] She said she had not a friend in the world, and prayed that God would take her from her sufferings. Others too could be mentio[ned] who were happy in the love of God. Then one is led to think of the reverse, the most sad sight of all, not because of their bodily sufferings (which were slight compared with others) but their spiritual darkness, knowing nothing of a Fathers love, and forgiveness, having no higher wish than to do their own will.

While walking through the corridors to special cases, I noticed a large number of wishful faces, and how readily they received a card (with a printed prayer & verses from Scripture) from us as we passed

18. 1 John 3:1.
19. This symptom came about from tuberculosis.

hurriedly along. Also how eagerly they listened to every word which was spoken to the one we went to visit, it seemed as if some were hungering for the "Bread of Life,"[20] one could not help but wish for time to speak to each one personally.

Wednesday 24th

Time table. 9.30. "First Aid to the Wounded." Sister Ruth questioned us on the 1st chapter, number & names of bones. 11.15 a.m. Preparation for Theological Lecture. Visiting the whole of the afternoon, no special case, but felt greatly bless'd in the work. At 8 o/c went to Gordon Hall for Preaching service, Mr. Chase was appointed to preach, he and I were the only ones there until 8.30, Mr. Ferguson and two others came so we had a prayer meeting. It was suggested that instead of ordinary Preaching, a Mission Service should be held, thinking it would be more likely to attract the working men.

Thursday 25th

Time table until 9.30. Lesson on the "Political divisions of Canada and their products." 10.30 private devotion. Afterwards preparation for Pastoral Lecture. Called at 10 different homes during afternoon, rather discouraging, it being so difficult to get an entrance inside, first time of calling with the majority, but in some cases received a hearty welcome. A nurse from the "Chest Hospital"[21] came to tea with us; and accompanied Miss Fordham and I to "Welcome Lodging House,"[22] she read the last parable in the XV. chapter of St. Luke's Gospel,[23] sang a solo, and gave her "Maiden Speech."[24] Said she, My dear brothers, I address you thus, because I am only just groping my way in the darkness. Two years ago I came to the "Chest Hospital" as a probationer nurse because I did not like the idea of living an aimless life, and I thought to be a nurse was noble & good. It was very different to what I had expected, the "patients" very much tried me, the Matron would speak cross, all seemed dark; until I met Sister Caroline Gregory, she led me into the light. Since then my life has been much brighter, and instead of being

20. John 6:35.
21. Tuberculosis sanatorium.
22. An inexpensive, pay-by-night hostel with many beds crowded into each room.
23. Parable of the Prodigal Son.
24. The first speech given by a person.

discontented and irritable, I now do all my work as I think would please Jesus Christ; will you men try and do the same? She then closed with an earnest appeal that they would love God, and live for Him. Miss Fordham sang "Come unto Me,"[25] also spoke from those words. Gods Spirit was working powerfully, one man wished for prayer to be offered up on his behalf. I would fain to have stayed longer, but was obliged to close the meeting because of the late hour. . . .

Wednesday 7th

Time table. Medical practice. Private devotion. Preparation for Theological Lecture. District visiting. One house out of the nine I visited, gave me special interest. The Mother, (an elderly person) seemed so thankful for a little spiritual intercourse. Her three daughters were making the uppers of boots and shoes, for which they received 1d¼ per pair. The three working very hard could manage 6 dz in a day. The eldest daughter had married a man in good way of business; he died leaving her with two children. She struggled hard and carried on the business for four years when she was obliged to give it up at a great loss; and come back to her own trade. The younger sister was engaged to a soldier, now in Africa. Notwithstanding the cloud of darkness overhead, love was in the "home," after speaking to them of a greater Love, they said they would try to attend service at Gordon Hall. Afterwards visited a young woman with child about twelve months old, her face was quite disfigured with crying. Her husband had left a few days previous, being summoned to the "War."[26] I felt it a great privilege to be sent to deliver a few words of comfort in time of need. . . .

Tuesday 13th

Time table. Bible lesson by Sister Elizabeth. Medical lesson, circulation of blood, sinews &c.

Visited Fire Station. Mrs. Lambert & Mrs. Burgess were out, but was greatly bless'd visiting the other four. Mrs Herm promised that her little girl shall go to Sunday school with me. Mrs. O was just in the midst of washing & changing her dress when baby awoke, so I nursed the little one until her Mother was ready to take her, then read from my Testament. Leaving the Fire Station, I was led towards James St; I knocked at 15 Landsdale Place. Mrs. Blackmon was her name, she was not in the habit of attending a place

25. Matt 11:28.
26. The Boer War (1899–1902).

of worship, but her boy (who was at home ill) had been a scholar in G. [ordon] Hall Sunday School for 4 ½ years. He first stayed away through ill health, was not visited, therefore was easily persuaded by a companion to attend Church, where he was invited to join the choir.

Returning home I passed a young woman standing on a door step when I was strongly impressed to speak to her, so went back offered her a paper, and invited her to the service on Sunday, she replied I don't believe in any religion. I said have you ever tried the religion of the Lord Jesus? Blushing she said, I went to Sunday school when a child and belonged to the Band of Hope & have kept my pledge.[27] After a little talk she gave consent for me to visit her again, saying she would be at home any afternoon.

Mr. White invited me to his class members annual Tea as he wanted a player to make the meeting brighter, we had a great deal of singing, solos, Testimonies, and prayers. After the meeting I had the pleasure of pointing a sinner to Christ. She was a very respectable young woman, her husband was wounded in battle Dec 15, left for 10 hours in the sun. Boers had stripped him of everything.[28] He is now in a convalescent home in Jersey; and his wife had the bullet in her purse that was cut out of his thigh. Noticing the expression on her face during the meeting, I felt certain she was in trouble about her soul, and although not knowing her, was led to pray for her salvation. While the friends were going home, I said to Mr. White, do you know if that young woman is a Christian? because I'm afraid she is not, he had the same impression and spoke to her, then she said I will give myself to Christ now. The Light soon came, and with a thankful heart praised God, and prayed for the salvation of her husband. . . .

Good Friday 13th

About 8.30 went to Approach Road Schoolroom to help prepare the Breakfast. By 9.30 the poor & aged came in large numbers. Mr. Tunbridge had a quantity of eggs given him from some Lincolnshire farmers; some had 2 & 3 each. Mrs. Tunbridge was kept busy boiling the eggs. There was also a plentiful supply of hot cross buns & bread & butter. The tables were decorated with flowers, which we had sent from our homes for the occasion. They all had a bouquet to take away with them. After breakfast followed a bright meeting, addresses were given by Rev. F. Tunbridge & Mr.

27. See 155n7.
28. See n26.

Lock, the latter said if there were any present that do not possess a Bible, would they give their names to Sister Frances when the meeting was over, and he would supply them with one. "Blind Charlie" greatly helped by his singing & playing. Although naturally blind he can see spiritually. I shall never forget hearing his earnest appeal to the people, followed by singing "There is sunlight in my soul."[29] It was most inspiring. . . .

Tuesday 22nd

Visited 6 of the most distressed homes in our district, no doubt the pouring rain added to the dreariness & gloom. In one attic was a delicate Mother, eight children, eldest daughter looked very ill as she sat in the midst of dirt & rags helping to make matchboxes. A quantity were in front of the fire to dry, a little child of three years was placing the boxes together. Another woman I have visited several times during her illness, wept bitterly while she told me of her past life. When a girl she had Christian training & married comfortably. Having all she desired in this life, she neglected the house of God and gradually drifted away. One trouble after another came, her husband died. It was not until earthly joys had faded away that she returned unto God for salvation. She has found the peace long sought for, & a few weeks ago became a member of Society at our Mission. I was greatly impressed by what she said, she simply neglected salvation, but her heart is filled with gratitude to God for his long suffering & lovingkindness towards her. . . .

Wednesday 13th

5 visits & 6 calls. First bought eggs &c to take to 3 special cases. Mrs. W. is over 70 yrs of age, but does not look much over 50, she has such a bright smiling face, one would think she is a stranger to trouble. But her husband is very infirm through old age and rheumatism. Her daughter (now over 30 yrs) has been an imbecile from 5 yrs of age, owing to an apoplectic fit, unable to do anything. Therefore the Mother has to work very hard to make ends meet. Mrs. H. has been confined to her room for many months through rheumatism, she is alone with the exception of her granddaughter who goes in at times to attend to her. I read a bright story, & for a few minutes she seemed to forget her sufferings, &

---

29. The lyrics for this hymn, "There Is Sunshine In My Soul Today," were composed by Eliza Edmunds Hewitt (1851–1920).

laughed quite heartily. 6 to 7.30 household duties. Played harmonium for Preaching Service. . . .

Tuesday 26th

Miss Sinclair[30] went with me visiting this afternoon. Mrs. Osborn was the first. We called to see if she would have her baby christened on Sunday. She readily consented. Mrs. T & her daughter were (as usual) busy making match boxes for 2 ¼ per gross; by working very hard & help from the children they can make 6 or 7 gross daily. Her little boy 2 ½ yrs was in such a dreadful temper that he turned black in the face & every minute we expected to see him in a fit. The Mother said neither she nor her husband could manage him. Thought that was a sad state of things. It was impossible to have prayer, so I just spoke a few words of counsel & comfort. After visiting Mr. C. we went to the fire station. Class Meeting at 8 p.m. . . .

August 9th

After a months holiday, one feels glad to go back to work once again. . . . After spending many happy hours in the old "Homestead" with my lov'd ones, and breathing in the pure country air, I came back with fresh vigour to enter into the many duties that were awaiting me. I was glad to receive a letter of welcome from our Sister in charge as she was away for her holidays. Miss Sinclair & the two other Sisters gave me a hearty reception. The next morning I set to work with such earnestness & brightness that Sister Ethel remarked "She did not believe I was the heart-home sick." It seemed strange being so few in number for 3 weeks, but we were busy with a great variety of domestic duties so as to have the house thoroughly cleaned before our Sister returned. Therefore did not visit regularly each afternoon although there were several special cases that required a great deal of attention. One of our Mothers who is far gone in consumption, was lying on a chair bedstead by the side of a broken window. The bed linen one would think had never been washed. Everywhere was in a most filthy condition. I asked if she would allow one to go the next morning to clean up. At first the poor woman consented then afterward asked me not to, as her married daughter had promised to come the following day. I tried to show her the necessity of a clean room as she required all the

---

30. As noted in the Introduction, Isabel Sinclair came from New Zealand to do her deaconess training at Mewburn House.

pure air she could get. The next time I called it was pleasure to see the change that had taken place even the grate was cleaned and the hearth stone whitened. Ms S. said it would have been cleaned before but they were afraid it would give her cold until she assured her daughter that Sister said it would be far better for her health. I have been in several times sense to give her nourishment and necessary attention as her husband and daughter are away at work until evening. Arthur her youngest boy, who is about 10 yrs of age; is a very delicate lad but always carries sunshine in his face. He does his best to help his Mother between & after school hours; were it not for him she would be alone all day. Each evening was taken up with meetings there being several extra ones to attend during the absence of other "sisters." We had a most successful "Social" at Gordon Hall on the 20th and Sister Grace gave her farewell address. Mr. Houseman thanked her for the help she had given in the Sunday School & especially for the class of girls she had tutored for a Scripture exam . . . one had gained a prize & two received certificates. Therefore she had the assurance her labour had not been in vain. . . .

We had the pleasure of entertaining Sister Dorothy for a few days. Then there was the homecoming of Sister Elizabeth which gave joy to us all. The following week was one continual excitement and rush. Sisters coming for a day or two. Some only for a few hours busy packing their boxes and saying "Good bye" before leaving us to go to their different appointments in circuit work. . . .

Wednesday 24th

Paid 17 visits on a block of buildings & 5 calls. For one room sat 3 women making the uppers of boots, complete with buttons & buttonholes for which they are paid 2 ½ per pair, instead of 10 as when they first commenced. Seeing how very busy they were I gave them a [sic] (or rather repeated & invited them to service on Sunday. In another room were 2 sisters, on entering I said you are busy! one replied that's just why we ask you in because we dare not hinder from our work. Their past life had been a sad one. They earn their livelihood by tailoring. The younger one of the two is evidently in consumption besides a weak heart sometimes obliged to keep to her bed. Mrs. N goes out to work putting the padding in tea cosies which is injurious to one with such a weak chest. Her husband spends most of his earnings in drink & cruelly treats his wife. Today she was too ill to go to her work. She wept bitterly as she looked at her poor children.

Mrs. R had a babe in her arms only 3 weeks old & 5 little ones which she grieved over because she had not bodily strength to attend to them. A young girl about 19 yrs of age works for the press her hours are from 1.30 am until 10 o/c. I was glad to have such a Saviour & friend as our Lord Jesus to recommend to those who are crushed by sickness, sorrow, & poverty for He alone can make the wounded spirit whole....

Friday 2nd

For sometime "Mother" McDougal has not been able to attend our missionary prayer mtg at 5.30 so Sister Elizabeth arranged for us to each take our turns in leading it; commencing with Sister Isabel Sinclair. She read a report from Sister Christian[31] in New Zealand which was followed by earnest prayers & singing....

Tuesday 11th

After leading the Ladies Class, to my surprise a farewell meeting had been arranged in the school room. A large number of members were present. At the close they presented me with a testimonial & leather writing satchel. I felt too overcome to say much. The whole of the week was a continual strain, with saying "goodbye."[32] ...

January 1901

Friday 4th

Received a letter from Dr. Stephenson informing me that I was stationed at Denaby, Yorks.[33] It was full of Christian sympathy & friendly counsel. Wrote to the Minister at once!...

---

31. Sister Christian Hughes, WDO deaconess, was sent by Thomas Bowman Stephenson to help establish Methodist deaconess work in New Zealand. Hughes was responsible for sending New Zealanders Isabel Sinclair and Frances Cannon to Mewburn House. Graham, *Saved to Serve*, 212–16.

32. This entry gives the information that Pitts completed her training at Mewburn House and would soon be sent out to work at a local church. At the end of this entry, the words, "Fare Well," are written in the margin in a different handwriting from Pitts's.

33. The town of Denaby, where Pitts was assigned to circuit work, is in south Yorkshire.

Saturday 12th

Left home at 11:30 a.m. We saw H.R.H. The Prince of Wales[34] at Kettering Station about 1:30.

Arrived at Sheffield soon after 4 p.m., wrote home while in the waiting room. I posted it at the station. Reached Conisbrough Station about 6 p.m. Miss H— came to meet me. While walking from the station I wondered what kind of hole I had landed in. The road was rough, up hill & down hill, fearfully dirty & very dark. But as soon as I entered the house, I felt at home with such a warm welcome.

Sunday 13th

New experience attending chapel in my first circuit. Attended prayer meeting at 5:30 p.m.

After preaching service, was introduced to the members of the congregation, so had to mount the rostrum & say a few words. A young man decided for Christ on his way home from chapel. . . .

Thursday 17th

I was very much amused with the blunt manner of the people; one woman said, "Come on in, I've heard about you," and another, "Well, I like the looks on you & believe you're just the one for here." . . .They [the Catholics] are strong in numbers therefore the work is not easy amongst such a class, & the majority do not attend a place of worship. Class meeting at 7 p.m. . . .

Wednesday 23rd

Rev. Mr. S— came about 4 o/c so as to have a little conversation about the work before tea.

At 6 p.m. I commenced a Catechumen Class. 14 present. They stayed to the Preaching Service & greatly helped with the singing. Mr. S— appropriate sermon for the occasion, referring to the sad bereavement the nation were now passing through in the death of our much-beloved Queen[35] & gave some interesting incidents from her home life & love for Methodism. . . .

---

34. Albert Edward, the Prince of Wales and the heir to the British throne, would become King Edward VII upon the death of Queen Victoria on January 22, 1901, only 10 days after Pitts saw him at the train station.

35. Queen Victoria (1819–1901).

October 1903

... Our little society has had a hard struggle the last 18 months. During the 12 mo[nth] strike,[36] many left, others came & went the population still seems very unsettled. Some do not like the place, others cannot stand the work. But the depression in the Glass Works these last few months seems to effect us even more than the strike. . . .

    Strike–scattered the people
    Poverty–still suffering

---

36. The Denaby Colliery Strike was "a dispute between the miners and the Management regarding what they got paid to remove waste material on the coal face." https://www.conisbroughheritage.com/bag-muck-strike.

Appendix B

DIARY EXTRACTS—
THIRZA MASTERS

Overview

MOST OF THE EXTRACTS from Thirza Masters's diary narrate her experiences while serving as a WDO deaconess in Cardiff, Wales, from 1893–1897. Her deaconess work takes place in the Cardiff dock area known as Tiger Bay, so named, according to Masters, "from the tigerlike propensities of some of the inhabitants." Descriptions of her outreach encounters with Tiger Bay inhabitants, like John W and his wife, Mrs W, are the most substantial parts of her diary.

Another noteworthy portion recounts the weeks she spent in the Birmingham Hospital, what she refers to as "the prison," while undergoing the infamous "rest cure," often prescribed for women in the late nineteenth and early twentieth centuries who had a nervous breakdown. These entries are brief yet poignant. Masters describes the debilitating impact of the prescribed total isolation; the one exception, "her sunbeam," is the massage nurse. "One day a sunbeam entered my room and day by day that Sunbeam came. It was my Massage nurse. She came like an Angel dropped from the skies. So bright, so pure, so fresh, so radiant."

Masters completes the rest cure; however, it is unclear whether her health ever fully returns. She re-enters deaconess work briefly, then she has to leave again for more rest. The diary ends with her deaconess appointment to Hednesford, a mining town in Staffordshire, which she clearly dislikes, describing it as "the dullest & ugliest of towns. No trees.

No birds. No falls. Uninteresting." Her diary ends in 1910 shortly after she arrives in Hednesford.

24 Londoun Square Oct 1st 1894[37]

[1893]

Dec. My first visiting of 'Tiger Bay' Cardiff Docks.[38] I entered a street a notably bad one being mostly houses of ill-fame—Peel St. A woman stood half-dressed with yellow hair streaming down her back, crying, "I am glad you have come to us as there is no one to care about our souls," some such words she said. "I'll come for you next Sunday to go to the service with me," I said. She promised to accompany me.

Sun. yes Mrs__the above was ready dressed to come with me. She wept aloud during the service. Tears of remorse more than penitence, for she continued her drinking ways & was there under the influence of Drink. (Found Mrs__a few days later in a sober state willing to give up Drink.

At the same service a notable bad character Dan Rees was led to come in being very miserable. He had figured in the great Streetcar case of the Hotel d'Marl[39] which gave the Police & Civil authorities such trouble.... He had been one of the ring-leaders of a gang of bad men....This night he heard the words of the Preacher "Come unto me & I will give you rest."[40] He came & was converted. It is not exaggerating that he has since been the reason of bringing hundreds into God's house.

Sat. Mrs__is going on better, quite reformed. "Speak to her," she said pointing to another woman in her house "ask her to give up Drink," she is in trouble, her husband has not arrived from sea & she fears mischief

---

37. This date is written on the first page of her bound diary; however, Masters actually began deaconess work in Cardiff a year prior in 1893. This earlier date is confirmed in her list of deaconess appointments on the diary's last page and by the following statement she wrote about halfway through the diary: "Oct. 1st 1894–It is just a year since I came to Cardiff to commence work in connection with the Loudonere Sq. Mission." I moved the 1893 portion of the diary to the beginning to put it in chronological order.

38. In the late nineteenth century, this area of Cardiff had the nickname, "Tiger Bay." With its proximity to the docks, sailors from around the world lodged there and frequented the many taverns, boarding houses, dancehalls, and brothels.

39. Local men in Cardiff devised the Hotel de Marl scheme in order to evade the 1881 Sunday Closing Act.

40. Matt 11:28.

that he has got into bad company. "Yes said Mrs Williams I fear he has lost his money." My pledge book was forthcoming. Mrs W signed pledge. I didn't know that she was an inebriate. A few days later I called at Mrs W's house in Peel St. It was too true. J. W. had been drugged at Hamburg [Germany] & robbed of £17. He managed to get home, but was penniless.

Sat. 16th I reasoned with him & he signed pledge. Calling during evening I found he was ready dressed to come to Temp.[erance] Concert. He walked along with me, I was a mite along side the tall, swarthy, fine, broad-shouldered Yankee.' He enjoyed Concert.

Sun. 17th Standing next morning in my sitting room a tall figure darkened window passing by. To any arrangement it was John W. dressed in his best going into morning service. In the evening his wife & he were at service the 1st time in their lives together. Before they had accompanied each other to the Public House. Both seemed impressed & when Rev. F invited anxious ones to come out into resting to my joy, John W stood up, looked at his wife to come along, but she was not willing, resisting the Spirit she remained seated & so he sat down again. As long as he was ashore he attended every service he could.

It was at a Lantern Service[41] on 'Angels,' when J.W. was present at his last service on shore. Calling at Peel St. I saw the packed trunk & an inquiry found that that there was a Bible inside & tracts & there followed a faithful promise to read these & pray. Prayer & good-by followed & I left a sober man & wife & changed house—two drunkards reformed. Never to see him again till we meet above.

30th J.W. sailed away this morning. As I heard afterwards, it was the first time he had gone away sober, the first time he had his wife to see him off at ship, the first time they had kissed on parting. They had both been drinking & sinning away the years of their married life & knew nothing of marital love or home happiness. Each absorbed in their life of sin. Now they really tasted of true love and happiness, they were to be parted, parted 'for-ever—no'. Only for this life. Standing on the shore she said to him, "John don't go, the ship leaks. I don't like the look of her." But he must go though it was a poor vessel, he thought of the empty cupboard & the debts not paid through his last money. Yes it was farewell to England!

41. See 155n8.

To-night at the Temperance Concert Mrs W sat by my side deeply agitated. At the close of meeting she said to me "Do you know what I came here for" "To give your heart to God" I said, "Yes," she said. We went out to the vestry, where she fell on her knees in an agony of soul, pouring out her heart in prayer for mercy & forgiveness. All the past weeks of hardening her heart against the Spirit, the power of God had broken down Satan's battlements now. "Victory through the Blood of Christ." She was "born again." The sinful Mary who had been indeed a Magdalene was transformed.[42] She had fought with men & overcome them. Many knew the strength of her wrists. All knew the strength of her eyes. Sailors on their return from sea would say "Mary come & have a Drink." They all knew her. She was a power. Had she been well-educated would have been a very intellectual woman.

On one occasion she did a little sewing for me in my room. Returning from my rounds I found her seated on the floor, crosslegged, as do tailors (she was a tailoress by trade), her work had dropped from her hands & she was buried in Milton's "Paradise Lost." She could enjoy reading Homer's Illiad & on one occasion presented me with a copy. Bright, witty, intelligent, conversant, she was an attraction to the opposite sex.

The next day she took her stand with our Mission Band in the street, in the midst of her old pals, & in view of her haunts of sin—the Public Houses. (She used to be out at 6 in mornings waiting for P. Houses[43] to open to get Brandy. It was her food once.

June 94 Mrs Williams is suffering terribly from "Drink Crave" & she has little appetite for food. Sometimes she has no strength to do her tailoring & has sat up part of the night to finish work for customers. She is laboring to pay off her debts. I read a letter she had written to her husband telling of her conversion. (He never saw it, I fear).

8th Mrs W's health is failing, lost flesh considerably. Devil and friends say it is through giving up Drink. She is fiercely tempted by her neighbours. Her nerves seem completely shattered.

Mr T a skilled chemist advises plenty of fresh air & beef tea.[44]

9th Mrs W better to-night, after drinking quart of beef-tea. . . .

42. See 74n7.
43. A bar where alcoholic beverages are sold.
44. A medicinal broth made by steeping cuts of beef in hot water.

APPENDIX B: DIARY EXTRACTS—THIRZA MASTERS

14th A great Public meeting at Routh Road Chapel. I related Mrs W's conversion, & was not aware that she was present hiding behind a Pillar. She endorsed all I said afterward, & was grateful that it was told to the glory of God. On entering the street of her home, she was mobbed by a crowd of dissolute women, who taunted her. No police to protect her she narrowly escaped injury of life—extricated herself from them & entered & locked her door. "The power of God kept me"[45] she said "or I should have felled some of them."

18th Mrs W's nerves are in such a shattered state that she is keeping her bed to-day.

24th Took Mrs W a country walk to Lllandaff.[46] She was grateful, & derived benefit from the fresh air. Concerned that she has no news of husband

30th Mrs. W has gone through a fire of persecution lately. Neighbours are disappointed at her continued loyalty to Christ. They speak bitterly of me (Sister Thirza) & say I bribe her & pay her rent. She is getting plenty of work. Health is improving King Alcohol & his effects are dying fast on her.

April 4th Hearing Mrs W. had had bad news I hastened to Peel St it was between 10 & 11 o'clock. Early in the evening she ran to the "Western Mail Office" without thought of hat, shawl, or jacket. It was a long distance from her house through the streets to the Office, but she was unconscious of anyone or anything save that she wanted a Paper & that there was something in about the "Lord Lytton" her husband's ship. She seized the paper & read that the "Lord Lytton" was in the Insurance Market. Frantic with grief, she turned along the street. God only knew her agony of mind. She came to a hotel, the Drink crave came suddenly upon her, she started to ascend the steps to take something to drown her grief. She stopped herself when she thought of me & my words. It was the dear Savior who prevented her. No human power could conquer such fierce temptation as then assailed her. "Jesus is stronger than Satan & Sin."[47]

---

45. 1 Pet 1:5.
46. Llandaff is in the northwest corner of Cardiff about an hour's walk from Loudoun Square.
47. This hymn is also known from its refrain as "Jesus Saves Me Now."

I sat a long time trying to comfort and pacify her. John W had gone to sea a changed man. Comfort dawned on her soul when the assurance secured given her from heaven that her husband was with Christ & that she would meet him again.

She related me a very vivid dream which she had had a few weeks previous, when she had had a vision of a ship tossed with a fearful storm in the Bay of Biscay. "It was that night," she said. "I saw my John struggling in the waves." She treasured the few lines which came from him as he passed out of the Bristol Channel.

5th I passed a 'brothel' in Peel St. One watching me used my name in scorn accompanied with vile language. (She was one of the devil's agents, & feared I should enter that house in which her interests lay. This woman & such as her make a market on the souls of the poor fallen girls. The Queen as Mrs Merrick is called was once an attender at the Cornish Class Meeting.[48] Now she is the ringleader of the most vicious women of Cardiff. A policeman who inspected her house was struck with ornaments and barely escaped with his life.) In the meantime Mrs W. knowing of my peril amongst such women stood watching me & ready to protect me from insult. Now on every occasion that I enter this street Mrs W. stands at her door or loiters till she sees I have safely passed these houses or brothels. When I can gain admittance I go in, but that is seldom. As I come out Mrs W is still standing as 'my guardian angel'" . . .

Oct. 1st 1894 – It is just a year since I came to Cardiff to commence work in connection with the Loudonere Sq. Mission. A year not lost, for God has owned and blessed any work. . . .

2nd A girl 18 years of age whose mother asked me to try and use my influence over her, being very fond of the theatre and novel reading, called of my house this evening. She accompanied us to the Girl's Parlour[49] and worked as a monitor. She tells us she intends to give up her companions

---

48. See 18n14.

49. Also known as a Girls' Club, it was a safe place for girls and young women to spend time during the day, away from temptations and harm, to learn how to cook, knit and sew, to borrow books to read, and to come in contact with the gospel. Masters described it in a talk she gave: "One remedy to the spread of vice and the advancement of social, moral, and spiritual good, is a large bright Parlour for girls' benefit. . . . It is to some a haven of rest from the vile oaths of a drunken parent, and has proved itself to be a real necessity to many." Masters, "Perils of Young Women," 188.

and be different. In connection with the National Vigilance Association[50] we held our first winter meeting. As we sought to bring in these fallen women, fearful sights met our eyes. We succeeded in bringing in twelve; these listened to words spoken by several of us, & and seemed touched, while they joined in the singing most heartily. Two were led off with our friends to the Rescue Home. . . .

6th Yesterday took to a S.A. [Salvation Army] Rescue Home a young girl 17 yrs of age. Mother died a fortnight ago leaving her an orphan. Consumption[51] had laid its hand upon her mother, who fought against the disease in working almost up to the last, because of extreme poverty. A son 23 yrs seems to have been an indolent fellow. After funeral he led his sister to Cardiff, the home being broken up at Blaenavon. His intention seems to have been to leave her with a married sister here. Not finding her, he & his sister sheltered at a friends house. The next day Sunday he led her from there to the Docks & left her upon the streets, first taking his orphan sisters black shawl from her shoulders. The poor girl wandered up & down. The first to speak to her was a publican, & prostitute the former gave her 6 for a lodge, the latter led her off to a brothel; but would not allow the mistress of this house to retain the girl to have her ruined. How I've shuddered to think of the peril that surrounded this poor child! Thanks to be to God for interposing. Our Mission is making itself felt in this neighborhood for one though a sinner herself will not see another lured to the evil life without trying to prevent. Nelle C. who brought her from the street said, "let her go to Mrs. W. Now Mrs. W. is one of our converts & has great influence over Nellie C. Nellie knew how Mrs. W & we at the Hall hate this sinful life which is commonly lived about here, & how we try to save the poor fallen ones. At 10 o'clock Sunday Eve, the orphan is brought to Mrs. W. by a brothel keeper saying, "I don't want this girl to be ruined in my house." Perhaps this woman thought she was doing a religious act for once; anyway let us rejoice. The next morning Monday found me leading a wretched clad girl along the street with a timid frightened gaze at every one. Her face bearing no trace of happiness. Now in the hands of Staff Capt. Goldsmith what will she be in the future? . . .

50. This social purity association was established in the UK in 1885 to combat prostitution.
51. Older name for tuberculosis.

10th Missed train to Penarth[52], walked through boisterous wind & rain, arriving in a not very prime condition at my friends house. What a relief to body and mind, to sit around the fire & chat with genial friends! I have been taken out of myself, & come back to the dreary Docks refreshed. . . .

8th An oil cooking stove has been given by a gentleman for the Girl's Parlour. This morning I tried a little cooking- Puddings[53] and Beef tea; & after dinner sailed out to deposit the good things in the sick-chambers. Nellie T. one of our Girls lay in a cheerless room, with scanty bed clothes coughing. She has many complaints. Her mother is ill, they are very poor, & it is very little attention the poor girl gets. Thank you Sister, she feebly said, as she drew the few clothes around her. Sickness & Poverty are around me. Whole families are crying for bread, while the breadwinner in vain seeks for employ. To-night I found Mrs B ready dressed to accompany me to the Temperance Concert. She said, my husband is as pleased as though any had given him £5. . . .

Five month's this poor diary has been forgotten & neglected. I will try to do better & write scraps after.

May 10th Much has transpired since I last wrote in this book. The best to be said is that the work of our mission is still progressing. While some who gave up drink have returned to it again; others who gave it up & took Christ instead are standing as monuments of his power to save. This shows that it is difficult, & sometimes impossible for men to refrain from this cursed stuff without the aid of Christ. The converted tailoress is still true. After her conversion her husband got drowned, the drink craze came upon her fiercely; a shebean[54] was prosecuted in the street in which she resided, her neighbours regarded her as a tell-tale, mobbed the house fought her, & being used to fighting men or women she would have raised her hand, but the Spirit of God resisted her so doing; a loaded revolved was ready in the house to shoot the next one who interfered with her peace, but God sent me to stop a dreadful work for I was led to go and see her one night at 11 o'clock. Not knowing of the revolver business I thought from a little she said to me she was in a furious mood, & especially as neuralgia was attacking her fiercely. "Try & be more patient & ask God to control your temper. Let us pray to Him." I said, & we

52. A town near the coast about four and a half miles from Cardiff.
53. Desserts.
54. Unlicensed drinking establishment.

kneeled down. Since that incident she told me that I had been the means of intervening an awful circumstance—murder. Entire victory over temper is not to be found in every Christian. It can be got if sought. Now she by God's help is getting stronger. A month or two ago the woman who was first to strike her in the mob sent for her to pray with her as she lay sick. The other week she induced several sailors who had been paid off to bank their money lest they squandered it with publicans and harlots. They did so. I accompanied her to see a sick woman she had known in her evil days. The sick woman had been a typical Tiger Bay woman & since she had left the Bay & been married her life had been no better. Married women at Cardiff Docks are sometimes given to get their living by keeping prostitutes & themselves are answerable for the wrecked lives of many dear girls. Sailors wife's will do wickedly in the absence of their husbands. It was a scene when the two women recognized each other. Mary & Minnie they called each other. "What the Lord has done for me he can do for you said the converted one." The sick woman wept bitterly & looked at me & said "I have been very very wicked ever since my husband's been away Will God forgive me" she said. I said "You have as much right to forgiveness as me." After reading messages from the Bible & praying we had the joy of leaving her trust in the power of Jesus to save. Since I have found her happy & enjoying the peace of soul that comes from Jesus. Two girls of the Parlour have given their hearts to Jesus & have joined my Society Class while several others come as seekers. . . .

Sept 22nd 1896 A young mother dying with consumption, baby lies at foot of bed gives a cry, patting on back and quickly he goes off to sleep, & turning to its mother a mere skeleton, I asked her why she could be certain that she was going home to rest & heaven. "A month ago I was praying so long, it got so bright about me & I saw the gates ajar." She gasped, & I said "for you." "Yes" she said "for me & since then I have been so happy. I should be happy all the time but children come to me crying for bread & I can do nothing, my husband gets no work. While there the children came home from school to dinner but only an empty cupboard, giving the little girl money she quickly ran to shop & brought back two loaves of bread in great delight. The room was indeed a den, bed in filthy plight, & swarms of flies.

[There are a few entries about her deaconess work in Camborne and Wolverhampton, where she was assigned after Cardiff. Then, on January

31, 1900, she wrote: "Ordered to take an appointment at London by Dr. Gregory."[55]]

Feb. 17th 1900 London. Leysian Mission[56]

<table>
<tr><td colspan="5">Weekly Plan of Work</td></tr>
<tr><td>Mon__</td><td>Visitation</td><td>- Play Hr.</td><td>- Public Meetings</td><td></td></tr>
<tr><td>Tues__</td><td>"</td><td>- Children Lantern Ser.[57]</td><td></td><td>- Girls Social</td></tr>
<tr><td>Wed__</td><td>"</td><td>- Play Hr.</td><td>- Relief Com.</td><td>- Address</td></tr>
<tr><td></td><td></td><td colspan="3">(Mother Mtg. once a month)</td></tr>
<tr><td>Thurs__</td><td>Off day.</td><td></td><td></td><td></td></tr>
<tr><td>Fri__</td><td>Medical Mission</td><td>- Junior Cl[ass].</td><td>- Prayer Mtg.</td><td></td></tr>
<tr><td>Sat__</td><td colspan="4">Special invitation to Sun. Serv.</td></tr>
<tr><td></td><td colspan="4">Concerts during winter</td></tr>
</table>

April. Continuing house to house visitation. People shew civility, but great reserve to me.

13th Address at Gray's Essex – Mission Band

21st Deaconess Convocation
Read Paper "How a Deaconess should live & lodge"
Continued house to house visitation.

May   "   "   "   "

June–Country holiday work starts–
Arranging for S.S. [Sunday School] Scholars journey to sea or country for 2 wks during summer. . . .

July–C. Country Holiday Work

14th Holidays at Evesham[58] till Aug. 8th . . .

---

55. See 223fn1.

56. The Leysian Mission, opened in 1886 in London's East End, provided a range of services, such as medical care, prayer meetings, and Bible classes. WDO deaconesses began working there in the 1890s.

57. For more on lantern shows, see 155n8.

58. Her home was in this West Midlands town.

Children's Country Holiday Report for Magazine 1900.[59]

The children like the sparrows are always with us & we can well ask what would London be without them? During the dark days of the past spring & winter in the history of the [Boer] war, they did much to hearten city life. We do not forget the sham fights, ambulance displays, & processions. Stern business men were forced to smile at their little maneuvers. The gallant bearing of the mock soldier lads, & the serious little faces of the mock nurses as they paraded the principal streets, won for them the swirling approval of hundreds. Yes, they played their part well. The children have so many ways of appealing to our sympathies, & their thin warm faces make the loudest appeal to us. Brave boys there are in this big city! One little fellow whose father had just gone to war, saw his mother crying & said "I'll be father" & her tears were quickly wiped away. It is now a common sight during the months of July & Aug to see bands of boys & girls with parcels under their arms wending their way to some Railway Sta. Off to the sea! Off to the country! Imprisoned in the heart of the city all the year round with the streets for their play-ground & no change of view, no wounder they look so happy at the prospect of new surroundings.

Some are about to look at the sea for the first time, & these assume an air as though the most important day in their life has arrived. It is good to see the pale faces light up in glowing expectation of what is coming; that we who witness are priviledged to see with Consumption & a fortnight of fresh air for these put a check on the run of disease. The orphan, cripple & fatherless children are to be found in our Holiday groups. The clean, tidy, smart appearance of some, tell us of mothers who have sat up late at night making & repairing clothes in order to shew that their children are of respectable origin. Many such mother's know nothing of a holiday themselves. They have toiled hard to scrape together the necessary means for the children to go, & now they are proud to start them off neatly dressed. A group of Mother's desired to pass to the Departure Platform "What sort of heart should I have" said the genial porter "if I did'nt let you pass."

There are plenty of people with hearts in London, & these do not forget to smile at the children. The children know who love them, & are lavish in their affection to such. So demonstrative are they sometimes that they will embrace us with hands full of bread & jam or butter or with the traces of mud-puddings on them. On their return they give

---

59. Also known as Fresh Air Work. See 29n52.

ample evidence that they have been on Holiday. Ruddy cheeks–increased appetites & damaged clothes speak for themselves. Tongues are let loose as they relate all they have seen & done. . . .

[There are a number of blank pages at this point. The year, 1903, is listed without any entries The next entries in 1904 focus solely on her health, since she had a complete breakdown.]

1904—Secured Sister Ruth to do my work for 2 months.[60] Taking my usual month's holiday & so obtaining a three months rest.

July 1st Left London for Evesham.

4th To Birmingham to consult a Physician about my weak state of health. Dr. Saundby_ Charles St B.ham[61] advised their Mitchell Treatment "The Rest Cure"[62] & nothing short of two months of treatment would be of any effect to render any good & even then he would not be sure of health being completely restored. For he said damage had been done by continuing on at work in unfit condition; that could never be undone. It was one of the worst cases of Nervous Prostration.

7th Agreed with my friends to have the Treatment recommended.

11th The New Leysian Mission opened by the Princess of Wales.[63] I was too prostrate to journey to London to this important Ceremony; but strange to say Dr Saundby chose this very day for me to enter my Prison. So I came to the General Hospital Birmingham where my Physician engaged a Private Ward. Here I spent a solitary existence for 9 weeks—not permitted to see a soul save Doctor & nurses. No conversation with either. Neither did any one stay in my room longer than was

60. Most likely, Sister Ruth refers to Ruth Norcroft, who was consecrated a deaconess in 1892 and remained active for over thirty years until her retirement in 1923. In 1902, she was the first WDO deaconess to receive the 12 year award, which was a "star pendant with the word 'true'" on it. Graham, *Saved to Serve*, 374.

61. Dr. Robert Saundby (1849–1918) studied medicine at the University of Edinburgh, then began working at Birmingham General Hospital in 1876.

62. The rest cure was "a strictly enforced regime of six to eight weeks of bed rest and isolation, without any creative or intellectual activity or stimulation. It was often accompanied by massage and electrotherapy, as well as a fatty diet, rich in milk and meat." "From Nerves to Neuroses."

63. Mary of Teck (1867–1953) was the wife of King George V and Queen of the United Kingdom from 1910–1936.

necessary. Though there was a Heat Wave for 3 wks yet my windows were continually closed, as not to be ever opened. Artificial Ventilation by Machinery continuously at work giving a buzzing sound as though one was on board a ship. With my bed turned that I could not see out of windows, & these looking out upon the roof of the Chapel. Not a bird to sing to me. Even the noises of the street would have been welcome. Nothing but a dead silence. Nellie Rogers, the Ward maid would make droll remarks when she passed my door when she was sure nurse was far away. Perhaps no one felt more than she did, of any rate she was determined to relieve the dull monotony for me if she could. No Good-night kiss from my mother. God only knows what that awful loneliness was to me. Sometimes I felt I should go mad.[64] And when I continued the weeks of endurance still before me. Yet with it all I never desired to get up. I was too weak & this Rest the Body had long craved for & been denied. Not a letter from home or from any one—this pleasure denied me.

Diet—5 pints of milk daily—compulsory

Treatment—General Massage & Faradism or Electric Battery[65]

One day a sunbeam entered my room and day by day that Sunbeam came. It was my Massage nurse.[66] She came like an Angel dropped from the skies. So bright, so pure, so fresh, so radiant. A glance from her dark blue eyes, with deep frayed lashes, told me there was wondrous depths of feeling. A few words told me she has a big heart that struck a chord with mine. Had God sent her to me? Yes, I felt sure he had. How I counted the moments till she came, & dreaded the going. She dared to tell me a little about her life (though this was not permissible for a Weir Mitchell Patient.[67]) Born in India (North) orphaned of both parents when a child—brought up by her eldest Brother. What a face! Open and frank. Sincerity stamped on every feature. Complexion—Pink made one think of Roses & Lillies. Hair curly Golden brown. Her laughter was as music &

---

64. The female character in Charlotte Perkins Gilman's short story, "The Yellow Wallpaper," did go mad during her rest cure. The title comes from the isolation room's yellow wallpaper, which became the focal point of the woman's obsession. Gilman underwent this same rest cure.

65. This is a therapeutic treatment through the application of a current of electricity.

66. Her name was Nurse Beynon, and Masters called her "My Sunbeam."

67. Silas Weir Mitchell was the physician who developed the rest cure; Charlotte Perkins Gilman was his patient. See n64 above.

when she laughed she shewed pearly teeth. There her step was light and free as a Fairy. This was my Massage nurse—my Angel. . . .

Weighed 6 stone 9lbs[68] in my dressing gown when I entered Hospital.

July

17th	gained	2 lbs.
24th	"	2 "
31st	"	2 "
Aug 7th	"	0 "
14th	"	2 "
21st	"	1 "
28th	"	2 "
Sept 4	"	0 "
9th	"	1 ½ "

Sept 8th allowed to sit up a little

10th My sweet sister Nancy came to fetch me. What a meeting! I feared Hysteria but burst into tears & saved myself. Then emerging from my Prison, the sights & sounds after the stillness—my hearing for a time seemed defective. All the noises seemed mixed so. My very eyes seemed blurred. What a new world of sight & noise as I passed down Corporation St. that bright Sept. morning. How strange to be dressed & sitting by my sister's side. Perhaps strangest of all was the feeling of the air on my face. I just took deep inspiration & felt it good to feed on fresh air after the artificial that I had imbibed for 9 wks.

Yet singular to say my appetite was always keen for milk. And, strange again through 9 wks of lying on my back there was not the faintest suspicion of soreness. What sustained me in these weeks of trial & loneliness. I had with me my Manual of Devotion "My Counsellor" & stole texts from it daily when nurse was away. Prayer was my chief sustenance & God's Grace was sufficient for me.[69] I felt often that it would have

---

68. She weighed 93 pounds.
69. 2 Cor 12:9.

been easier to bear bodily pain. I never once slept in day-time & often lay awake at night tossed with acute head-ache.

[Masters returned to deaconess work at the Leysian Mission; however, on July 11, 1908, she once again became ill and had to take another break from deaconess work to recuperate.[70] In 1910, she was assigned to Hednesford, a mining town in Staffordshire. She describes her initial, extremely negative impressions of the town in these clipped phrases: "the dullest & ugliest of towns. No trees. No birds. No falls. Uninteresting. The Climate exceedingly bleak as the place is 500 ft above sea level. The people generally have little thought of much else but Business, Pleasures & self. The skating Rink & concerts come first with many of the sons & daughters of the leading Wesleyans. These are quite proficient at Card Playing, & enjoy the Card Party in preference to Class [meetings].[71]

After several months of brief entries followed by many blank pages, the diary ends with this list of her deaconess appointments:

Sister Thirza Masters (Deaconess)

Training Home	Mewburn House London
Entered Sept 1891	Left Sept 1892
Consecration or Recognition	July 1893
Truro Sept 1892	Left Sept 1893
Cardiff Sept 1893	Left June 30th 1897
Camborne Sept 1897	Left June 30th 1899
Wolverhampton Sept 1899	Left Jan 31st 1900
Leysian Mission Feb 1900	_ _ _ _
	Left July 11, 1908
At Evesham for Health & Home Claims	
Hednesford Staff	Appointed Sept 1, 1910

70. Graham, *Saved to Serve*, 13.
71. See ch. 18n14.

BIBLIOGRAPHY

Archives

Bridwell Library, Southern Methodist University
Camden Theological Library
Harris Memorial College
John Rylands Research Institute and Library
Kei Muri Māpara/Methodist Church of New Zealand
Library of the Wesley Historical Society
Martha-Maria-Verein
Methodist Archives and History Center of the United Methodist Church, Drew University
Methodist Library, Special Collections & Libraries, Drew University Libraries
Scarritt Bennett Center–Laskey Library and Archives
Styberg Library, Garrett-Evangelical Theological Seminary
Vennard College Collection, Marge Smith Archives, MidAmerica Nazarene University

Primary Sources

50 Jahre Diakonissenarbeit 1874–1924. Martha-Maria-Verein für allgemeine Krankenpflege.
"Afro-American Cullings." *Cleveland Gazette* (July 6, 1912) n.d.
Ames, A. H. "Lucy Webb Hayes National Training-School." In *Nineteenth Annual Report of the General Board of Managers of the Woman's Home Missionary Society of the Methodist Episcopal Church, For the Year 1899–1900*, 135–38. Cincinnati: Western Methodist Book Concern, 1900.
Annual Report of the Deaconess Society of the Methodist Church and the Toronto, Hamilton, Manitoba, Montreal, Newfoundland, Nova Scotia, New Brunswick and Prince Edward Island, Bay of Quinte, London, Saskatchewan, Alberta, and British Columbia Conferences (1909–1910).
Barraclough, Sister Elizabeth. "The Privilege & Responsibility of Our Vocation as Deaconesses." *Flying Leaves* 8–9 (1902) 100.
Bigham, R. J. "The Scarritt Bible and Training School." *Methodist Review* 42 (2:1898) 261–67.
Booth, Maud. "Salvation Army Work in the Slums." *Social News* (1911) 3.

Briggs, Emilie G. "The Restoration of the Order of Deaconesses." *The Biblical World* 41 (1913) 382–90.
Burns, W. H. "Methodism in Transition." *Northwestern Christian Advocate* (August 22, 1877) 6.
Butt, Israel L. *History of African Methodism in Virginia, or Four Decades in the Old Dominion*. Hampton, VA: Hampton Institute, 1908.
"Deaconess Conference Sets Rules for Deaconess Homes." In *Notes Concerning Management of Deaconess Home*, 1–4. New York: Methodist Book Concern, 1889.
Deaconess Institute Minute Book 1906–1917. The John Rylands Research Institute and Library.
"Deaconess Training-School for Colored Girls." In *Twentieth Annual Report of the General Board of Managers of the Woman's Home Missionary Society of the Methodist Episcopal Church, For the Year 1900–1901*, 151. Cincinnati: Western Methodist Book Concern, 1901.
"Deaconess Work in Salford." *Highway and Hedges: The Children's Advocate, The Organ of the Children's Home* 86 (1895) 38.
Diekmann, J. A. "Lucy Rider Meyer." Unpublished essay, n.d.
"A Dinner-Hour Service." *Highways and Hedges: The Children's Advocate, The Organ of the Children's Home* 131 (1898) 260.
Dougherty, Mary Agnes. "The Deaconess Story." Video produced by the UMC General Commission of Archives and History.
"Dr. Parkhurst's New Word." *Medical Arena* 4 (1895) 27.
Dreyer, Margaretha. "German Deaconess Echoes." *The Message and Deaconess World* 9 (1893) 7–8.
The Early History of Deaconess Work and Training Schools for Women in American Methodism, 1883–1885, With Supplement Answering Certain Objections. Detroit: Hines Press for the Woman's Home Missionary Society, Methodist Episcopal Church, 1912.
An Exhibit of the Industrial Homes, Missions, and Deaconess Homes of the Woman's Home Missionary Society of the Methodist Episcopal Church: Souvenir of the Twentieth Anniversary, 1880–1900. Cincinnati: Western Methodist Book Concern, 1900.
Fifth Annual Report of the Woman's Home Missionary Society of the Methodist Episcopal Church, For the Year 1885–86. Cincinnati: Western Methodist Book Concern, 1886.
Fry, Susan M. D. "Ancient and Modern Sisterhoods." *The Ladies Repository* 32 (1872) 241–45.
German Methodist Deaconess Home and Bethesda Hospital, 14th Annual Report, 1909–1910.
"A Halleluiah Lassie." *Zion's Herald* 69 (1891) 118.
Harbord, Lena. "Girls' Clubs." *Highways and Hedges: The Children's Advocate, The Organ of the Children's Home* 121 (1898) 19–20.
Highways and Hedges: The Children's Advocate, The Organ of the Children's Home 129 (1898) 212.
Holding, Elizabeth E. *Joy the Deaconess*. Cincinnati: Jennings & Graham, 1898.
"In Perils Oft. By a Wesley Deaconess." *Flying Leaves* 73 (1908) 201.
Jahreiss, Christian, ed. *Schwestern erzählen: Ein Buch von irdischer Not und helfender Liebe*. München: Anker Verlag, 1948.
James, Myrtle. "Tributes from Deaconesses and Missionaries." *The Missionary Voice* 12 (1922) 308.

Jones, Mrs. I. D. "Colored Deaconess Work." In *Twenty-Third Annual Report of the Board of Managers of the Woman's Home Missionary Society of the Methodist Episcopal Church, For the Year 1903-1904*, 150. Cincinnati: Western Methodist Book Concern, 1904.

Journal of the Forty-Ninth Annual Session of the Texas Conference of the Methodist Episcopal Church, Held at Clarksville, Texas, Dec. 17 to 21, 1914, In Saint Paul Church. Houston: Western Star, 1915.

"A Letter from Leeds." *Flying Leaves* 70 (1907) 154.

Masters, Thirza. "Lives of Wesley Deaconesses. Sister Thirza Masters." *Flying Leaves* 23 (1903) 168.

———. "Perils of Young Women, and Efforts to Save Them." *Highways and Hedges: The Children's Advocate, The Organ of the Children's Home* 116 (1897) 187–90.

Methodist Episcopal Church. *Journals of General Conference, Vol. I, 1796-1836*. New York: Carlton & Phillips, 1855.

Meyer, Lucy Rider. "Assorted Writings of Lucy Rider Meyer." Archives, Styberg Library, Garrett-Evangelical Theological Seminary.

———. "Deaconesses and the Need." *The Message* 5 (1890) 9.

———. *Some Little Prayers*. Cincinnati: Jennings and Graham, 1907.

Minutes of the Fifty-Third Session of the Texas Annual Conference of the Methodist Episcopal Church, Held in Lee Tabernacle M.E. Church, Navasota, Texas, November 20-24, 1918. Houston: Western Star, 1915.

"Minutes of the First Meeting of the General Committee, held in the Church Parlour of the Oxford Place Chapel, Leeds, on Tuesday, 25th of September 1906, at 3:15 p.m. Special Matter of Discipline—the Case of Sister May Keeling." The John Rylands Research Institute and Library.

Minutes of the Forty-Third Session of the St. Louis Annual Conference of the Methodist Episcopal Church, Held in Mountain Grove, MO, March 22 to 26, 1911. Warrensburg, MO: Perry E. Pierce, 1911.

Minutes of the Thirty-Ninth Session of the St. Louis Annual Conference, Held in Clinton, MO, March 20th to 25th, 1907. Clinton, MO: Republican, 1907.

"The Mission Field at Home & Abroad: Notanda." *Highways and Hedges: The Children's Advocate, The Organ of the Children's Home* 118 (1897) 232.

"Much the Same in America." *Highway and Hedges: The Children's Advocate, The Organ of the Children's Home* 127 (1898) 164.

Nightingale, Florence. *The Institution of Kaiserswerth on the Rhine for the Training of Deaconesses Under the Direction of the Reverend Pastor Fliedner, Embracing the Support and Care of a Hospital, Infant and Industrial Schools, and a Female Penitentiary*. London: London Ragged Colonial Training School, 1851.

"The Order of Service for the Ordination of Deaconesses." Library, Wesley Historical Society.

"Our American Sisters." *Highways and Hedges: The Children's Advocate, The Organ of the Children's Home* 60 (1892) 234.

"Our Bible Reading Table for 1906." *Flying Leaves* 50 (1906) 14.

Parkhurst, Charles. "Andromaniacs." *The Ladies' Home Journal* 12:3 (1895) 15.

———. "College Training for Women." *The Ladies' Home Journal* 12:6 (1895) 15.

———. "True Mission of Woman." *The Ladies' Home Journal* 12:5 (1895) 15.

"A Pathetic Incident." *Flying Leaves* 32 (1904) 85.

"Personals." *Inasmuch* 1 (1905) 8. Vennard College Collection, Marge Smith Archives, MidAmerica Nazarene University.
Pratt, Rugby. *The Story of the South Island Methodist Orphanage and Children's Home, Christchurch*. Christchurch: Bascands, 1934.
Ransom, Reverdy. *The Christian Recorder* (July 14, 1898) n.p.
"A Recognition Service." *Highways and Hedges: The Children's Advocate, The Organ of the Children's Home* 57 (1892) 178.
Robinson, Jane Bancroft, and Henrietta A. Bancroft. "Bureau for Deaconess Work." In *Nineteenth Annual Report of the General Board of Managers of the Woman's Home Missionary Society of the Methodist Episcopal Church, For the Year 1899–1900*, 134. Cincinnati: Western Methodist Book Concern, 1900.
Rust, Elizabeth (Mrs. R. S. Rust). "Letters from Friends." In *First Annual Report of the Board of Managers of the Woman's Home Missionary Society of the Methodist Episcopal Church, For the Year 1881–82*. Cincinnati: Western Methodist Book Concern, 1882.
———. "Woman's Home Missionary Society." *Methodist Review* 69 (1887) 653.
Scarritt College Folder 1880–1892. Scarritt Bennett Center-Laskey Library and Archives.
Searle, Elise. "Notes from Norwich." *Highways and Hedges: The Children's Advocate, The Organ of the Children's Home* (June 1895) 118–19.
———. "A Unique Congregation." *Highways and Hedges: The Children's Advocate, The Organ of the Children's Home* 91 (1895) 136.
"Some Wesley Deaconesses and Their Work." *Flying Leaves* 98 (1910) 77.
Stephenson, Dora. "What Is a Deaconess?" *Highways and Hedges: The Children's Advocate, The Organ of the Children's Home* 95 (1895) 219–20.
"A Student's View of College Life. By a Student." *Flying Leaves* 109 (1911) 73.
Third Annual Session of the Woman's Conference of the Philippine Islands Mission of the Methodist Episcopal Church, Manila, February 17–23, 1907.
Thoburn, James. "Deaconesses and the Church." *The Message* 5 (1890) 6.
Tigert, Jno. J., ed. *Journal of the 14th General Conference of the MEC, South, Held in Dallas, TX, May 7–26, 1902*. Nashville: MEC South, 1902.
"True." *Flying Leaves* 33 (1904) 102.
Vennard, Iva Durham. "An Appeal to Young Women." *Inasmuch* (1906) 8.
———. "The Deaconess of Today." In *A Report on Deaconess Work*, 10–12. The Committee on Co-operation, 1908.
———. "Editorial." *Deaconess Advocate* (August 1906) 6.
———. "Epworth Settlement." *Inasmuch* 1 (1905) 5–6.
———. "'Help Those Women': XIV. The Evangelistic Department of Deaconess Work." *Inasmuch* 2 (1906) 8. Vennard College Collection, Marge Smith Archives, MidAmerica Nazarene University.
W. J. W. "Sister Isabel Sinclair." *The New Zealand Methodist Times* (May 27, 1922) 14.
Wardle, Addie G., comp. *A Report on Deaconess Work*. Chicago: Methodist Deaconess Association, 1908.
Weaver, Elisha. "The Roanoke Deaconess Home." *The Christian Recorder* (March 21, 1901) n.p.
Wells-Barnett, Ida B. "Rev. R. C. Ransom, D.D." *The Christian Recorder* 47 (1900) 1.
Wesley Deaconess Order, 1904–1905. The John Rylands Research Institute and Library.
Wesley Deaconess Order Pamphlet. Library, Wesley Historical Society.

"The White-Striped Veil." *Flying Leaves* 54 (1906) 71.
"Why the Title, *Flying Leaves*?" *Flying Leaves* 3 (1902) 5.
Willing, Jennie Fowler. "The Home." *Guide to Holiness* (January 1895) 20.
———. "The Mother's Power in Evangelism." *Guide to Holiness* (December 1896) 220.
"World-Wide Deaconess Notes." *The Message and Deaconess World* 10 (1894) 7.
"World-Wide Deaconess Notes. Deaconesses in Australia." *The Message and Deaconess World* 10 (1894) 4.

Secondary Sources

Abell, Aaron. *The Urban Impact on American Protestantism, 1865–1900*. London: Archon, 1962.
Aitchison, Ronald J. "The Overseas Mission of the Wesley Deaconess Order: Theological Aberration or Inspiration?" PhD diss., Potchesfstroomse Universiteit vir Christelike Hoër Onderwys, 2003.
Albanese, Catherine L. "Horace Bushnell among the Metaphysicians." *Church History* 79 (2010) 614–53.
AMEC Sunday School Union. *The Doctrine and Discipline of the African Methodist Episcopal Church, 2004-2008*. Nashville: AMEC Sunday School Union, 2005.
Ammerman, Nancy. *Studying Lived Religion: Contexts and Practices*. New York: New York University Press, 2021.
Andersen, Arlow W. *The Salt of the Earth: A History of Norwegian-Danish Methodism in America*. Nashville: Parthenon, 1962.
Armstrong, Anthony. *The Church of England, Methodists and Society, 1700–1850*. London: University of London Press, 1973.
Arthur, Linda B. "Introduction: Dress and the Social Control of the Body." In *Religion, Dress, and the Body*, edited by Linda B. Arthur, 1–7. New York: Berg, 1999.
Beck, Michael Adam, and Jorge Acevedo. *A Field Guide to Methodist Fresh Expressions*. Nashville: Abingdon, 2020.
Bendroth, Margaret Lamberts. *Fundamentalism and Gender, 1875 to the Present*. New Haven, CT: Yale University Press, 1993.
Bennett, David H. *The Party of Fear: From Nativist Movements to the New Right in American History*. New York: Vintage, 1988.
Binney, Amos, and Daniel Steele. *Binney's Theological Compend Improved*. 2nd ed. Cincinnati: Curts & Jennings, 1875.
Black, J. Anderson, and Madge Garland. *A History of Fashion*. New York: William Morrow, 1975.
Bloedt, Mareike. "The Pioneering Deaconess Movement in Germany." In *Women Pioneers in Continental European Methodism, 1869–1939*, edited by Paul Chilcote and Ulrike Schuler, 48–64. London: Routledge, 2018.
Blue, Ellen. *St. Mark's and the Social Gospel: Methodist Women and Civil Rights in New Orleans, 1895–1965*. Knoxville: University of Tennessee Press, 2014.
———. *Women United for Change: 150 Years in Mission*. New York: United Methodist Women, 2019.
Bowie, Mary Ella. *Alabaster and Spikenard: The Life of Iva Durham Vennard, D.D., Founder of Chicago Evangelistic Institute*. Chicago: Chicago Evangelistic Institute, 1947.

Bradfield, William. *The Life of the Reverend Thomas Bowman Stephenson, B.A., LL.D., D.D.* London: Charles H. Kelly, 1913.
Brekus, Catherine. *Strangers and Pilgrims: Female Preaching in America, 1740–1845.* Chapel Hill: University of North Carolina Press, 1998.
Brereton, Virginia Lieson. "Protestant Sunday Schools and Religious Education." In *Encyclopedia of Women and Religion in North America*, edited by Rosemary Skinner Keller and Rosemary Radford Ruether, 2:906–12. Bloomington: Indiana University Press, 2006.
———. *Training God's Army: The American Bible School, 1880–1940.* Bloomington: Indiana University Press, 1990.
Breward, Christopher. *The Culture of Fashion: A New History of Fashionable Dress.* New York: Manchester University Press, 1995.
Brown, Daniel Alan. "A Comparative Analysis of Bible College Quality." PhD diss., University of California, Los Angeles, 1982.
Buenker, John D., ed. *The Gilded Age and Progressive Era, 1877–1920.* Sources of the American Tradition. Acton, MA: Copley, 2002.
Bushnell, Horace. *Discourses on Christian Nurture.* Boston: Massachusetts Sabbath School Society, 1847.
Campbell, Barbara Kuhn. *The "Liberated" Woman of 1914: Prominent Women in the Progressive Era.* Studies in American History and Culture 6. Ann Arbor, MI: UMI Research Press, 1979.
Chambers, Wesley A. *Not Self-But Others: The Story of the New Zealand Methodist Deaconess Order.* Proceedings 48. Auckland, NZ: Wesley Historical Society, August 1987.
Cherry, Conrad. *Hurrying Toward Zion: Universities, Divinity Schools and American Protestantism.* Bloomington: Indiana University Press, 1995.
Chilcote, Paul. *John Wesley and the Women Preachers of Early Methodism.* ATLA Monograph Series, 25. Metuchen, NJ: Scarecrow, 1991.
Chilcote, Paul, and Ulrike Schuler, eds. *Women Pioneers in Continental European Methodism, 1869–1939.* London: Routledge, 2018.
Clapp, Elizabeth J. *Mothers of all Children: Women Reformers and the Rise of Juvenile Courts in Progressive Era America.* University Park: Pennsylvania State University Press, 1998.
Clark, David. "The Hallmark of the Methodist Diaconal Order—Its Life as a Religious Order—and Some Implications for the Future of Methodism." *Theology and Ministry* 2 (2013) 6.1–18.
Clarke, Edward H. *Sex in Education; or, A Fair Chance for the Girls.* Boston: James R. Osgood, 1873.
Crum, Mason. *The Negro in the Methodist Church.* New York: The Editorial Department of the Board of Missions and Church Extension of the Methodist Church, 1951.
Curry, Jane. *Marietta Holley.* Twayne's United States Authors Series 658. New York: Twayne, 1996.
Curts, Lewis, ed. *The General Conferences of the Methodist Episcopal Church from 1792 to 1896.* Cincinnati: Curts & Jennings, 1900.
Deen, Edith. "Lucy Webb Hayes—Faithful First Lady (1831–1889)." In *Great Women of the Christian Faith*, 245–48. New York: Harper & Brothers, 1959.
Deichmann, Wendy J. "Forging an Ideology for American Missions: Josiah Strong and Manifest Destiny." In *North American Foreign Missions, 1810–1914: Theology,*

Theory, and Policy, edited by Wilbert R. Shenk, 163–91. Grand Rapids: Eerdmans, 2004.

Dickerson, Dennis. *The African Methodist Episcopal Church: A History.* New York: Cambridge University Press, 2020.

———. "Theologizing Rosa Parks." *The AME Church Review* 124 (2008) 29–37.

Dieter, Melvin. *The Holiness Revival of the Nineteenth Century.* 2nd ed. Studies in Evangelicalism 1. Lanham, MD: Scarecrow, 1996.

Dietz, Susanne Malchau. "The Deaconess Movement and Professional Nursing. International Demographics and Danish Deaconess Settlements at Home and Abroad 1836–1914." In *Deaconesses in Nursing Care: International Transfer of a Female Model of Life and Work in the 19th and 20th Century*, edited by Susanne Kreutzer and Karen Nolte, 117–34. Stuttgart: Franz Steiner, 2016.

Diner, Steven J. *A Very Different Age: Americans of the Progressive Era.* New York: Hill and Wang, 1998.

Dorr, Rheta Childe. *What Eight Million Women Want.* Boston: Small, Maynard & Co., 1910.

Dougherty, Mary Agnes. "The Methodist Deaconess, 1885–1919: A Study in Religious Feminism." PhD diss., University of California, Davis, 1979.

———. "The Meyers: Josiah Shelley and Lucy Jane Rider." *Methodist History* 37 (1998) 48–58.

———. *My Calling To Fulfill: Deaconesses in the United Methodist Tradition.* New York: Women's Division, General Board of Global Ministries, The United Methodist Church, 1997.

———. "The Social Gospel According to Phoebe: Methodist Deaconesses in the Metropolis, 1885–1915." In *Perspectives on American Methodism: Interpretive Essays*, edited by Russell E. Richey, et al., 356–68. Nashville: Kingswood, 1993.

Douglas, Ann. *The Feminization of American Culture.* New York: Alfred A. Knopf, 1977.

Douglass, Paul. *The Story of German Methodism: Biography of an Immigrant Soul.* New York: Methodist Book Concern, 1939.

Dulles, Foster Rhea. "A Historical View of Americans Abroad." *The Annals of the American Academy of Political and Social Science* 368 (1966) 11–20.

Dwyer-McNulty, Sally. *Common Threads: A Cultural History of Clothing in American Catholicism.* Chapel Hill: University of North Carolina Press, 2014.

Edwards, Jo. "What Is a Fresh Expression?" http://freshexpressions.org.uk/about/what-is-a-fresh-expression/.

Eicher, Joanne B. "Clothing, Costume and Dress." In *The Berg Companion to Fashion*, edited by Valerie Steele, 151–52. Oxford: Bloomsbury Academic, 2010. https://www.bloomsburyfashioncentral.com/products/berg-fashion-library/encyclopedia/the-berg-companion-to-fashion/clothing-costume-and-dress.

Evans, Christopher H. "'The Noblest Ideals of Service': Sister Jeanie Banks's Sojourn in London's East End, 1888–1893." *Methodist History* 56 (2018) 197–210.

Evenson, Sandra Lee, and David J. Trayte. "Dress and the Negotiation of Relationships Between the Eastern Dakota and Euroamericans in Nineteenth-Century Minnesota." In *Religion, Dress, and the Body*, edited by Linda B. Arthur, 95–116. New York: Berg, 1999.

Ewing, Elizabeth. *Women in Uniform: Through the Centuries.* Totowa, NJ: Rowman and Littlefield, 1975.

Field, Clive D. "The Social Structure of English Methodism: Eighteenth to Twentieth Centuries." *British Journal of Sociology* 28 (1977) 199–225.

Fischer, Gayle V. "Dressing to Please God: Pants-Wearing Women in Mid-Nineteenth-Century Religious Communities." *Communal Societies* 15 (1995) 55–74.

Flanagan, Maureen. "Gender and Urban Political Reform: The City Club and the Woman's City Club of Chicago in the Progressive Era." *The American Historical Review* 95 (1990) 1032–50.

Ford, Stephen V. R., ed. *The Methodist Year Book 1909*. Cincinnati: Jennings & Graham, 1909.

Freedman, Estelle. "Separatism As Strategy: Female Institution Building and American 'Feminism, 1870–1930." *Feminist Studies* 5 (1979) 512–29.

———. "Separatism Revisited: Women's Institutions, Social Reform, and the Career of Miriam Van Waters." In *U.S. History as Women's History*, edited by Linda K. Kerber et al., 170–88. Chapel Hill: University of North Carolina Press, 1995.

"From Nerves to Neuroses." Science Museum, June 12, 2019. https://www.sciencemuseum.org.uk/objects-and-stories/medicine/nerves-neuroses#the-rest-cure.

Fry, Ruth. *Out of the Silence: Methodist Women of Aotearoa, 1822–1985*. Christchurch: Methodist Publishing, 1987.

Furnish, Dorothy Jean. "Women in Religious Education: Pioneers for Women in Professional Ministry." In *Women and Religion in America, Volume 3: 1900–1968*, edited by Rosemary Radford Ruether and Rosemary Skinner Keller, 310–17. San Francisco: Harper & Row, 1986.

Geary, Patrick J., et al. "Germany: The Economy, 1890–1914." *Encyclopedia Britannica*. https://www.britannica.com/place/Germany/The-economy-1890-1914.

Gifford, Carolyn De Swarte, ed. *The American Deaconess Movement in the Early Twentieth Century*. New York: Garland, 1987.

Gill, Sean. *Women and the Church of England: From the Eighteenth Century to the Present*. London: SPCK, 1994.

Gjelsness, Rudolph. "Centenary of Samantha: Marietta Holley, who was 'Josiah Allen's Wife,' Achieved Fame as a Humorist." *The New York Times* (July 19, 1936) 9.

Golder, Christian. *The Deaconess Motherhouse, in its Relation to the Deaconess Work*. Pittsburgh: Pittsburgh Printing, 1907.

———. *History of the Deaconess Movement in the Christian Church*. New York: Eaton and Mains, 1908.

Gomez-Jefferson, Annetta. *The Sage of Tawawa: Reverdy Cassius Ransom, 1861–1959*. Ashland, OH: Kent State University Press, 2013.

Gordon, Linda. "Gender, State and Society: A Debate with Theda Skocpol." *Contention* 2 (1993) 139–89.

Graham, Dorothy. *Saved to Serve: The Story of the Wesley Deaconess Order, 1890–1978*. Werrington: Methodist Publishing, 2002.

Grant, Abraham. *Deaconess Manual of the African Methodist Episcopal Church*. A.M.E. Church, 1902.

Hammond, Geordan. *John Wesley in America: Restoring Primitive Christianity*. New York: Oxford University Press, 2014.

Hancock, Bethany. *A History of the Methodist Deaconess Order in South Australia*. Malvern, SA: Uniting Church Historical Society (SA), 1995.

Harper, William Rainey. "Shall the Theological Curriculum Be Modified, and How?" *The American Journal of Theology* 3 (1899) 45–66.
Hartley, Benjamin L. "Salvation and Sociology in the Methodist Episcopal Deaconess Movement." *Methodist History* 40 (2002) 182–97.
Hatch, Nathan. *The Democratization of American Christianity.* New Haven, CT: Yale University Press, 1989.
Hempton, David. *Methodism: Empire of the Spirit.* New Haven, CT: Yale University Press, 2005.
Herfarth, Margit. "The European Roots of the American Methodist Deaconess Movement." In *Women Pioneers in Continental European Methodism, 1869–1939,* edited by Paul Chilcote and Ulrike Schuler, 65–82. London: Routledge, 2018.
Higginbotham, Evelyn Brooks. *Righteous Discontent: The Women's Movement in the Black Baptist Church, 1880–1920.* Cambridge, MA: Harvard University Press, 1993.
Hofstadter, Richard, ed. *The Progressive Movement, 1900–1915.* Englewood Cliffs, NJ: Prentice-Hall, 1963.
Holding, Elizabeth E. *Joy the Deaconess.* Cincinnati: Jennings & Graham, 1898.
Holifield, E. Brooks. *God's Ambassadors: A History of the Christian Clergy in America.* Grand Rapids: Eerdmans, 2007.
Holley, Marietta. *Samantha Among the Brethren.* New York: Funk & Wagnalls, 1892.
———. *Samantha At Saratoga, or, "Flirtin' with Fashion."* Philadelphia: Hubbard Brothers, 1887.
Horton, Isabelle. *The Builders: A Story of Faith and Works.* Chicago: The Deaconess Advocate, 1910.
———. *The Burden of the City.* New York: Fleming H. Revell, 1904.
———. *High Adventure: Life of Lucy Rider Meyer.* New York: The Methodist Book Concern, 1928.
Hume, Lynne. *The Religious Life of Dress: Global Fashion and Faith.* New York: Bloomsbury, 2013.
Hunt, Beverly W. *Walking in the Power of Purpose: Deaconess Handbook, African Methodist Episcopal Zion Church.* Rev. ed. Charlotte, NC: Christian Education Department, AME Zion Church, 2013.
Hurty, Kathleen S. "Protestant Women's Colleges in the United States." In *Encyclopedia of Women and Religion in North America,* edited by Rosemary Skinner Keller and Rosemary Radford Ruether, 2:912–23. Bloomington: Indiana University Press, 2006.
Ingersol, Stan. "The Deaconess in Nazarene History." *Herald of Holiness* 81 (1992) 36.
Joselit, Jenna Weissman. *A Perfect Fit: Clothes, Character and the Promise of America.* New York: Metropolitan Books, 2001.
Joseph, Nathan. *Uniforms and Nonuniforms: Communication Through Clothing.* Contributions in Sociology 61. New York: Greenwood, 1986.
Jürisson, Cynthia A. "The Deaconess Movement." In *Encyclopedia of Women and Religion in North America,* edited by Rosemary Skinner Keller and Rosemary Radford Ruether, 2:821–33. Bloomington: Indiana University Press, 2006.
Keller, Rosemary Skinner. "Belle Harris Bennett and Lucy Rider Meyer." In *Something More than Human: Biographies of Leaders in American Methodist Higher Education,* edited by Charles E. Cole, 9–23. Nashville: United Methodist Board of Higher Education and Ministry, 1986.
———. "Creating a Sphere for Women." In *Women in New Worlds,* edited by Hilah F. Thomas and Rosemary Skinner Keller, 1:246–60. Nashville: Abingdon, 1981.

———. "The Deaconess: 'New Woman' of Late Nineteenth Century Methodism." *Explor* 5 (1979) 33–40.

———. "Leadership and Community Building in Protestant Women's Organizations." *Union Seminary Quarterly Review* 57 (2003) 40–56.

———. "Women and the Nature of Ministry in the United Methodist Tradition." *Methodist History* 22 (1984) 99–114.

Kerber, Linda K. *Toward an Intellectual History of Women: Essays by Linda K. Kerber.* Chapel Hill: University of North Carolina Press, 1997.

Klassen, Pamela E. "The Robes of Womanhood: Dress and Authenticity Among African American Methodist Women in the Nineteenth Century." *Religion and American Culture: A Journal of Interpretation* 14 (2004) 39–82.

Koven, Seth, and Sonya Michel. "Womanly Duties: Maternalist Politics and the Origins of Welfare States in France, Germany, Great Britain, and the United States, 1880–1920." *American Historical Review* 95 (1990) 1076–1108.

Kreutzer, Susanne, and Karen Nolte. "Deaconesses in Nursing Care: A Transnational History." In *Deaconesses in Nursing Care: International Transfer of a Female Model of Life and Work in the 19th and 20th Century*, edited by Susanne Kreutzer and Karen Nolte, 7–15. Stuttgart: Franz Steiner, 2016.

Kreutziger, Sarah Sloan. "Going on to Perfection: The Contributions of the Wesleyan Theological Doctrine of Entire Sanctification to the Value Base of American Professional Social Work through the Lives and Activities of Nineteenth-Century Evangelical Women Reformers." DSW diss., Tulane University, 1991.

Le Zotte, Jennifer. "'Be Odd:' The Contradictory Use of Dress in the Gilded Age Salvation Army." *Winterthur Portfolio* 47 (2013) 245–66.

Lee, Elizabeth M. *As Among the Methodists: Deaconesses Yesterday, Today and Tomorrow.* New York: Woman's Division of Christian Service, Board of Mission, Methodist Episcopal Church, 1963.

Legath, Jenny Wiley. *Sanctified Sisters: A History of Protestant Deaconesses.* New York: New York University Press, 2019.

Lehnert, Gertrud. "Gender." In *Berg Encyclopedia of World Dress and Fashion: West Europe*, edited by Joanne B. Eicher, 8:452–61. https://www.bloomsburyfashioncentral.com/encyclopedia-chapter?docid=b-9781847888570&tocid=b-9781847888570-EDch8075&st=Gender.

Library of Congress. "The Gibson Girl's America: Drawings by Charles Dana Gibson." https://www.loc.gov/exhibits/gibson-girls-america/the-gibson-girl-as-the-new-woman.html#:~:text=Writers%20in%20the%201890s%20and,ideal%20of%20this%20new%20phenomenon.

———. "Teacher's Guides and Analysis Tools." https://www.loc.gov/programs/teachers/getting-started-with-primary-sources/guides/.

Lindley, Susan Hill. *"You Have Stepped Out of Your Place:" A History of Women and Religion in America.* Louisville, KY: Westminster John Knox, 1996.

Lloyd, Jennifer M. *Women and the Shaping of British Methodism: Persistent Preachers, 1807–1907.* Manchester: Manchester University Press, 2010.

Macleod, David I. *Building Character in the American Boy: The Boy Scouts, the YMCA, and their Forerunners, 1870–1920.* Madison: University of Wisconsin Press, 1983.

Mangiduyos, Gladys P. "Filipino Deaconess Receives Peace Award." *UM News*, April 22, 2024. https://www.umnews.org/en/news/filipino-deaconess-receives-peace-award.

Mangion, Carmen M. "Women, Religious Ministry and Female Institution-Building." In *Women, Gender and Religious Cultures in Britain, 1800–1940*, edited by Sue Morgan and Jacqueline deVries, 72–93. London: Routledge, 2010.
Marty, Martin. *Protestantism in the United States: Righteous Empire*. Chicago: University of Chicago Press, 1986.
Mathews, Shailer. *The Faith of Modernism*. New York: Macmillan, 1924.
———. *New Faith for Old: An Autobiography*. New York: Macmillan, 1936.
McCarthy, Kathleen D. *Noblesse Oblige: Charity & Cultural Philanthropy in Chicago, 1849–1929*. Chicago: University of Chicago Press, 1982.
McConnell, Sherri-Lynne. "Canadian Deaconess and Missionary Education for Women Training to Live the Social Gospel: The Methodist National Training School and the Presbyterian Deaconess and Missionary Training Home, 1893–1926." MA thesis, University of Winnipeg, 2003.
McCulloh, Gerald O. *Ministerial Education in the American Methodist Movement*. Nashville: United Methodist Board of Higher Education and Ministry, 1980.
McDannell, Colleen. *The Christian Home in Victorian America, 1840–1900*. Bloomington: Indiana University Press, 1986.
———. *Material Christianity: Religion and Popular Culture in America*. New Haven, CT: Yale University Press, 1995.
McDowell, John Patrick. *The Social Gospel in the South: The Woman's Home Mission Movement in the Methodist Episcopal Church, South, 1886–1939*. Baton Rouge: Louisiana State University Press, 1982.
McFadden, Margaret H. *Golden Cables of Sympathy: The Transatlantic Sources of Nineteenth-Century Feminism*. Lexington, KY: University Press of Kentucky, 2009.
McGill, Jenny. "The Legacy of Anna E. Hall, African American Missionary to Liberia." *International Bulletin of Mission Research* 46 (2022) 92–103.
McKinley, Edward H. *Marching to Glory: The History of the Salvation Army in the United States, 1880–1992*. Grand Rapids: Eerdmans, 1995.
Meeker, Ruth Esther. *Six Decades of Service, 1880–1940: A History of the Woman's Home Missionary Society of the Methodist Episcopal Church*. Cincinnati: The Woman's Home Missionary Society, 1969.
Merritt, Jonathan. *Learning to Speak God from Scratch: Why Sacred Words Are Vanishing—And How We Can Revive Them*. New York: Convergent, 2018.
Mesaros-Winckles, Christy. *Silenced: The Forgotten Story of Progressive Era Free Methodist Women*. Lanham, MD: Lexington, 2023.
Meyer, Lucy Rider. *Deaconess Stories*. Chicago: Hope, 1900.
———. *Deaconesses, Biblical, Early Church, European, American: With the Story of The Chicago Training School, For City, Home and Foreign Missions, and The Chicago Deaconess Home*. 2nd ed. Chicago: The Message, 1889.
———. "Deaconesses and Their Work." In *Woman in Missions: Papers and Addresses Presented at the Woman's Congress of Missions, October 2–4, 1893, in the Hall of Columbus, Chicago*, compiled by E. M. Wherry, 182–98. New York: American Tract Society, 1894.
———. *Mary North: A Novel*. Chicago: Fleming H. Revell, 1903.
———. "The Mother in the Church." *Methodist Review* 83 (1901) 716–32.
Michel, Sonya. "Maternalism and Beyond." In *Maternalism Reconsidered: Motherhood, Welfare and Social Policy in the Twentieth Century*, edited by Marian van der Klein et al., 22–37. New York: Berghahn, 2012.

Miller, Glenn T. *Piety and Profession: American Protestant Theological Education, 1870–1970*. Grand Rapids: Eerdmans, 2007.

Morgan, David. *The Thing About Religion: An Introduction to the Material Study of Religions*. Chapel Hill: University of North Carolina Press, 2021.

Morley, William. *The History of Methodism in New Zealand*. Wellington: McKee, 1900.

Morris, Calvin S. *Reverdy C. Ransom: Black Advocate of the Social Gospel*. Lanham, MD: University Press of America, 1990.

Muncy, Robyn. *Creating a Female Dominion in American Reform, 1890–1935*. New York: Oxford University Press, 1991.

Ninde, W. X. "The Deaconess Movement." In *Proceedings of the Second Ecumenical Methodist Conference, Held in the Metropolitan Methodist Episcopal Church, Washington, October 1891*, edited by Arthur B. Sanford, 276–78. New York: Hunt & Eaton, 1892.

Nolte, Karen. "Deaconesses' Self-Understanding and Everyday Nursing Practice in the First Deaconess Community in Kaiserswerth, Germany." In *Deaconesses in Nursing Care: International Transfer of a Female Model of Life and Work in the 19th and 20th Century*, edited by Susanne Kreutzer and Karen Nolte, 19–35. Stuttgart: Franz Steiner, 2016.

Nordby, Lars-Erik. "Maria Bagger: Scandinavian Pioneer Nurse and Deaconess." In *Women Pioneers in Continental European Methodism, 1869–1939*, edited by Paul Chilcote and Ulrike Schuler, 205–7. London: Routledge, 2018.

O'Brien, Anne. *God's Willing Workers: Women and Religion in Australia*. Sydney: University of New South Wales Press, 2005.

Oehler, Carolyn Henninger. "Femininity and Religious Anxiety: Gender Trouble in the United Methodist Church." PhD diss., Northwestern University, 1997.

Oldham, William F. "Thoburn—Mystic, Seer, Prophet, Missionary." *Methodist Review* 39 (1923) 185–93.

Olson, Jeannine E. *Deacons and Deaconesses through the Centuries*. Rev. ed. St. Louis, MO: Concordia, 2005.

Orton, Andrew. "The Diverse and Contested Diaconate: Why Understanding this Ministry is Crucial to the Future of the Church." *International Journal of Practical Theology* 16 (2013) 260–84.

———. "Editorial." *Theology and Ministry* 2 (2013) 1.1–2.

Patterson, Louis Dale. "The Ministerial Mind of American Methodism: The Courses of Study for the Ministry of the Methodist Episcopal Church, The Methodist Episcopal Church, South and The Methodist Protestant Church: 1890–1920." PhD diss., Drew University, 1984.

Plant, Rebecca Jo, and Marian van der Klein. "Introduction: A New Generation of Scholars on Maternalism." In *Maternalism Reconsidered: Motherhood, Welfare and Social Policy in the Twentieth Century*, edited by Marian van der Klein et al., 1–21. New York: Berghahn, 2012.

Pope-Levison, Priscilla. *Building the Old Time Religion: Women Evangelists in the Progressive Era*. New York: New York University Press, 2014.

———. "Expanding the Historiography of Methodist Settlement Work." *Methodist Review* 12 (2020) 169–90.

———. "The Role of Deaconess Training Schools for American Women Missionaries, 1885–1895." In *Methodist Mission at Home and Abroad: Proceedings of the European Methodist Historical Conference, 6–9 September 2023, Velletri, Italy*, edited by Judit Lakatos and Michael Wetzel, 105–19. Budapest: World Methodist Historical Society, European Section, 2025.

———. "Single Vision, Separate Spheres: Iva Durham Vennard and the Methodist Episcopal Church." In *The Radical Holiness Movement in the Christian Tradition*, edited by William Kostlevy and Wallace Thornton, 97–109. Lexington, KY: Emeth, 2016.

———. *Turn the Pulpit Loose: Two Centuries of American Women Evangelists*. New York: Palgrave Macmillan, 2004.

Prelinger, Catherine M., and Rosemary Skinner Keller. "The Function of Female Bonding: The Restored Diaconessate of the Nineteenth Century." In *Women in New Worlds*, edited by Rosemary Skinner Keller et al., 2:318–37. Nashville: Abingdon, 1982.

Putnam, Robert D. *Bowling Alone: The Collapse and Revival of American Community*. New York: Simon & Schuster, 2000.

Rack, Henry D. "Wesleyan Methodism 1849–1902." In *A History of the Methodist Church in Great Britain*, edited by Rupert Davies et al., 3:119–66. London: Epworth, 1983.

Ransom, Reverdy. *The Pilgrimage of Harriet Ransom's Son*. Nashville: Sunday School Union, 1949.

Richey, Russell E. *Formation for Ministry in American Methodism: Twenty-first Century Challenges and Two Centuries of Problem-Solving*. Nashville: General Board of Higher Education and Ministry, The United Methodist Church, 2014.

Richey, Russell E., et al., eds. *The Methodist Experience in America: A History, Volume I*. Nashville: Abingdon, 2010.

———. *The Methodist Experience in America: A Sourcebook, Volume 2*. Nashville: Abingdon, 2000.

Riess, Steven A. *Touching Base: Professional Baseball and American Culture in the Progressive Era*. Rev. ed. Chicago: University of Illinois Press, 1999.

Robert, Dana L. *American Women in Mission: A Social History of Their Thought and Practice*. Macon, GA: Mercer University Press, 1997.

Robertson, Alice. "What Is Deaconess Work?" *Methodist Review* 35 (1919) 357–65.

Robinson, Jane Bancroft. *Deaconesses in Europe and Their Lessons for America*. New York: Hunt and Eaton, 1889.

Robledo, Liwliwa Tubayan. "Gender, Religion and Social Change: A Study of Philippine Methodist Deaconesses, 1903–1978." PhD diss., The Iliff School of Theology and University of Denver, 1996.

Robledo, Liwliwa Tubayan, and Phebe Gamata Crismo. *Celebrating A Century of God's Faithfulness: Harris Memorial College and the Deaconess*. Rizal: Harris Memorial College, 2003.

Rosenberg Library Museum. "Magic Lanterns." https://www.rosenberg-library-museum.org/treasures/magic-lanterns#:~:text=By%20the%201800s%2C%20magic%20lantern,were%20among%20the%20most%20common.

Rowe, Kenneth E. "The Ministry of Deacons in Methodism from Wesley to Today (1998)." *Quarterly Review* 19 (1999–2000) 343–46.

———. "New Light on Early Methodist Theological Education." *Methodist History* 10 (1971) 58–62.

Rubinstein, Ruth P. *Dress Codes: Meanings and Messages in American Culture*. San Francisco: Westview, 1995.

Rury, John L. *Education and Women's Work: Female Schooling and the Division of Labor in Urban America, 1870-1930.* Albany: State University of New York Press, 1991.

Sapiro, Virginia. *Women in American Society.* 2nd ed. Mountain View, CA: Mayfield, 1990.

Schmidt, Jean Miller. *Grace Sufficient: A History of Women in American Methodism, 1760-1939.* Nashville: Abingdon, 1999.

Schmidt, Leigh Eric. "'A Church-Going People are a Dress-Loving People': Clothes, Communication, and Religious Culture in Early America." *Church History* 58 (1989) 36–51.

Scott, Martin J. *Convent Life: The Meaning of a Religious Vocation.* New York: Kennedy & Sons, 1919.

Shaver, Lisa J. "The Deaconess Identity: An Argument for Professional Churchwomen and Social Christianity." In *Mapping Christian Rhetorics: Connecting Conversations, Charting New Territories,* edited by Michael-John DePalma and Jeffrey M. Ringer, 203–21. Florence: Taylor & Francis, 2014.

Shaw, Anna Howard. *Anna Howard Shaw: The Story of a Pioneer.* The William Bradford Collection, edited by Barbara Brown Zikmund. Repr. Cleveland: Pilgrim, 1994.

Sider, Ronald J., et al. *Churches That Make a Difference: Reaching Your Community with Good News and Good Works.* Grand Rapids: Baker, 2002.

Sklar, Kathryn Kish. *Florence Kelley and the Nation's Work: The Rise of Women's Political Culture, 1830-1900.* New Haven, CT: Yale University Press, 1995.

———. "Hull House in the 1890s: A Community of Women Reformers." *Signs: Journal of Women in Culture and Society* 10 (1985) 658–77.

———. "Two Political Cultures in the Progressive Era: The National Consumers' League and the American Association for Labor Legislation." In *U.S. History as Women's History: New Feminist Essays,* edited by Linda Kerber et al., 36–62. Chapel Hill: University of North Carolina Press, 1995.

Smaby, Beverly Prior. "'Only Brothers Should be Accepted into this Proposed Council:' Restricting Women's Leadership in Moravian Bethlehem." In *Pietism in Germany and North America, 1680-1820,* edited by Jonathan Strom et al., 133–62. Burlington, VT: Ashgate, 2009.

Smith, Henry. *Ministering Women,* 3rd ed. London: Henry Hooks, 1923.

Staton, Maurice. "The Development of Diaconal Ministry in the Methodist Church in Britain." *Theology and Ministry* 2 (2013) 3.1–14.

Steele, Valerie. "Dressing for Work." In *Men and Women. Dressing the Part,* edited by Claudia Brush Kidwell and Valerie Steele, 64–91. Washington, DC: Smithsonian, 1989.

Steinbach, Susie. "Victorian Era." *Encyclopedia Britannica.* https://www.britannica.com/event/Victorian-era.

Stephenson, Thomas Bowman. *Concerning Sisterhoods.* London: C. H. Kelly, 1890.

Stevenson, William Fleming. *Praying and Working, Being Some Account of What Men Can Do When in Earnest.* New York: Thomas Whittaker, 1892.

Strong, Josiah. *Our Country.* 1891 ed., edited by Jurgen Herbst. Cambridge, MA: Harvard University Press, 1963.

Sulkunen, Irma. "An International Comparison of Women's Suffrage: The Cases of Finland and New Zealand in the Late Nineteenth and Early Twentieth Century." *Journal of Women's History* 27 (2015) 88–111.

Taiz, Lillian. *Hallelujah Lads and Lasses: Remaking the Salvation Army in America, 1880-1930.* Chapel Hill: University of North Carolina Press, 2001.

Taves, Ann. *Fits, Trances, and Visions: Experiencing Religion and Explaining Experience from Wesley to James*. Princeton, NJ: Princeton University Press, 1999.

———. "Women and Gender in American Religion(s)." *Religious Studies Review* 18 (1992) 263–70.

Tennant, Margaret. "Pakeha Deaconesses and the New Zealand Methodist Mission to Maori, 1890–1940." *Journal of Religious History* 23 (1999) 309–26.

———. "Sisterly Ministrations: The Social Work of Protestant Deaconesses in New Zealand, 1890–1940." *New Zealand Journal of History* 32 (1998) 3–22.

Thoburn, James Mills. *The Church of Pentecost*. Cincinnati: Jennings & Pye, 1901.

———. *The Deaconess and Her Vocation*. New York: Hunt & Eaton, 1893.

———. *My Missionary Apprenticeship*. New York: Phillips & Hunt, 1884.

Tholin, Phyllis. "Samantha and Her Sisters: Images of Women in the Writings of Marietta Holley." In *Rethinking Methodist History: A Bicentennial Historical Consultation*, edited by Russell E. Richey and Kenneth E. Rowe, 204–11. Nashville: Kingswood, 1985.

Thomas, John D. "Servants of the Church: Canadian Methodist Deaconess Work, 1890–1926." *Canadian Historical Review* 65 (1984) 371–95.

Thompson, Betty Jane. *Adventure in Building Brotherhood: Methodist Women and Race*. Cincinnati: Woman's Division of Christian Service, 1946.

The University of Chicago Library. "Shailer Mathews (1863-1941): Theology." https://www.lib.uchicago.edu/collex/exhibits/university-chicago-centennial-catalogues/university-chicago-faculty-centennial-view/shailer-mathews-1863-1941-theology/.

Vicinius, Martha. *Independent Women: Work and Community for Single Women, 1850–1920*. Chicago: University of Chicago Press, 1985.

Walters, W. D. "Methodist Brotherhoods and Sisterhoods." In *Proceedings of the Second Ecumenical Methodist Conference, Held in the Metropolitan Methodist Episcopal Church, Washington, October 1891*, edited by Arthur B. Sanford, 278–81. New York: Hunt & Eaton, 1892.

Warner, Laceye C. "Methodist Episcopal and Wesleyan Methodist Deaconesses in the Late Nineteenth and Early Twentieth Centuries: A Paradigm for Evangelism." PhD diss., University of Bristol, 2000.

———. "'Toward the Light': Methodist Episcopal Deaconess Work Among Immigrant Populations, 1885–1910." *Methodist History* 43 (2005) 169–82.

———. "Wesley Deaconess-Evangelists: Exploring Remnants of Revivalism in Late 19th Century British Methodism." *Methodist History* 38 (2000) 176–90.

Waugh, Norah. *The Cut of Women's Clothes, 1600–1930*. New York: Theatre Arts, 1968.

Wellings, Martin. "'A Time to be Born and a Time to Die'? A Historian's Perspective on the Future of Methodism." In *Methodism and the Future: Facing the Challenge*, edited by Jane Craske and Clive Marsh, 148–57. London: Cassell, 1999.

Wesley, John. "On Visiting the Sick." Edited by Chris Dinter et al. 1872. https://wesley.nnu.edu/john-wesley/the-sermons-of-john-wesley-1872-edition/sermon-98-on-visiting-the-sick/.

West, Janet. "A Recipe for Confrontation: Female Religious Orders and the Male Hierarchy in Nineteenth Century Australia." In *Long Patient Struggle: Studies in the Role of Women in Australian Christianity*, edited by Mark Hutchinson and Edmund Campion, 71–87. Sydney: Centre for the Study of Australian Christianity, 1994.

Wheeler, Henry. *Deaconesses Ancient and Modern.* New York: Hunt & Eaton, 1889.

Williams, Patricia. "The Crackerbox Philosopher as Feminist: The Novels of Marietta Holley." *American Humor: An Interdisciplinary Newsletter* 7 (1980) 16–21.

Willing, Jennie Fowler. *The Potential Woman: A Book for Young Ladies.* Boston: McDonald & Gill, 1886.

Wilson, Robert L. *Attitudes of the United Methodist Deaconess, 1970.* New York: Department of Research and Survey, National Division, Board of Missions, United Methodist Church, 1970.

Winston, Diane. "Living in the Material World: Salvation Army Lassies and Urban Commercial Culture, 1880–1918." In *Faith in the Market: Religion and the Rise of Urban Commercial Culture*, edited by John M. Giggie and Diane Winston, 13–36. New Brunswick, NJ: Rutgers University Press, 2002.

———. *Red-Hot and Righteous: The Urban Religion of the Salvation Army.* Cambridge, MA: Harvard University Press, 1999.

Winter, Kate H. *Marietta Holley: Life with 'Josiah Allen's Wife.'* Syracuse, NY: Syracuse University Press, 1984.

Wisbey, Herbert A. *Soldiers Without Swords: A History of the Salvation Army in the United States.* New York: Macmillan, 1955.

Wood, Ann Douglas. "'The Fashionable Diseases': Women's Complaints and Their Treatment in Nineteenth-Century America." In *Clio's Consciousness Raised: New Perspectives on the History of Women*, edited by Mary Hartman and Lois W. Banner, 1–22. New York: Harper & Row, 1974.

Wood, Joseph. "Diaconal-Dilemmas—The Development of the Diaconate in the Church of the Nazarene." *Theology and Ministry* 2 (2013) 5.1–17.

Woodworth, Maria Beulah. *The Life, Work, and Experience of Maria Beulah Woodworth.* St. Louis, MO: Commercial, 1894.

World Council of Churches. *The Deaconess: A Service of Women in the World of Today.* World Council of Churches Studies 4. Geneva: World Council of Churches, 1966.

Wright, Don. *Mantle of Christ: A History of the Sydney Central Methodist Mission.* St. Lucia: University of Queensland Press, 1984.

Wuthnow, Robert. *Boundless Faith: The Global Outreach of American Churches.* Berkeley: University of California Press, 2009.

Zink-Sawyer, Beverly. *From Preachers to Suffragists: Woman's Rights and Religious Conviction in the Lives of Three Nineteenth-Century American Clergywomen.* Louisville, KY: Westminster John Knox, 2003.

SUBJECT INDEX

Africa, 4, 9, 31, 229
African Methodist Episcopal Church
 (AME), 8, 23, 27, 33–34, 38,
 168, 194–95, 199–205
 bishops, 194–95, 199–201
 Deaconess Manual, 34, 38, 189,
  194–95, 199–205
 deaconesses, 8, 33–34, 38, 108, 201
 General Conferences, 8, 33, 168
 missions, 200
 Sunday School Union, 8
 training school, 34
African Methodist Episcopal Zion
 Church (AMEZ), 8
American Bible Society, 89
Ames, A. H., 148
andromania, 189–95, 197–98
Asbury, Francis, 40
Asia, 9
Australia, 3–4, 8, 22–23, 40, 96, 115
 deaconesses, 8, 16, 27
 Sydney, city of, 3, 16–17, 22, 27, 213
 Sydney Central Methodist Mission,
  115
 See also Francis, Laura; Taylor, W. G.
Austria, 28, 163
 Vienna, city of, 21, 163

Bagger, Marie, 18
Band of Hope, 155, 230
Banks, Jeannie, 18, 176
Bennett, Belle Harris, 22, 27

Bible, 28, 43, 45, 51, 89–90, 131, 144–
 45, 168–69, 184, 195, 200, 202,
 221, 231, 239, 245
 Deborah, 200–201
 Hannah, 184
 Jesus Christ, 74–75, 156, 179, 181–
  82, 200, 229
 Lydia, 200
 Mary Magdalene, 74, 240
 Paul, 21, 42, 87–88, 112, 140, 169,
  200
 Phoebe, 15–16, 21, 165, 184,
  200–201
 Priscilla, 200–201
 study of, 70–71, 79, 81–82, 84–85,
  88, 91, 99, 144, 166, 213, 223
 teaching, 19, 28, 70–71, 79, 81,
  84–85, 89–90, 122, 156, 166,
  226, 246
Bible Christian Connexion, 15
Black deaconesses, 14, 18–19, 30–31,
 41, 63, 139, 166, 191. *See also*
 African Methodist Episcopal
 Church (AME); African
 Methodist Episcopal Zion
 Church (AMEZ); Hall, Anna;
 Parks, Rosa; Riley, Walter;
 Simpson, Rosa; Slater, Sarah
Blakeley, Jane, 17
Bradfield, William, 99
Boer War, 229, 247
Boston University School of Theology,
 80, 87, 92
Bovey, Margaret, 20

SUBJECT INDEX

Bryn Mawr College, 5, 61, 191
Bushnell, Horace, 212

Canada, 6–8, 23, 112, 228
    deaconesses, 3, 6, 17, 28, 36–37, 171
    Montreal, city of, 29
    Toronto, city of, 6–7, 17, 29, 37, 171, 213
    Toronto Deaconess Home and Training School, 17. *See also* Massey, H. A.
Cannon, Frances, 2, 234
Catholicism (Roman), 10, 83, 87, 103, 191
    anti-Catholicism, 34, 39, 115–16
    convents, 39
    habits, 105, 114, 116
    nuns, 39, 114–16
celibacy, 39, 83
charity, 42, 114, 186, 200, 203, 263
Chicago Evangelistic Institute (CEI), 174. *See also* Vennard, Iva Durham
Chicago Training School (CTS), 2, 17, 27, 35, 60, 66, 84, 143–44, 149, 173–74, 221
    curriculum, 84–88
    evangelism, 65–66
    practical work, 22, 89–90
    See also Meyer, Josiah Shelley; Meyer, Lucy Rider
children, 121, 138–40, 142–44, 148, 155–56, 219–20, 225, 231–33, 245, 247
    care for, 29, 63, 66, 69, 71, 89, 111
    evangelism of, 30, 65, 74, 122, 125
    homes, 3, 63, 163, 225
    See also Band of Hope; Fresh Air Work; girls' clubs; lantern shows; motherhood.
Church of England, 20, 106, 121, 214
church history, study of, 74, 81, 85, 87, 213
Church of the Nazarene, 7
Church of the United Brethren in Christ, 7
Clarke, Edward, 81
class meetings, 18, 140, 232, 235

clergymen, 26, 37–40, 70–71, 110, 137, 145, 147–48, 163, 166–68, 170, 190, 194–96
Coke, Thomas, 40
conversion, 67, 75, 172, 211–12, 240–41, 244
course of study, 84–85, 90, 196
Crump, Grace, 19

deaconess
    anti-Catholicism, 39, 115–16
    bonnet, 32, 103, 108, 112–14, 120–21, 124–25
    calling, 45, 67, 169, 179–82, 194, 196, 198–201, 203, 211–12, 221
    conflict with clergymen, 37–39, 189–98, 202–3
    consecration, 75, 127–28, 148, 180–81, 212, 251
    ceremony, 6, 194, 176, 189, 199–201
    distinctive dress (*see* deaconess uniform)
    early church, 5, 20, 87, 168, 176, 200, 263
    hairstyle, 108, 130
    homes, 15, 27, 33, 61, 67, 143–45, 147, 171, 213, 215, 222, 254
    Motherhouses, 21, 27, 46, 50–52, 163
    movement, international, 7, 15, 25, 27–28, 34, 36, 71, 141, 222
    Office of, 8, 15, 22–23, 27, 33, 137, 141, 150–51, 162, 164–65, 191, 195, 199
    role and boundaries, 8, 15, 20, 24–25, 33, 36–40, 66, 69, 105, 194–97, 199
    superintendents, 2, 3, 10, 17, 28, 144–45, 148, 170
    training schools, 15, 79–80, 82, 84, 87, 89–91, 93, 166, 213
    curriculum, 19, 66, 69, 71, 79, 81, 83–93, 196, 212–13
    practical work, 79, 83, 88–92, 196, 213, 223
    uniform, 6, 32, 39, 73, 99, 103, 105, 110–13, 115, 117, 164, 215

SUBJECT INDEX 271

vows, 39, 115, 145
work, 35–36, 38–39, 58, 64–65, 91, 195, 217, 220
  evangelism, 65, 218–19
  hospitals, 8, 18, 28–29, 32, 50, 59, 89–90, 136, 144, 156, 171, 203, 213, 216, 219 (*see also* nursing)
  orphans, 136, 144–45, 148, 153, 175, 198, 243, 247
  sickroom, 8, 19–20, 74, 190, 202–3, 205, 209 (*see also* nursing)
  visitation, 2, 8, 19–20, 28, 89, 175, 203, 209–10, 246
Deaconess College (at Ilkley), 2, 78–79, 94–100, 108, 164, 213
Deaconess Stories, 133–34, 142. See also Meyer, Lucy Rider.
Denmark, 18, 23
devotion, 31, 49, 83, 145, 228–29, 250
  Bible reading, 43, 45, 51, 85, 88, 130–31, 144–45, 221, 245
  personal prayer, 42–43, 46, 53, 90, 95–96, 130–31, 140, 211, 216, 221, 250
diaconate, 8, 15, 31, 170, 193, 215
Do Without Band, 216
Dollaga, Norma P., 9
domesticity, 87, 138
Dougherty, Mary Agnes, 7, 16–17, 31, 58–59, 61, 66
dress, 19, 40, 103–17, 120, 128, 130, 145, 209, 215
  fashionable, 105–10, 116, 215
  plain, 113, 116
  nuns' habit, 39, 105, 114, 116, 229
  Salvation Army, 105, 111–12
  uniform, 10, 32, 73, 83, 86, 110, 112, 128, 165, 180, 212, 215
  See also deaconess bonnet; deaconess uniform

education, 66, 80, 82–83, 126–27, 192, 196. *See also* course of study; deaconess training schools; seminary; theological education; women's education
Edward VII, King, 235
Eliot, George, 96, 155

Elizabeth Gamble Deaconess Home, 22
Epworth Evangelistic Institute (EEI), 68–71, 79, 84, 87, 89, 165, 174, 194. *See also* deaconess training schools; Vennard, Iva Durham.
Epworth League, 73, 122
Evangelical Alliance, 24
Evangelical Association, 7
evangelism, 6, 25, 58, 64–70, 164, 169–70, 175–76, 194–95, 211–12, 216–18. *See also* deaconess evangelism

family, 39, 48–49, 87, 123, 136, 139, 144–45, 174, 184, 215
female institution building, 58, 62–64, 148
feminism, 3–4, 149, 184. *See also* women's rights.
Fliedner, Mina, 215
Fliedner, Theodore, 21, 175–76, 193
France, 5, 96, 231, 262
Francis, Laura, 13, 16, 27, 115
Franco-German War, 114, 164
Free Methodist Church, 7
Freedman, Estelle, 58, 62, 148, 260
Fresh Air Work, 29, 247
Fresh Expressions, 220
Fry, Susan M., 83, 254
fundraising, 171. *See also* Do Without Band

Gamble, James, 171
Gatdula, Fidela, 19
gender, 138, 194
  borders, 177, 192–95, 197–98
  dress, 106–7
  roles, 58, 64–65, 72, 138, 149, 163, 186, 192, 201, 205. *See also* women's separate spheres
George V, King, 248
German Methodism, 16, 21–22, 91
  Bethany Association, 21
  deaconesses, 5, 21–22, 38, 61, 163. *See also* Martha-Maria Deaconess Organization

United States, in, 22, 28, 38, 61, 163, 196, 254. *See also* Golder, Christian; Golder, Louise
Germany, 3, 7, 14, 16–17, 21–22, 24, 27–28, 163, 170, 221, 266
    Dusseldorf, city of, 21, 163
    Elberfeld, city of, 21
    Frankfurt am Main, city of, 21, 27, 163, 213
    Magdeburg, city of, 21
    Munich, city of, 21
    Nuremberg, city of, 16, 21, 28, 126, 131
    Stuttgart, city of, 17, 259, 262, 264
GI Bill, 80–81
Gibson Girl, 183
Gibson, Maria Layng, 83
Gifford, Carolyn De Swarte, 3, 65–66, 136–37, 148
Gilman, Charlotte Perkins, 249
girls' clubs, 219, 242, 254
Golder, Christian, 5, 26, 61, 161, 163, 170, 176–77, 183–86, 190–91, 193
Golder, Louise, 17, 22, 196
Gordon Hall, 223–25, 230
Gorham, Sarah, 200
Graham, Dorothy, 3, 24
Greek, study of, 15, 86–87
Gregory, A. E., 223, 246
Gregory, Caroline, 228

Hall, Anna, 18, 24, 31, 139, 187
Harper, William Rainey, 92
Harris Memorial Training School, 9, 19, 173, 213
Harris, Norman Waite, 172–73
Hartley, Benjamin, 80, 92
Hayes, Lucy Webb, 139
Heidner, Elise, 16
Helping Hand Mission, 17
Hendrix, Eugene, 27, 164
Holding, Elizabeth, 136, 144. See also *Joy the Deaconess*
Holiness movement, 7, 100
Holley, Marietta, 109, 149, 151
Holy Spirit, 46, 91, 167–69, 186, 195, 201, 211

Horton, Isabelle, 66, 104
hospitals, 28, 33, 126, 210, 226, 250
    Bethesda Hospital, 17
    Birmingham General Hospital, 237, 248
    Chest Hospital, 228
    Children's Hospital, 227
    Christ Hospital, 17, 171
    See also deaconess work, hospitals; nursing
Hughes, Christian, 234
Hughes, Hugh Price, 16, 115
Hughes, Katherine, 16
Hull House, 62
humanitarianism, 217–18

immigration, 24, 36, 57, 175
India, 23
Indonesia, 9

jails, 8, 28, 32, 89, 204, 213
Jamaica, 4
Jeffrey, Olive, 207
Johnson, John (Jack) Arthur, 32
Joy the Deaconess, 136–37, 144–45, 152, 167, 254, 261
juvenile courts, 69, 89

Kaiserswerth, 21–22, 163, 165, 175–76, 193, 215, 221, 226. *See also* Fleidner, Theodore
Keeling, May, 108
Keller, Rosemary Skinner, 3, 60, 63, 149, 152
King, Sarah, 6, 17
King's Daughters, The, 122–23

labor, 24, 26, 58, 66, 89, 150–51, 153, 180, 200, 214
lantern shows, 155, 219, 239
Lathrop, Julia, 63
Legath, Jenny, 15–16, 31, 36, 39, 110, 112, 114–15
Lucy Webb Hayes National Training School, 31, 148
Luther, Martin, 46

Malaysia, 9

Martha-Maria Deaconess Organization, 14, 16, 21, 28, 42–53, 103, 126–31, 214–15
Mary North, 137, 142–47, 152, 263. See also Meyer, Lucy Rider
Massey, H. A., 171
Masters, Thirza, 29, 210–12, 238–51
maternalism, 10, 39, 135–45, 147, 149, 151–52, 193, 262–64. *See also* motherhood
McKendree College, 59, 144
Methodist Episcopal Church (MEC), 22, 194
   annual conferences, 23, 85, 150, 163, 198
   Norwegian-Danish, 26
   Texas, 19, 32
   bishops, 5, 16, 18, 22–23, 25, 84–85, 113–14, 140, 161, 163–65, 167, 169, 178, 195
   deaconesses, 25, 32, 35, 38, 165, 221
   General Conferences, 22–23, 32, 37, 59, 61, 137, 139, 141, 150, 165–66, 195, 199
   See also Woman's Foreign Missionary Society (WFMS); Woman's Home Missionary Society (WHMS)
Methodist Episcopal Church South (MECS), 23, 27, 37, 77, 164
   bishops, 27, 162, 164
   deaconesses, 18, 27, 83, 164, 171–72, 188
   General Conferences, 27, 37, 162, 171
Methodist history, 20, 81
Methodist Protestant Church (MPC), 15
Mewburn House, 1–2, 164, 209, 223–24, 232, 234, 251
Meyer, Josiah Shelley, 22, 59, 173–75. *See also* Chicago Training School (CTS); Meyer, Lucy Rider
Meyer, Lucy Rider, 2, 5–7, 22, 55, 67, 69, 71, 118–125, 135, 137, 144, 153, 162, 167–68, 171, 173, 222
   dress, 32, 103–10, 112–14, 116
   education, 65, 84–86, 90

evangelism, 65–66, 69
maternalism, 136, 140–41, 144–46, 149
politics (church), 27, 59, 61–62, 141, 152
See also Chicago Training School (CTS); *Deaconess Stories*; *Mary North*; Meyer, Josiah Shelley
Mildmay Mission, 165
missionaries, 15, 19, 23–24, 29, 31, 82–84, 90, 143, 166, 171–72, 186, 200, 254, 264
Mitchell, Silas Weir, 249. *See also* rest cure
Moravians, 20, 170
motherhood, 39, 57, 71, 121, 135, 138–39, 141–46, 150, 184–85, 194. *See also* maternalism
music, 74–76, 98, 121–22, 155, 213, 219, 249
   hymns, 11, 18, 53, 74–75, 95, 103, 108, 112, 129, 144, 194, 211, 217, 219, 225, 231, 241

Nacpil, Emerito P., 197
National Vigilance Association, 243
New England Deaconess Training School, 18, 31, 86–87, 92
New Zealand, 1–2, 4, 8, 19, 23, 36–37, 40, 154
   Auckland, city of, 17
   Christchurch, city of, 3, 17, 19
   deaconesses, 1–2, 8, 17, 19, 28, 36–37, 136, 207, 232, 234. *See also* Sinclair, Isabel
   Dunedin, city of, 28
   Wellington, city of, 2, 17, 154. *See also* Tory Street Mission
Nightingale, Florence, 22
Ninde, W. X., 5
Nineteenth Amendment, 23, 191
Norcroft, Ruth, 248
Northwestern University, 59–60
Norway, 18
nursing, 15, 17, 21–22, 65–66, 83, 88, 90, 124, 142, 144, 177, 209, 228, 248–50

Ocean Grove Camp Meeting
    Association, 168, 214
Oldham, William, 164–67, 264
ordination, 15, 37, 71, 162, 165–66, 185,
    195
orphanages, 3, 39, 59. See also deaconess
    work

Panama Canal, 1
Parkhurst, Charles, 190–93, 255. See
    also andromania
Parks, Rosa, 8
pastoral care, 38, 182
Philippines, 3, 8–9, 14, 23, 27, 40, 173,
    197, 213
    deaconesses, 8–9, 19. See also
        Dollaga, Norma P.; Gatdula,
        Fidela; Harris Memorial
        Training School
    Manila, city of, 9, 19, 27, 173, 213
Pitts, Elizabeth Ann, 1–2, 210, 223–24,
    234–35
political reform, 62–63, 216
poverty, 15, 24, 28, 48, 80, 124–25, 148,
    154, 193, 214, 220, 234, 243–44
prayer, 74–75, 89–90, 116, 122, 145,
    148, 167, 179, 194, 209, 216,
    219, 226–27, 229–30, 232, 239–
    40, 244–45.
    family, 144
    meeting, 224, 228, 235, 246
    See also devotion, personal prayer
preaching, 25, 36, 50, 71, 84, 148,
    169–70, 175–76, 180, 195, 198,
    209, 217, 228
    defense of female, 87–88, 167,
        169–70
    female, 18, 20, 38, 40, 67, 70, 146,
        162, 180, 193–94
Primitive Methodist Connexion, 15
Progressive Era, 57–58, 62, 148, 260,
    266
prostitution, 17, 69, 74–75, 205, 243,
    245.
    See also women, fallen
Public Houses, 239–40

racism, 30, 150
Ransom, Reverdy, 33–34, 168

rest cure, 210, 237, 248
revivalism, 67, 69–70, 167, 208, 210–11,
    213, 220
Riley, Walter, 30–31, 166
Robertson, Alice, 35, 265
Robinson, Jane Bancroft, 5, 22, 27, 56,
    58, 60–64, 67–68, 71–72, 87,
    104, 114–15, 161
Robledo, Liwliwa T., 197

sacraments, 8, 151, 165
salvation, 49–50, 95, 142, 145, 230–31
Salvation Army, 16, 103, 111–12, 116,
    212
    slum sisters, 105, 111–12. See also
        dress
Saundby, Robert, 248
Scarritt Bible and Training School,
    18, 77, 83, 144, 171–72, 253.
    See also Bennett, Belle Harris;
    Gibson, Maria Layng; Holding,
    Elizabeth; Scarritt, Nathan
Scarritt, Nathan, 171–72
Schmidt, Jean Miller, 66
Schneider, Louise, 16
Searle, Elise, 17–18, 206, 216–17
seminary, 10, 79–81, 83, 85–86, 90,
    92–93. See also course of study;
    deaconess training schools;
    theological education
Semple, Louise, 196
settlement houses, 3, 57, 63, 89, 191, 213
Shaw, Anna Howard, 80
sickness, 38–39, 52, 126, 202, 204, 210,
    216, 234. See also deaconess
    work; hospitals
Simpson, Matthew, 22
Simpson, Rosa, 12, 19, 32–33
Sinclair, Isabel, 1–3, 136, 154–57, 210,
    232, 234
Singapore, 9
sisterhood, 63, 83, 115, 149, 164, 215
Sisters of Charity, 114
Sisters of the People, 115
Slater, Sarah, 34
Smith, Hannah Whitall, 211
Smith, Henry, 38
social work, 34, 36, 56, 58, 64–66,
    69–70, 88–90

SUBJECT INDEX

South Africa, 4
Stanton, Elizabeth Cady, 184
Stephenson, Dora, 159, 212, 225
Stephenson, Thomas Bowman 6–7, 22, 26, 110, 114, 120, 162–64, 172, 175–77, 210, 222, 225, 234. *See also* Wesley Deaconess Order (WDO)
Strong, Josiah, 24
Sunday school, 35, 37–38, 59, 82, 84–85, 89–90, 141, 156, 213, 229–30, 233
Swarthmore College, 67
Sweden, 23, 170
Switzerland, 5, 7, 61, 163, 170

Taiwan, 9
Taylor, W. G., 16, 22, 115
temperance, 30, 57, 139, 149, 240, 244. *See also* Band of Hope; Women's Christian Temperance Union (WCTU)
tenements, 57, 69, 142, 144, 215. *See also* deaconess visitation
testimony, 49, 114, 164, 179, 181, 202, 230
Thayer Industrial School, 18, 139. *See also* Hall, Anna
theological education, 10, 79–81, 83–85, 87–93, 196, 229. *See also* course of study; deaconess training schools; seminary
theology, study of, 70–71, 79–80, 87, 90, 92, 145, 166–67, 223. *See also* course of study; deaconess training schools; seminary
Thoburn, Isabella, 22, 144, 171
Thoburn, James, 16, 22–23, 25, 84, 111, 140, 161, 163–65, 169, 175, 177, 179–82, 195–96
Thompson, Alice, 6, 17
Tory Street Mission, 2, 135, 154
training schools. *See* deaconess training schools

United Kingdom, 1, 4, 248
Bradford, city of, 99, 213, 220
Cardiff, city of, 237–38, 241–45, 251
Denaby, city of, 223–24, 234, 236
Liverpool, city of, 219
London, city of, 1–2, 6, 16, 18, 26, 209, 213, 219, 223–24, 246–48
Norwich, city of, 17, 216
Nottingham, city of, 219
Scotland, 18, 176, 248
United Methodist Church (UMC), 8, 90, 166, 197
annual conferences, 197
deaconesses, 8–9, 38, 197–98
United States, 4, 35, 57, 101
Boston, city of, 18, 80, 87, 92, 146, 213
Chicago, city of, 22, 33–34, 57, 62–63, 89, 92, 104, 143, 146, 168, 172–74, 213–14
Dallas, city of, 32
Galveston, city of, 32
Georgia, 20, 139
Atlanta, city of, 18–19, 31, 139
Kansas City, city of, 144
Minneapolis, city of, 32
New York, city of, 3, 25, 57, 67, 73, 111, 169, 181–82, 190, 213
Ohio, 17, 22, 28, 30, 33, 56, 164, 167–68, 171
Cincinnati, city of, 17, 22, 27–28, 30, 166, 171, 196
Roanoke, city of, 33–34
St. Louis, city of, 71, 84
Texas, 19, 32–33
Washington, D.C., 61
United States government, 80
Commissioner of Education, 82
University of Chicago, 86, 92
urbanization, 24, 41, 105

Van Cott, Maggie Newton, 37
Van Waters, Miriam, 63
Vennard, Iva Durham 25–26, 54, 56, 58, 67–73–76, 164–65, 167–68, 173–74, 194, 196, 256–57. *See also* Chicago Evangelistic Institute (CEI); Epworth Evangelistic Institute (EEI); Vennard, Thomas

Vennard, Thomas, 174–75. *See also* Vennard, Iva Durham
Victoria, Queen, 235
Vincent, John Heyl, 140
vital piety, 211–14, 222
vocation 10, 19, 25, 39–40, 46, 105, 111, 149, 169, 176, 179–85, 197, 200. *See also* deaconess, calling
voluntary organizations, 63

Wandera, Leah, 9
Warner, Laceye, 3, 162, 176
Wellesley College, 67, 191
Wells-Barnett, Ida B., 34
Wesley, Charles, 179
Wesley Deaconess Order (WDO), 2, 8, 36, 99, 120, 175, 217, 221
  deaconesses, 2, 18, 159, 206, 211–12, 215–16, 218–19, 224, 234, 237, 246, 248
  dress, 108, 110, 117
  See also Deaconess College; Masters, Thirza; Mewburn House; Pitts, Annie; Stephenson, Thomas Bowman
Wesley, John, 20, 40, 225
Wesley, Susannah, 179
Wheeler, Henry, 168–69, 177, 194
Willard, Frances, 87
Willing, Jennie Fowler, 37
Wittenmyer, Annie, 22

Woman's Foreign Missionary Society (WFMS), 9, 23, 27, 138, 165, 173. *See also* Harris Memorial Training School
Woman's Home Missionary Society (WHMS), 5, 18–19, 25, 27–28, 30–32, 60–62, 67, 136, 138–40, 147–48, 253–55. *See also* Robinson, Jane Bancroft
women/women's
  clubs, 57, 63
  education, 15, 23, 81, 92, 191
  fallen, 17, 75, 205
  professionalization, 34–35
  rights, 152, 177, 183–84
  in the church, 137, 141
  suffrage, 23, 150, 191, 211
  separate spheres, 26, 30, 36, 60, 62–63, 71, 87, 135, 137, 148–52, 176, 184–86
  See also female institution building
Women's Christian Temperance Union, 57, 211
Woodworth-Etter, Maria, 69
World War I, 7, 14, 34–35, 41, 116
World War II, 80
Wright, Mattie, 18, 27, 164

Young Men's Christian Association, 173
Young Women's Christian Association, 3

SCRIPTURE INDEX

Genesis
1:24 — 177

Judges
4–5 — 200

1 Samuel
1–2 — 184

1 Kings
19:12 — 202

2 Kings
4:8 — 195

1 Chronicles
29:17a — 42

Psalms
19:9–10 — 214
19:14 — 90
63:7 — 42
68:6 — 145
130:4 — 44
139:23–24 — 42

Proverbs
27:6 — 99

Isaiah
6:8 — 196
9:6 — 75
40:1 — 204

Joel
2:28–29 — 169

Micah
3:8 — 44

Matthew
9:36 — 154
9:37–38 — 179
11:28 — 203, 229, 238
18:15–18 — 129

Mark
12:41–44 — 46

Luke
1–2 — 200
2:14 — 125
8:2 — 74
8:2–3 — 181

Luke (continued)

10:25–37	204
14:23	203
15:1–7	147
15:11–32	204, 228
21:1–4	46

John

1	95
6:35	228
11:9	225

Acts

2	95
2:1–21	169, 179
2:17–18	169–70
6:3	170
16	200
16:9–15	88
18	200
20:35	75
21:9	169, 179

Romans

8	95
8:38–39	91
16:1	21, 165, 184
16:1–2	15, 200
16:1–7, 12–15	88
16:3–4	200

1 Corinthians

1:16–19	200
9:22	112
10:31	130
11:5	169
14:33b–35	87
14:34–35	185
15	95
16:19	200

2 Corinthians

8:9	214

Galatians

3:28	21, 185
6:10	140

Ephesians

1:16–19	42
5:23	185

Philippians

4:3	153

Colossians

3:17	43
3:12–17	129

1 Timothy

2:1–3	43
2:9	130

2 Timothy

1:5	200
4:19	200

Hebrews

13:14	45

James

1	95
4:11	129

1 Peter

1:5	241

1 John

3:1	227

Revelation

5:5	74
22:16	204